Sylvia Linan-Thompson
Sharon Vaughn

Research-Based Methods of
Reading
Instruction
for English
Language Learners

Grades K–4

Association for Supervision and Curriculum Development ~ Alexandria, Virginia USA

Association for Supervision and Curriculum Development
1703 N. Beauregard St. • Alexandria, VA 22311-1714 USA
Phone: 800-933-2723 or 703-578-9600 • Fax: 703-575-5400
Web site: www.ascd.org • E-mail: member@ascd.org
Author guidelines: www.ascd.org/write

Gene R. Carter, *Executive Director*; Nancy Modrak, *Director of Publishing*; Julie Houtz, *Director of Book Editing & Production*; Ernesto Yermoli, *Project Manager*; Georgia Park, *Senior Graphic Designer*; Sarah Plumb, *Production Specialist*. For EEI Communications: Renee Dexter, *Project Manager*.

All Web links in this book are correct as of the publication date below but may have become inactive or otherwise modified since that time. If you notice a deactivated or changed link, please e-mail books@ascd.org with the words "Link Update" in the subject line. In your message, please specify the Web link, the book title, and the page number on which the link appears.

PAPERBACK ISBN: 978-1-4166-0577-5   ASCD product #108002   s9/07
Also available as an e-book through ebrary, netLibrary, and many online booksellers (see Books in Print for the ISBNs).

Quantity discounts for the paperback edition only: 10–49 copies, 10%; 50+ copies, 15%; for 1,000 or more copies, call 800-933-2723, ext. 5634, or 703-575-5634. For desk copies: member@ascd.org.

Library of Congress Cataloging-in-Publication Data
Linan-Thompson, Sylvia, 1959–
  Research-based methods of reading instruction for English language learners, grades K–4 / Sylvia Linan-Thompson and Sharon Vaughn.
    p. cm.
  Includes bibliographical references and index.
  ISBN 978-1-4166-0577-5 (pbk. : alk. paper) 1. Reading (Elementary)—United States. 2. English language—Study and teaching (Elementary)—Foreign speakers. I. Vaughn, Sharon, 1952- II. Title.

LB1525.V337 2007
372.41'6—dc22

2007014306

18 17 16 15 14 13 12 11 10 09 08   2 3 4 5 6 7 8 9 10 11 12

Research-Based Methods of
Reading Instruction
for English Language Learners, Grades K–4

Acknowledgments v

Preface vii

1   Research-Based Practices for English Language Learners 1

2   Phonemic Awareness 9

3   Phonics and Word Study 31

4   Fluency 57

5   Vocabulary Instruction 87

6   Comprehension 113

7   Questions and Answers for Teachers 145

Glossary 151

References 161

Index 173

About the Authors 183

Acknowledgments

IN THE LAST FEW YEARS WE HAVE HAD THE OPPORTUNITY TO WORK WITH MANY talented people who have an interest in improving educational outcomes for English language learners, and these interactions have contributed to our own growth.

We would like to thank our colleagues at the Vaughn Gross Center for Reading and Language Arts who have worked side by side with us on many of our projects: Leticia Martinez, Kathryn Prater, Jessica Mejia, Elizabeth Portman, Peggy Hickman, Barbara Scholer, and Elizabeth Villareal.

We would also like to thank our colleagues at other institutions who have collaborated with us on a number of projects, in particular our colleagues at the University of Houston: Elsa Cardenas Hagan, David Francis, and Coleen Carlson. There are many teachers, principals, and students who have participated in our studies. We appreciate the excellent advice and feedback they have provided.

We appreciate the support we receive from the Dean of Education's office at the University of Texas at Austin, in particular Dean Manuel Justiz and Associate Dean Marilyn Kameen.

Finally, we would like to thank Mark Goldberg. You have done it again. Thank you for your time, commitment, feedback, and unwavering support.

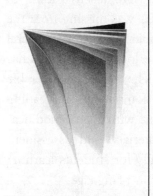

Preface

THIS BOOK PROVIDES TEACHERS WITH CLEAR GUIDANCE AND PRACTICAL CLASSROOM lessons for teaching initial reading instruction to English language learners (ELLs) in kindergarten through 5th grade. English language learners are students whose first language is other than English and who are not yet proficient in English. We focus on ELLs who are young enough to profit from the research-based methods of teaching initial reading detailed in this book.

We are not aware of another short, helpful book for teachers that adequately acquaints them with the background and practices they need to do their work. Parts of books, articles, and other materials are available, but too often they are not research based and end up being of little help to classroom teachers.

Classroom teachers do not usually have the resources to search for excellent materials and put them together in a way that is both comprehensive and helpful, particularly since much of this information resides in places that appeal more to researchers than working teachers. Teachers of ELLs have asked us again and again to do a comprehensive book, and we now have the research and practices that allow us to offer this book to teachers.

Without question, the need for sound ELL materials is urgent and growing. In Johanna Haver's 2003 book, she said that in 1999–2000 the number of limited English proficient students was 4,148,997. No one has an exact number for ELLs, but we do know that the demand is great, and new ELLs show up to register in our schools every day.

The goal of the No Child Left Behind Act (2001) is to ensure that all students read on grade level by 3rd grade. Of course, if a student enters school in the 2nd or 3rd grade with little knowledge of English, the goal must become the 4th or 5th grade. A danger with too many English language learners who may have had inappropriate or insufficient reading instruction is that they are regarded as needing special education (Donovan & Cross, 2002). In fact, they frequently have no learning disability but do need proper, sustained, and focused reading instruction, albeit with special attention to and specific methods for engaging ELLs. Research and practice tell us that the components and methods in this book can be used with children as young as 5 or 6 and as old as 11.

Individual reading studies, syntheses of studies, and national panels on reading conducted in the 1990s affirmed that the components of initial reading instruction for monolingual English-speaking children are phonemic awareness, phonics and word study, fluency, vocabulary, and comprehension. Of course, comprehension is the whole point of reading, and this includes understanding age-appropriate reading materials of high quality.

Solid research on how to teach reading to English language learners was missing from the original studies and books. In the past several years, a knowledge base for these students has been created, one in which we have considerable confidence. The basic components of reading listed above remain, but with many modifications in approach, materials, and assessment tools designed specifically for students learning English as a second or third language.

This book complements the authors' earlier ASCD book, *Research-Based Methods of Reading Instruction: Grades K–3* (2004). The new book focuses sharply on English language learners. Most of the classroom lessons are new, meaning they were not used in the 2004 book. Other lessons have been altered with ELLs in mind. The research-based background material in this book is not as extensive as in the earlier ASCD book, with, of course, special attention to the needs of ELLs. Teachers who wish to read much more about reading research should consult the earlier book.

—*Mark Goldberg*

◆   ◆   ◆

1 Research-Based Practices for English Language Learners

CAROLYN DERBY HAS TAUGHT EITHER 2ND OR 3RD GRADE FOR THE PAST 10 YEARS IN A district in the Northwest. The district she teaches in draws from a community that is both rural and suburban in character. Carolyn comments: "I would really like to feel more confident about teaching the growing number of students in my class whose parents speak a language other than English in the home. Initially, new students were primarily Spanish speaking, although now some students speak languages such as Vietnamese, Croatian, and Russian. I have learned a great deal in the last few years about the customs of these families and have integrated my learning into my classroom, but I still worry that I may not be using the best practices for teaching—especially teaching reading."

Carolyn is not alone. She is among many teachers instructing English language learners (ELLs), who are found in every state in growing numbers. ELLs come from families with a wide range of education, from the highly educated to those with very limited or no formal education. They are represented in every socioeconomic level and speak more than 470 different languages, although Spanish is the home language for at least 75 percent of these students. Despite these differences, researchers have identified effective instructional and assessment practices for beginning readers who are ELLs.

As with all reading instruction, the ultimate goals are reading for understanding, learning, and interest. In the early grades, with most students, the focus is on moving to meaning after assuring that students have foundational skills such as phonemic awareness, phonics, fluency, and vocabulary. How do these goals differ for English language learners? The broad goals of reading are the same for all students. An additional goal with ELLs is to simultaneously build oral language skills. While building oral language skills is important with all students, it is even more essential for English language learners. Although we do not include a chapter dedicated exclusively to oral language, ways of building oral language are referred to in each chapter and are integrated into the activities.

Many ELLs are learning a new language as they acquire and develop literacy skills, especially vocabulary, in English. The integration of practices for English as a second language (ESL) with effective reading instructional practices can provide students the support they need to develop both language and literacy skills in a cohesive manner. The most effective teachers integrate instructional objectives seamlessly (Baker, 2003) in teaching the elements of reading and use language- and meaning-based approaches (Goldenberg & Gallimore, 1991; Goldenberg & Sullivan, 1994).

Fortunately, the similarities in the cognitive processes involved in learning to read different alphabetic languages have been documented (Fitzgerald & Noblit, 2000). These similarities provide researchers and educators a starting point in identifying effective instructional practices in the teaching of reading.

What Are the Most Effective Instructional Practices for Teaching English Language Learners?

After reviewing 33 studies of effective or exemplary schooling for ELLs, August and Hakuta (1997) identified seven classroom attributes associated with positive student outcomes. In these studies, teachers provided explicit skill instruction, student-directed activities, instructional strategies that enhanced understanding, opportunities to practice, systematic student assessment, and a balanced curriculum either alone or in combination. Often these practices were integrated to enhance student learning.

Student understanding of new concepts may be enhanced through instruction that uses routines, embeds redundancy in lessons, provides explicit discussion of vocabulary and structure, and teaches students metacognitive skills (August & Hakuta, 1997). Although not specific to reading instruction, these practices can be used in the teaching of reading.

More recently, an observational study conducted in 20 classrooms serving English language learners from 10 language groups identified a variety of reading instructional practices used by effective classroom teachers of ELLs. Effective teachers—those whose students had the strongest academic outcomes—used effective instructional practices such as explicit teaching, monitoring student progress, and opportunities to practice. They also incorporated strategies that supported student acquisition of English language skills (Graves, Gersten, & Haager, 2004; Haager et al., 2003).

Which instructional practices should you incorporate into teaching reading to ELLs? We will describe three broad instructional practices, explicit teaching, providing practice, and adjusting the language of instruction, which are integrated into the lessons in this book found at the ends of Chapters 2–6.

What Is Meant by Explicit Skill Instruction?

Explicit instruction refers to task-specific, teacher-led instruction that overtly demonstrates how to complete a task and can be used to teach students both basic and higher-order reading skills. Elements of explicit teaching include setting and articulating learning goals, illustrating or modeling how to complete a task, and assessing student understanding and ability to complete the task independently (Tikunoff, 1983). The routines and consistent language used in explicit teaching provide ELLs clear, specific, and easy-to-follow procedures as they learn not only a new skill or strategy but also the language associated with it (Calderon, Hertz-Lazarowitz, & Slavin, 1996; Edelsky et al., 1993; Hernandez, 1991; Muniz-Swicegood, 1994; Saunders et al., 1996).

Explicit skill instruction has been shown to be effective with ELLs who are in the beginning stages of learning to decode English texts. Explicit instruction assists students in identifying and using the structural and visual cues present in words. English language learners can use unique features of words, word patterns, or similarities to other known words as an aid in decoding unknown words (Au, 1993). In fact, when given explicit instruction on phonemic awareness and decoding, many ELLs acquire these skills at the same rate as monolingual English speakers (Chiappe, Siegel, & Wade-Woolley, 2002; Geva, Yaghoub-Zadeh, & Schuster, 2000).

Teachers who teach explicitly also make relationships obvious among concepts, words, or ideas to help students see the link between prior learning and new learning. During reading instruction, for instance, you might remind students of the meaning of a particular vocabulary word in a different context, extend their knowledge by providing additional meanings of multiple-meaning words, or help them see similarities in previously learned spelling patterns. Another example is to teach a new concept such as subtle word distinctions—say, the differences among downpour, drizzle, and sprinkle to describe the fall of precipitation.

In addition, during vocabulary and comprehension instruction, explicit instruction can be used to teach ELLs metacognitive skills and strategies so they think about and prepare for a task and learn to regulate their own learning and understanding (Dianda & Flaherty, 1995). A teacher who teaches a skill explicitly—by modeling, explaining, and demonstrating the skill in context—provides students insight into the thinking processes (metacognition) that proficient readers use. The teacher models skills and strategies step by step, provides students opportunities to practice, and teaches students to use the skills and strategies independently. For example, in teaching students to make predictions prior to reading a text, you would first tell students what you are going to do and why. Then, model the process step by step using think-aloud instruction. Finally, guide students as they make their own predictions and prompt them as needed.

How Do You Provide Opportunities to Practice?

All students, but English language learners in particular, need many and varied opportunities to practice their skills with assistance from the teacher as well as independently (Grabe, 1991; McLaughlin, 1987). Effective teachers have several ways to provide students additional practice and review. During instruction they make sure that there are enough practice items so that students have multiple opportunities to use the target skill and receive feedback as needed. Other methods that provide students multiple opportunities to respond and engage students are choral response and all-response activities. They provide ELLs a low-risk setting for practicing new skills while simultaneously providing teachers an efficient way of providing all students adequate practice. Students who have received explicit instruction and guided practice can then practice the skills and strategies they have learned through student-directed activities such as peer tutoring and cooperative learning (Calderon et al., 1996; Muniz-Swicegood, 1994).

How Do You Adjust Instructional Language?

Ensuring that the input or instruction that English language learners receive is comprehensible is an indispensable practice in teaching ELLs. For instruction to be meaningful, students must understand the essence of what is said to them. Teachers who adjust their level of English and vocabulary scaffold ELLs' acquisition of new skills and strategies during reading instruction as well as their acquisition of English language skills. Two ways in which you can modify your language to enhance instruction are to adjust the level of the vocabulary you use and to use language consistently.

First, you can adjust the level of English vocabulary during instruction by using clear, explicit language when you introduce a new concept. Identifying the instructional objective will help you stay focused on the most critical directions needed to complete a task and reduce the amount of talk you use. If the goal of a lesson is to have students segment phonemes in words, before modeling the task, tell students what they will be doing directly, using words they understand. In addition, use explicit discourse markers, such as first, second, and finally, to help students organize information.

Explicit discourse markers are particularly effective if you pair them with visual prompts, such as holding up your fingers or writing each step. For example, in introducing a lesson on segmenting words, a teacher who is mindful of language might say, "Today you will learn to separate the sounds in a word. To separate the sounds in a word, you say each sound." Discourse markers are also helpful in giving directions for activities—for example, "First, I will say the sounds of a word, and then you will tell me the word."

A second effective practice is to use consistent language. Consistent language provides students a model for talking about the new concept. In addition, the use of consistent language allows

ELLs to focus on the task rather than trying to figure out the meaning of new words. For example, when teaching students to segment words into phonemes, choose just one word to explain the concept of segmenting, such as stretch, separate, or divide. Students can then associate the task with the target word, and they will know what to do when they hear you use the target word. Furthermore, using teaching routines consistently will minimize student dependence on language they may not yet know.

How Do the Critical Elements of Reading Contribute to the Reading Development of English Language Learners?

A balanced curriculum requires instruction in all the elements of reading. Reading instruction for ELLs is most effective when both basic and higher-order skills are included on a daily basis. English language learners can benefit from sound reading instruction even before they are fully proficient in English as long as the instruction is comprehensible (Geva, 2000; Hudelson, 1984; Linan-Thompson et al., 2003).

Phonological awareness is an important early reading skill for all students. A number of studies have found that students that have phonemic awareness in their home language can often transfer that knowledge to a second language (Gersten & Geva, 2003). However, when they are receiving beginning reading instruction in a new language, children will be learning some phonemes that may not exist in their home lan-

guage, and they will need explicit instruction in producing these sounds and may need additional practice to identify them readily. If students have not yet developed phonemic awareness skills, participation in carefully designed activities will help them develop such skills and familiarize them with the sounds of English (Gersten & Geva, 2003).

In addition to the new sounds that students may need to learn in order to participate in phonemic awareness activities, they may also need to learn new letter-sound correspondences, new orthographic patterns, and which orthographic representations are most important in English (Durgunoglu, Nagy, & Hancin-Bhatt, 1993). Explicit instruction in these differences contributes to the development of appropriate decoding skills (Fashola et al., 1996).

Although many English language learners develop phonemic awareness and decoding skills, their fluency development tends to lag behind. Improved fluency and automatic word recognition will allow students to focus on understanding and analyzing the content of the text. Repeated reading activities provide the practice these learners need to develop automatic recognition of English phonemes, high-frequency words, and word patterns, which in turn increases reading rate and accuracy (Grabe, 1991; McLaughlin, 1987).

Vocabulary development is perhaps the most critical element of literacy instruction for English language learners. Vocabulary knowledge is necessary for reading comprehension, and for ELLs it is also necessary to develop English oral language skills. It is not possible to directly teach

ELLs all the vocabulary they will need; therefore, teaching students strategies for learning new vocabulary is essential so they can acquire new vocabulary on their own.

Strategy instruction is also a key component of comprehension instruction. ELLs use the same cognitive strategies as native English speakers to comprehend the text they read. Grabe (1991) found that providing ELLs a framework for using strategies prior to, during, and after reading helped students comprehend text.

Comprehensive reading instruction taught explicitly and systematically builds both reading and English language skills. Specific factors that contribute to instructional efficacy are the explicit teaching of English letter-sound correspondences; word patterns and spelling rules; vocabulary development that emphasizes relationships between and among words to build oral language skills; instruction in when, where, and how to use comprehension and vocabulary strategies; and introduction of skills in isolation and practice in context.

What Assessments Are Appropriate for English Language Learners?

Research on effective reading instruction for ELLs has documented the importance of assessing students' progress in reading (Chamot & O'Malley, 1994). To ensure that students are learning and understanding the instruction they receive, effective teachers monitor progress both daily and periodically and provide students opportunities to evaluate their own progress according to predetermined goals and objectives (Chamot & O'Malley, 1994). Daily assessment occurs as part of instruction; it is naturally necessary to monitor student understanding of the lesson. Checking in frequently with students during instruction allows you to determine whether or not students understand and can complete the instructional task. Effective teachers correct student errors and give corrective feedback about tasks on an ongoing basis to ensure that students are practicing the new skills they are learning correctly.

Most reading measures cannot tell you the cause of a student's difficulty. However, if a student does not meet a benchmark, he or she needs more instruction in that particular area. Screening measures in 1st grade are valid for identifying students who need intensive early intervention, but students' oral language proficiency is not a valid predictor of reading success or failure. Assess all ELLs using benchmarks and progress-monitoring measures to identify students at risk for difficulties, and provide supplemental instruction. Systematic assessment and continual progress monitoring are critical components of instruction that have been validated with ELLs acquiring English literacy skills. We will provide several assessment possibilities in later chapters.

Our intention is that this book will provide guidance to teachers who, like our composite Carolyn Derby, are committed to improving their instruction for ELLs. Some teachers will feel confident in expanding many of the effective practices they are already using and applying some of the new ideas from this book. Other teachers may find this book a valuable resource for altering their practices, and still others will blend some of the instructional practices from this book with other excellent resources they have discovered.

Chapters 2–6 in this book will provide background information and short examples of the five major components of teaching reading and other literacy skills to English language learners. Most important to teachers, each chapter has a lengthy final section of fully developed, effective classroom lessons that incorporate the material in the chapter and focus clearly on the reading components under discussion.

◆ ◆ ◆

2

Phonemic Awareness

TEACHERS OF ENGLISH LANGUAGE LEARNERS (ELLS) ARE OFTEN CONCERNED ABOUT the value and importance of teaching phonemic awareness to students who are just acquiring English. How can we expect them to manipulate the smallest units of a language they do not speak? These are valid concerns. However, we do know that phonemic awareness is an important component in the acquisition of literacy and, therefore, it is critical that English language learners acquire this skill as early as possible. The benefits and role of phonemic awareness in the development of reading skills are well documented across both alphabetic and nonalphabetic languages (Goswami & Bryant, 1990; Gottardo et al., 2001; Lundberg, Olofsson, & Wall, 1980; Wagner, Torgesen, & Rashotte, 1994). In addition, once children have acquired this skill in one language, they can apply it to another (Cicero & Royer, 1995; Comeau et al., 1999).

Furthermore, there is evidence that phonemic awareness in one language predicts reading ability in another (Durgunoglu et al., 1993; Lindsey, Manis, & Bailey, 2003; Quiroga et al., 2002). For children acquiring initial literacy skills in a second language, phonemic awareness helps them learn the sounds of the new language. In this chapter we discuss phonemic awareness: what it is, how to assess it, and how to design instructional activities to promote phonemic awareness in children who are learning English as a second language.

What Is Phonemic Awareness?

Phonemes are the smallest sound units of spoken language. Phonemic awareness is the understanding that the sounds of a language can be identified, isolated, and manipulated. Instruction in phonemic awareness includes helping students develop a range of skills to identify, segment, blend, and manipulate phonemes. Identification is the easiest of these skills. Identification of the initial sound is easiest, followed by final sounds and, finally, medial sounds, those in the middle of words. The segmentation and blending of phonemes is most often associated with phonemic awareness instruction. Segmentation requires students to produce the individual sounds heard in a word. For example, given the word *mat*, students would produce /m/ /a/ /t/. In blending activities, students will respond to a prompt of the sounds by providing the word. If given the sounds /f/ /a/ /n/, they would produce *fan*.

Manipulation of sounds includes several tasks, such as deleting, substituting, or adding sounds to a word. Deletion tasks require students to produce a word after deleting either the beginning or ending sound as requested. Conversely, students can add sounds to the beginning or end of a word as directed by you. Finally, students might change sounds at the beginning, middle, or end of a word to form different words or even nonwords.

Although these tasks seem easy, they are not always so, particularly when the language is unknown or when that sound does not occur in the student's first language. If you have ever tried to learn another language, you know that sometimes it is difficult to determine where one word ends and another begins. Identifying individual sounds in words is much harder, and to help your students complete these tasks, you will need to pronounce the words or sounds you use in these activities clearly.

In addition, there is not always a one-to-one correspondence between letters and sounds in words. In some words, each letter is represented by one sound. For example, the word *sat* has three letters and three phonemes: /s/ /a/ /t/. Two letters can represent one sound, as in the word *ship*. *Ship* has three phonemes but four letters because the /sh/ sound is represented by two letters. *Rack* also has three phonemes but four letters. In this case, the sound k is represented by the letters /ck/. In some words, such as those with r-controlled vowels like *bird*, sounds are co-articulated, making them difficult to isolate (Adams et al., 1998).

The students' ability to engage in these types of activities demonstrates that they are aware of the sounds in language and can produce and manipulate them. This ability will facilitate learning to read and write. There are many activities provided at the end of the chapter that you can use to assist English language learners in understanding and manipulating the sounds in words. Remember that many of the simple words you use for these activities may not be part of their speaking or even their listening vocabulary. The use of pictures or brief definitions can help in providing students context for the words they are manipulating.

Why Should I Teach Phonemic Awareness?

> Children who begin school with little phonological awareness have trouble acquiring alphabetic coding skill and thus have difficulty recognizing words. (Stanovich, 2000, p. 393)

Phonemic awareness is one of the best predictors of how well children will learn to read during their first two years of school (Learning First Alliance, 2000; National Reading Panel [NRP], 2000; National Research Council [NRC], 1998). Having an awareness of the sounds within words influences outcomes in word recognition within and across languages and ultimately enhances comprehension for all students. Phonemic awareness instruction also improves spelling for students, with the exception of those with established learning disabilities. Children who have poorly developed phonemic awareness skills at the end of their kindergarten year are likely to become poor readers. This is true for students learning to read in most languages, and it is true for students learning to read in a second language.

The good news is that most beginning readers, including ELLs and those who have early reading difficulties, can acquire these skills if they are given explicit instruction in phonemic awareness for even a brief amount of time each day (such as 15 minutes). Young English language learners can acquire age-appropriate phonemic awareness skills even when their English proficiency is not fully developed. In fact, there is some evidence that limited speech perception does not interfere with a child's ability to develop phonemic awareness skills (Chiappe et al., 2002). Although very recent immigrants with minimal to no exposure to English will have to develop some English language skills before engaging in phonemic awareness activities, it is important that teachers provide students opportunities to develop these skills as early as possible. Kindergarten students benefit from phonemic awareness instruction more than students who receive their first lessons in phonemic awareness in 1st or 2nd grade (Ehri et al., 2001). Those teaching 1st and 2nd grade will want to teach phonemic awareness to students who lack this skill (Ehri et al., 2001) and as a review for all students.

What Are the Phonemic Awareness Skills That Students Should Know?

The skills that have the most impact on later reading are blending and segmenting at the phoneme level. However, before students get to this level, there are other phonological awareness skills that will prepare them for these and other phonemic awareness tasks. Phonological awareness includes blending, segmenting, and manipulating, but with larger word parts such as syllables and onset-rimes. Words that can be divided into onset and rime are one-syllable words. The onset consists of the consonant or consonants before the vowel. The rime is the vowel and every sound after the vowel. For example, in the word *can*, /c/ is the onset, /an/ is the rime. In *scratch*, the onset is /scr/ and the rime is /atch/. Phonemic awareness is the most complex of the skills on the continuum of phonological awareness skills because you are working at the individual sounds level. Words of any length can be divided into phonemes or individual sounds. The more sounds, the more difficult the word is to segment into sounds.

Bender and Larkin (2003) suggest the following hierarchy of phonological awareness skills:

- Detecting rhyming sounds
- Identifying words with the same initial sound
- Isolating the initial sound
- Categorizing onsets and rimes
- Isolating middle and ending sounds
- Blending sounds into words
- Segmenting or dividing sounds
- Adding phonemes
- Deleting phonemes
- Substituting phonemes

The importance of each of these skills varies with grade level. A kindergarten teacher might begin the school year teaching students to manipulate the larger sound units in words: segmenting words into syllables and blending syllables into words and onset-rime. By the beginning of the second half of kindergarten, the teacher should explicitly teach students to segment words into phonemes and blend phonemes into words. For 1st grade students who lack phonemic awareness or who read fewer than 20 words per minute, the teacher should also explicitly teach segmenting words into phonemes and blending phonemes into words. This instruction should not take the place of teaching phonics and other reading components but should be included in reading instruction.

To determine which students need phonemic awareness instruction or to determine which skills to teach, use progress monitoring. A good progress-monitoring system will allow you to determine which of the three important aspects of phonemic awareness—deleting, segmenting, and blending—are problematic.

Progress monitoring in phonemic awareness assists in identifying those students who are at risk for failing to acquire phonological awareness skills, and in monitoring the progress students are making as phonemic awareness instruction is provided. There are two important aspects of progress-monitoring measures: (1) they should be predictive of later reading ability, and (2) they need to guide instruction. In the case of ELLs, however, progress-monitoring measures cannot tell you why the student is having difficulty. It may be just lack of exposure to English and English sounds, it may be lack of opportunity in engaging in phonemic awareness tasks, or it may be an indication of a reading difficulty. The important thing to remember is that English language learners need to acquire these skills to read English.

The following tests may be useful to teachers of ELLs as they make decisions about what measures they will use to monitor students' progress in phonemic awareness (Chard & Dickson, 1999).

Test of Phonological Awareness (TOPA). The TOPA is a test of students' awareness of sounds in words for grades K–2. It can be administered in groups or individually. This assessment is aimed at identifying students at risk for reading difficulties or detecting phonological deficits in students already experiencing reading difficulties. The kindergarten version consists of two subtests. First, students are asked to mark pictures (multiple choice) that begin with the same sound as a target word. Then, students must choose pictures that begin with a different sound. The elementary version consists of the same two subtests, but students are asked to mark pictures with the same or different ending sounds. Group administration time is approximately 15–20 minutes.

Comprehensive Test of Phonological Processing (CTOPP). The CTOPP is an individually administered test for identifying students who may need additional instruction in phonological awareness. Three areas are assessed: phonological awareness, phonological memory, and rapid-naming ability. The first version of the test is for ages 5 and 6 (kindergarten and 1st grade), and a second version is for ages 7–24. The phonological awareness subtests consist of blending words (e.g., /c/ /a/ /t/ = cat); deleting parts of words (e.g., "Say baseball without saying base"); and matching words with similar beginning or ending sounds. Students must choose pictures (multiple choice) that start or end with the same sound as a target word. Phonological memory tasks include recall of a series of digits and repetition of nonwords (e.g., "Say blit"). Rapid-naming tasks are timed and consist of naming colors and objects (5- and 6-year-olds) or naming digits and letters (7 years and up). These core subtests take approximately 30 minutes to administer. Supplemental subtests are also included to allow for more specific assessment of student strengths and weaknesses.

Phoneme Segmentation Fluency (Dynamic Indicators of Basic Early Literacy Skills [DIBELS]) (Kaminski & Good, 1996). There are 18 forms of this measure, with 10 words for each form. All forms have two or three phonemes for each of the 10 words. This measure is individually administered and timed. Students are given 60 seconds to get as many phonemes correct as possible. Students receive points for each correct phoneme even if the entire word is not correct. Students are not provided corrective feedback for errors.

When selecting screening measures for your students, consider the following important characteristics of the measure:

1. Has the measure been normed with English language learners?
2. Does the measure allow you to predict with accuracy if your ELLs will later have difficulties in reading?
3. Does the measure allow you to differentiate among high, average, and low performers?
4. Does the measure tell you what phonemic awareness skills you need to teach?
5. Does the measure have multiple forms, or is it designed so that you can administer it more than one time per year?

If you can answer yes to all of the above, use the measure with confidence. If you can answer yes to all except number 1, use it but be aware that you are comparing your English language learners to monolingual English students. If your students have been in the country only a short time and have limited English proficiency, not meeting a grade-level benchmark is an indication that they need more instruction. It does not mean that they have a learning difficulty. Progress is a better indicator of a student's ability to learn, so monitor student progress regularly and adjust instruction based on the students' response to instruction.

How Do I Teach Phonemic Awareness?

Recall that phonemic awareness has the most impact in the earliest grades, and all beginning readers benefit from instruction in phonemic awareness. It will be important to provide phonemic awareness in kindergarten and 1st grade. However, kindergarten or 1st grade students who can read more than 20 words per minute accurately or have phonemic awareness skills in their home language rarely need to have additional instruction in phonemic awareness. Older students who are just beginning English instruction and do not demonstrate phonemic awareness skill or those students who have had instruction and are still having difficulty benefit from phonemic awareness linked to print. We discuss this at the end of this section.

After you determine what your students know about phonemic awareness, you are ready to begin planning for instruction. Plan lessons that address the needs of most or all of the students. Provide small group activities to address the specific needs of selected students. Focus on one or two skills at a time, perhaps for a week, especially skills at the phoneme level. In addition, make sure you model each task and provide time for students to respond in groups and individually. For example, "Watch me; I'm going to say each of the sounds in the word *mast* separately, then I'm going to put them together and say the word. Watch my lips and fingers: /m/, /a/, /s/, /t/ [put one finger up for each sound until four fingers are up]. *Mast*. Now do it with me. *Mast*: /m/ /a/ /s/ /t/." Watch to be sure students hold up one finger for each sound. Finally, provide positive

and corrective feedback and many opportunities for practice to determine which students are making progress and which students need additional support (Bos & Vaughn, 2006; Smith, Simmons, & Kame'enui, 1998). To support students' acquisition of language, review the meaning of the words you use in these lessons. All of this can be done in 15 to 20 minutes a day.

If students have difficulty completing the tasks, you can support them by scaffolding their learning. If students are having difficulty segmenting sounds, use manipulatives, body movements, or fingers to make the auditory or oral tasks more visible. For example, "Watch me; I'm going to take one step sideways each time I say a sound in the word *cap*: /c/, /a/, /p/. Now you stand up. After I say a word, you say the sounds with me and take one step sideways for each sound in the word."

One thing you do not want to do is turn these activities into articulation or diction lessons. Just think back to the time you took a class in a foreign language and tried to trill the *r* in Spanish or produce the nasal *gn* in French and how—despite your best efforts—you were not able to produce those sounds, yet you understood them when you heard them. This might be the case for your students. To help with the pronunciation, provide support and explicit instruction on how to form the mouth to produce certain sounds, but do not spend a lot of time on this. Model once or twice and let students practice; then move on. Remind them of what you have taught them each time you come to that sound. Remember, the lesson's objective is to master phonemic awareness skills, not diction.

While many activities will be oral, as soon as possible, link sounds to letters and print—

particularly with 1st and 2nd grade students who are just learning English. Phonemic awareness training is most beneficial when it is combined with practice in connecting sounds to letters (Bradley & Bryant, 1985; Byrne, 1998; Share, 1995). Provide many opportunities for students to write the letters that represent the sounds they hear. Whenever possible, teach students these skills in small groups of four to six students. Students who are taught in small groups transfer their phonemic awareness skills to reading and spelling better than students who receive whole-class instruction or one-to-one instruction (Ehri et al., 2001).

It is valuable for teachers to ensure that students' progress with phonemic awareness provides opportunities for them to use letters to manipulate phonemes and to apply their knowledge of segmenting and blending when they read and write new words. When oral blending and segmenting are paired with letters, teachers can explicitly teach the alphabetic principle (Goswami, 2000; Greaney, Tunmer, & Chapman, 1997). You can assist students in linking the sounds of language to print by using some of the following activities.

- "I'm going to say some sounds that make a word. I want you to tell me the word. Listen: /p/, /o/, /t/. What is the word? Yes, the word is *pot*. Now write the first sound in *pot*. Now write the last sound in *pot*."
- "I'm going to say some sounds that make a word. After I say the sounds, put them together and say the word. Listen: /s/, /l/, /i/, /p/. What is the word? Yes, the word is *slip*. Now write the word *slip* without the /s/ sound."

- "I'm going to say four sounds separately. Write each sound after I say it. Listen: /f/, /i/, /s/, /t/. Now, say the word."
- "I'm going to say the last part of a word. You write a letter that could be added to the beginning to make a new word. Listen: *am*. Write a letter at the beginning to make a new word." Rapidly call on individual students to say their new word. If students say a nonword, say, "That is a make-believe word."
- "I'm going to say a sound. You write a word that begins with that sound. Listen: /m/."
- Provide each student with a small dry-erase board. Use a large dry-erase board to model. "I'm going to write each letter that represents the sound I say. Watch me." Say /s/ [write the letter *s* on the board], /t/ [write the letter *t* on the board], /e/ [write the letter *e* on the board], /p/ [write the letter *p* on the board]. "Now, what word is /s/, /t/, /e/, /p/? Yes, that's right; it is *step*. Now, I will say some sounds and I want you to write the letter that represents each sound. Then tell me the word."
- Provide each student with a small dry-erase board. Use a large dry-erase board to model. "I'm going to write each letter that represents the sound I say. Watch me." Say /s/ [write the letter *s* on the board], /p/ [write the letter *p* on the board], /i/ [write the letter *i* on the board], /n/ [write the letter *n* on the board]. "Now, what is that word? Yes, it is *spin*. Now write *spin* without the /s/ sound."

Some teachers have difficulty with identifying, segmenting, and blending speech sounds at a level required for explicit instruction (Moats, 2001). Teachers may be more willing and interested in teaching the critical elements of phonemic awareness if they have the confidence and skills they need to provide instruction. Teachers with little experience with phonemic awareness need time to practice and rehearse the skills they need to manipulate the sounds of language for instructional purposes. It may be useful for teachers to further understand the system of speech sounds that make up English and contribute to reading. This knowledge will be especially helpful for teachers of English language learners because it will help you explain the structure of English and make the tasks visible for students. In addition, clear pronunciation of sounds and words will help ELLs master the sounds of English. A good source for information on sounds is the Neuhaus Education Center (W. Oscar Neuhaus Memorial Foundation, 4433 Bissonnet, Bellaire, Texas 77401-3233; www.neuhaus.org).

What Are Some Useful Classroom Phonemic Awareness Activities?

The following activities are appropriate for all students in the second semester of kindergarten, 1st grade students weak in phonemic awareness, or any students who read fewer than 20 words per minute. English language learners in grades 2 or higher will begin literacy with phonics. The lessons are labeled to indicate whether it is a basic lesson for introducing a new skill or element or a follow-up lesson to

practice these skills. Word lists for all classroom activities are provided at the end of this section (see Figure 2.1 on. pp. 24–27).

Basic Lesson in Identification: What's the Sound?

Objective. Given a word, students will identify the target sound in the word.

Materials. Word list for teacher

Sequence. Initial sound, ending sound, middle sound

1. Tell students that they will identify the first sound they hear in the word you say.
2. Model the task. "Listen, the word is *mat*. The first sound is /m/."
3. Ask students to do the next word with you.
4. Ask students to identify the first sound in the next word. Have students respond as a group; then call on individual students.
5. If all students perform the task correctly, give students new words until you are convinced this skill has been mastered.
6. Review meanings of words with students.

Variation. Give the students two to three words with the same target sound.

Scaffolds. (1) Stretch or emphasize the target sound. (2) Ask students to say the word emphasizing the target sound. (3) Use words with the same initial sound or two different sounds.

Challenge. (1) Give students two words and ask them to determine whether the initial sounds are the same or different. (2) Change the target sound from initial to ending within one lesson.

Follow-up Lesson in Identification: Did You Hear It?

Objective. Given a word, students will determine whether or not the target sound is present in the beginning, middle, or end of the word as identified by the teacher.

Materials. Word list for teacher; a yes/no card for each student

Sequence. Sounds in the initial position, ending position, medial position, all three positions

1. Give each student a card with *yes* written on one side and *no* written on the other.
2. Review with students that words are made up of phonemes or sounds.
3. Tell students that they will listen for a specific sound at the beginning of the word. If they hear the sound at the beginning of the word, they will show the yes side of the card. If they do not, they will show the no side of the card.
4. Model the task. Use some words that meet the criteria and some that do not.
5. Give students two to three practice words to ensure they are completing the task correctly.
6. If all students perform the task correctly, continue giving students words from the word list for a short time.
7. Review the meanings of the words.

Variations. Give each student red and green slips of paper to hold up or ask them to hold up their thumbs.

Scaffolds. (1) Emphasize the target sound by elongating the sound as you say it. (2) Elongate the sound in the target position.

Challenge. Use words that have similar sounds, such as having students listen for /e/ and then use some words with /i/. Other similar-sounding letter pairs are /b/ and /d/, /m/ and /n/, /ch/ and /sh/.

Follow-up Lesson in Identification: The First Sound Is . . .

Objective. Given the label for an object, students will provide the initial sound of the word.

Materials. Bag, small objects (8 to 10)

1. Tell students they will identify the first sound of a word. Show them each object and name it. Ask them to repeat the name. Place the object in the bag.
2. Tell students that they will pull an object from the bag. You will name the object if they do not know it and they will say the sound with which it begins.
3. Model the task. Take an object out of the bag. Say, "This is a top. The first sound is /t/." Return the object to the bag.
4. Practice with students with two to three objects to ensure they can complete the task.
5. If all students can perform the task correctly, let students take turns pulling an object from the bag.
6. If students do not know the name of the object, say the name; then ask the student to repeat it before identifying the initial sound.

Variations. Use pictures instead of objects. Focus on ending sound.

Scaffolds. (1) Limit the number of objects in the bag. (2) Limit the number of sounds that objects begin with.

Follow-up Lesson in Identification: Which Word Is Different?

Objective. Given three words, students will identify the word that has a different vowel sound in the target position.

Materials. Word list for teacher

Sequence. Vowels in the initial position; vowels in the medial position; words with vowels that are dissimilar, such as /a/ and /i/; words with vowels that are more similar, such as /e/ and /i/

1. Tell students that you will say three words and they will identify the word that has a different vowel sound in the initial position.
2. Model the task. "Listen carefully to each of these words. Listen for the sound at the beginning of the word. Tell me the word that is different from the others. Listen: *ate*, *ape*, and *eye*. Which word begins with a different sound?" Stretch the vowels if you need to.
3. Give students two to three sets of words to ensure they can complete the task.
4. If all students perform the task correctly, continue giving students sets of words from the word list for a short time.
5. Review the meanings of words.

Variations. Use other minimal pairs, such as /ch/ and /sh/; use both long and short vowel sounds.

Scaffold. Use words with two distinct vowel sounds, such as /a/ and /i/.

Challenge. Use words with similar vowel sounds in the middle position.

Basic Lesson in Blending: What Did I Say?

Objective. When given a segmented word, students will blend the sounds and identify the word.

Materials. Word list for teacher

Sequence. CVC words (C = consonant; V = vowel), two-syllable words, words with blends and digraphs

1. Tell students they will listen carefully to the sounds you say and then tell you the word.
2. Model blending phonemes into words. "For example, /s/ /a/ /t/. What word is that? Yes, that word is *sat*." If students are having difficulty hearing the sounds and blending into words, stretch the sounds. If students still have difficulty, stretch the first sound (the onset) and say the last two sounds (the rime) as a syllable (/s/ /at/).
3. Have students go through several words with you. "For example, /c/ /a/ /n/. Say the word with me: *can*."
4. Give students two to three words to blend. Be sure students are performing the task correctly by asking each student to blend sounds into a word.
5. If all students are performing the task correctly, continue giving students words for a short time.

Variation. Let students provide the words.

Scaffolds. (1) Extend each sound, for example: /mmmm/aaaa/t/. (2) Extend the first sound /m/ (onset) and say the last two sounds as one syllable /at/ (rime). (3) Give students chips.

Model lining the chips up in a row, but apart from each other. Model moving the first chip into the second chip and into the third chip as students blend the sounds together. Have students use the chips as they blend words. (4) Use the Elkonin boxes (see p. 21). Have students touch the first box. Have students slide a finger across the boxes as they blend the sounds together to make a word.

Challenges. (1) Use words that are long but only have a few sounds, for example, tough, might. (2) Use sounds with blends, digraphs, and vowel blends.

Follow-up Lesson in Blending: Put It Together Chant

Objective. Given an onset and rime, students will blend to form a word.

Materials. Word list for teacher

1. Tell students that you will give them an onset and a rime and they will put them together to make a word.
2. Review that onsets are the initial consonant or consonant blend and that the rime is the word pattern that follows.
3. Model the task. Say, "It begins with /t/ and it ends with /op/. Put them together and they say *top*!"
4. Have students go through several words with you.
5. Give students two to three words to blend. Be sure students are performing the task correctly.
6. If all students are performing the task correctly, continue giving students a few more words.

7. Review the meanings of the words.

Variation. Let students provide the onset and rime.

Scaffold. Ask students to say each word part before blending.

Follow-up Lesson in Blending: Guess My Picture

Objective. Given the sounds of a word, students will blend the sounds and say the word.

Materials. Picture cards of common objects (10–15)

Sequence. CVC words (C = consonant; V = vowel), two-syllable words, words with blends and digraphs

1. Tell students that you will pick a card and look at it. You will say the sounds in the name of the object pictured and they will tell you the word.
2. Model the task. "My picture is of a /c/ /a/ /p/. What is it? *Cap*."
3. "Now do it with me." Practice with students two to three times, picking a different picture each time. Make sure students are performing the task correctly.
4. If all students are performing the task correctly, continue giving students words.
5. Review the meanings of the words.

Variation. Use objects in the class instead of pictures.

Scaffolds. (1) Ask students to say the sounds before they blend them. (2) Stretch the sounds.

Basic Lesson in Segmentation: Break It Up!

Objective. Given a word, students will separate the word into the specified unit (syllable, onset-rime, or phoneme).

Materials. Word list for teacher

Sequence. Syllables, onset-rime, phonemes

1. Tell students that they will learn to separate words into smaller parts: "I will say a word and you will say each sound separately."
2. Model the task. "Listen, the word is *sat*. The sounds are /s/ /a/ /t/."
3. Ask students to do the next word with you. Have students respond as a group; then call on individual students.
4. If all students perform the task correctly, give students new words until you are convinced this skill has been mastered.
5. Review meanings of words with students.

Variation. Separate students' names into syllables.

Scaffold. Students can use chips, tiles, or their fingers to help them keep track of word parts.

Challenge. Use longer words.

Follow-up Lesson in Segmentation: Two for One

Objective. Given a compound word, students will separate it into the two words.

Materials. Word list for teacher

1. Tell students that some words are two words put together. These are called compound words. You are going to say a compound word. They are going to tell you the two words separately.
2. Model separating compound words.
3. Have students segment words with you. "The word is *football*. Say the parts with me: foot, ball." Have students go through several examples with you to be sure they do the task correctly. If a student makes a mistake, have all the students watch you model it correctly. Have students repeat the word task with you.
4. Ask students to separate a compound word. Have students respond as a group; then call on individual students.
5. If all students perform the task correctly, give students new words until you are convinced this skill has been mastered.
6. Review meanings of words with students.

Scaffolds. (1) Students can use chips, tiles, or their fingers to help them keep track of segments. (2) Tell students how many segments a word has.

Follow-up Lesson in Segmentation: Syllable Split

Objective. Given a two-syllable or three-syllable word, students will separate the word into syllables.

Materials. Word list for teacher

Sequence. Two-syllable words, three-syllable words, words with four syllables or more

1. Tell students that words can be separated into syllables or parts and that each syllable contains a vowel.
2. Model separating words into parts or syllables. "The word is *airplane*. The parts are air and plane."

3. Have students segment words with you. Have students go through several examples with you to be sure they do the task correctly. If a student makes a mistake, have all the students watch you model it correctly.

4. Ask students to separate a compound word. Have students respond as a group; then call on individual students.

5. If all students perform the task correctly, give students new words until you are convinced this skill has been mastered.

Variation. Use student names for syllables.

Scaffolds. (1) Students can use chips, tiles, or their fingers to help them keep track of syllables. (2) Tell students how many syllables a word has.

Challenge. Use words with three or more syllables.

Follow-up Lesson in Segmentation: Elkonin Boxes

Elkonin boxes are boxes drawn together in a horizontal line, like this:

They can be drawn on a piece of paper or on an index card. Laminating the paper or index cards helps them to last longer.

One box represents one sound. For words with three phonemes, students have three boxes connected together; for four sounds, students have four boxes connected together. For each produced sound, students can put a marker into each box, touch the box, move a letter into the box, or write the letter(s) for the sound in the

box. For kindergarten students, it helps to put a green dot or a picture in the first box to reinforce that print moves from left to right.

Objective. Given a word, students will segment the word into phonemes.

Materials. Word list for the teacher; Elkonin boxes and chips for the students. The number of boxes in a row matches the number of phonemes. If students are learning to segment words with two phonemes, there are only two boxes in a row.

Sequence. Two-phoneme words, CVC words, CVCC words, CCVCC words (C = consonant; V = vowel)

1. Tell students that words can be divided into sounds.

2. Model segmenting a word into phonemes. Model moving a chip into a box as you say each sound. "For example, *go.* What sounds? /g/ [move a chip into the first box], /o/ [move a chip into the second box]."

3. Have students go through several with you. Watch to be sure students move a chip into a box for each sound. Listen to be sure students say the right sounds. If any student makes a mistake, stop and have the group watch you model; then have students segment the word and move chips with you. Continue having students go through the task with you until they are fairly successful.

4. Tell the students a word. Have students segment the word into its phonemes (sounds). Have students respond as a group. Call on individual students to be sure they are segmenting correctly. If any

student makes a mistake, stop and have the group watch you model; then have students segment the word and move chips with you. Continue with new words, having students respond without your model.

5. After students have mastered segmenting two-phoneme words, advance to three-, four-, and five-phoneme words.

Variations. (1) Use a puppet. Tell students the puppet's name is /m/ /a/ /t/ (*Matt*) or any other segmented one-syllable name. Tell students the puppet only understands slow talk. Tell students a word the fast way. Students will tell the puppet the word the slow (segmented) way. (2) After students have learned the corresponding sound for a letter, use that letter in place of a chip. Watch that students place the letter in the corresponding box. As students learn more letter-sound correspondences, use more letters in place of chips. Be careful not to have so many letters for students to choose from that you lose instructional time for teaching segmenting.

Scaffolds. (1) Stretch the word to help students identify the phonemes. (2) Tell students how many phonemes the word has. (3) If students are having difficulty identifying phonemes in CVC words even with prompts, do the activity at the onset-rime level.

Challenge. Use words with blends and digraphs. Use words with more than one syllable.

Basic Lesson in Manipulation: Add a Sound/Take Away a Sound

Objective. Given a word, students will either add or delete a phoneme to that word as directed.

Materials. Word list for teacher

Sequence. Add or delete phonemes in the initial position and final position

1. Review with students that words are made up of phonemes or sounds.
2. Tell them that they will be adding one phoneme or sound to a word to create a different word.
3. Model the task. "The word is *at*. I add /b/ and I get *bat*."
4. Give students two to three practice words. Be sure they are completing the task correctly before moving on to deleting the sound at the end of the word. Following is an example: "Listen to the sounds and tell me the word: /f/ /a/ /s/ /t/. That's right; the word is *fast*. Now drop the /f/ sound. What do you get? That's right, you get *ast*."
5. If all students perform the task correctly, continue giving students words from the word list for a short time.
6. Use this format to add or delete the final phoneme.
7. Review the meanings of the words.

Scaffold. Use manipulatives, such as plastic chips or tokens, so students can see and move the token with each sound. The plastic chips or tokens will also help students see how sounds are removed.

Variation. After students have learned a few letter-sound correspondences, use a word list with the learned letter sounds. Give each student a baggie containing four or five of the learned letter sounds (such as /a/, /m/, /t/, /s/, and /f/). Students will put the letters in a row at the top of their desks. Say, "Move the first sound you hear so it is in front of you." Say *mat*; the students move the /m/ in front of themselves. Say, "Change the /m/ to /s/." Students move the /m/ back and move the /s/ in front. Say, "What is the new word?" Students say *sat*.

Challenge. Substitute phonemes in all three positions and use longer words.

Follow-up Lesson in Manipulation: Deleting Syllables

Objective. One-syllable or two-syllable word; students will delete one syllable and say the word part that is left.

Materials. Word list for teacher

Sequence. Two-syllable words, three-syllable words, words with four syllables or more

1. Tell students that words can be separated into syllables or parts. You are going to tell them to take away one syllable and say the syllable that is left.

2. Model by saying the word, saying the part you will leave off, and saying the new word. Say, "The word is *tiger*. I will take away *ti*." Say *ger*.

3. Model, having students go through it with you. Have students do several with you to be sure they can do the task correctly before you go to the next step, which is having students respond without you. If students make a mistake, stop and have the whole group watch as you model. Have the group repeat the word and task with you.

4. Ask students to say the word, leave part of the word in their mind, and say the new word. Have students respond as a group, and then call on individual students.

5. If all students perform the task correctly, continue giving students new words.

6. Review meanings of the words.

Variations. Use student names; take away the last word part or syllable.

Scaffold. Students can use chips, tiles, or their fingers to help them keep track of syllables. Students cover up the chip that represents the word part that is being taken away.

Challenge. Use words with three or more syllables.

Follow-up Lesson in Manipulation: Do the Phoneme Shuffle

Objective. Given a word and directions to substitute a phoneme, students will substitute phonemes in words.

Materials. Word list for teacher

Sequence. Substitute phonemes in the initial position, ending position, medial position, all three positions

1. Review with students that words are made up of phonemes or sounds.

2. Tell them that they will be changing one phoneme or sound in a word to create a different word.

3. Model changing the phoneme in the initial position of two to three words. "The word is *hat*. I change the /h/ to /b/ and I get *bat*."

4. Ask student to go through the next one with you. "The word is *sit*; change the /s/ to /l/. What do you get? That's right, *lit*."

5. Give students two to three practice words. Be sure they are completing the task correctly before moving on to changing the sounds at the end of the word.

6. Changing sounds at the end of the word is harder than at the beginning of the word. Following is an example: "Listen to the sounds and tell me the word: /f/ /a/ /t/." After students respond, say "That's right, the word is *fat*." Proceed, "Now drop the /t/ sound. What do you get?" If students answer correctly, continue with "That's right, you get *fa*. Now add /n/ to the end of *fa*. What word do you get?" Respond with, "That's right, you get *fan*."

7. If all students perform the task correctly, continue giving students words from the word list for a short time.

Scaffold. Use manipulatives, such as plastic chips or tokens, so students can see and move the token with each sound. The plastic chips or tokens will also help students see how sounds are removed.

Variation. After students have learned a few letter-sound correspondences, use a word list

(continued on p. 28)

FIGURE 2.1 ➤ Word Types for Use in Activities

Compound Words			
sunshine	cowboy	bookcase	seesaw
baseball	cupcake	inside	cowgirl
someplace	outside	shoeshine	oatmeal
steamship	sometime	himself	daytime
cardboard	airplane	eyelash	playmate
football	herself	doorbell	upset
homework	housework	applesauce	bobcat
armpit	popcorn	spaceship	shapeless
birthday	highway	hallway	meatball
wristwatch	withdraw	doorknob	knothole
snowplow	somehow	handbook	snowball
bullfrog	cartwheel	ladybug	bulldog
backyard	bathtub	toothbrush	haystack

(continued)

FIGURE 2.1 ➤ **Word Types for Use in Activities (cont.)**

Two-Syllable Words				
bubble	mister	candy	person	rabbit
cartoon	funny	daddy	garden	barber
window	paper	magic	after	little
dentist	monkey	kitten	chicken	napkin
bashful	kettle	butter	mistake	empty
April	July	August	yellow	purple
needle	apple	teacher	student	buddy
spider	bamboo	panda	magnet	attic
eager	baker	invite	jolly	rusted
happen	lazy	baby	ladle	crayon
whisper	reply	quickly	nylon	zero
maybe	payment	away	purchase	hundred
thousand	compass	almost	walnut	fallen
author	country	glasses	number	problem
breakfast	vibrate	children	older	explain

Three-Syllable Words				
peppermint	carpenter	wonderful	buttermilk	understand
fisherman	forgetful	important	mistaken	September
valentine	October	November	December	excitement
Saturday	family	example	gasoline	capitol
rapidly	consider	property	popular	woodpecker
grandmother	vacation	potato	volcano	umbrella
magazine	hyena	energy	babysit	ladybug
handwriting	however	parachute	beautiful	rollerskate
microscope	telephone	museum	photograph	alphabet
neighborhood	employer	animal	different	gentleman
elephant	Indian	referee	dangerous	wonderful

(continued)

FIGURE 2.1 ➤ **Word Types for Use in Activities (cont.)**

		Two-Phoneme Words		
go	see	bay	sigh	on
no	knee	tie	say	me
bay	mow	bye	is	hi
each	my	ill	off	ate
oak	ease	ice	so	odd
aim	ace	up	age	he
day	an	may	new	eat
egg	we	by	ache	own
pie	it	zoo	be	if
ash	ape	low	us	ray

		Three-Phoneme Words		
man	dip	hop	men	sup
tip	bit	ran	bat	sun
ten	mop	bed	cup	fun
can	hit	top	let	fed
pup	whiff	pop	chop	less
bug	sit	big	shop	fan
dug	dim	shop	pen	pan
back	mug	web	wit	end
dash	and	fade	sash	hide
bite	fish	bone	date	joke
beat	nice	rush	math	lock
cane	shot	cape	seek	chat
beef	bus	bake	cuff	rice
poke	seen	home	light	cave
came	tone	feet	kite	side
cage	late	soak	act	slow

(continued)

FIGURE 2.1 ➤ **Word Types for Use in Activities (cont.)**

Four-Phoneme Words				
best	told	list	rent	catch
fact	mind	sold	cent	lunch
vast	task	pest	dance	bench
mist	kind	must	test	help
bend	past	lent	pant	rest
wind	gold	chant	lend	gift
band	mild	sent	last	cold
mend	fast	hand	yelp	lift
mask	bold	sift	cast	land
send	wild	sand	dust	milk
child	west	silk	lint	wisp
cast	since	went	bind	jump
find	pact	budge	bump	mold
just	shift	cinch	nest	lump
crab	bleach	step	tribe	slid
plug	price	bled	fried	spill
flies	drab	cluck	bread	slight
green	brick	fluff	fled	fright
blade	preach	sniff	brim	skin
pride	stuck	flab	speech	flight
sleet	grade	broke	smack	slime
fries	broom	plead	sled	spoon
slide	sneak	flop	grab	still
track	creek	bright	stop	scab
click	spade	please	skies	slope
bleed	glide	stage	sped	crack
played	speak	stick	blot	press
spoke	braid	grim	steal	black
club	steam	gloom	snail	plus

with the learned letter sounds. Give each student a baggie containing four or five of the learned letter sounds (such as /a/, /m/, /t/, /s/, and /f/). Students put the letters in a row at the top of their desks. Say, "Move the first sound you hear so it is in front of you." Say *mat*; the students should move the /m/ in front of themselves. Say, "Change the /m/ to /s/." Students move the /m/ back and move the /s/ in front. Say, "What is the new word?" Students say *sat*.

Challenge. Substitute phonemes in all three positions and use longer words.

◆   ◆   ◆

Annotated Bibliography

Adams, M. J., Foorman, B. R., Lundberg, I., & Beeler, T. (1998). *Phonemic awareness in young children: A classroom curriculum.* Baltimore: Paul H. Brookes.

This book provides phonological and phonemic awareness activities geared primarily for kindergarten and 1st grade students and some older students with special needs. The introduction provides a brief description of phonemic awareness and its importance. Includes a sequence of activities that provide adequate description to assist teachers in in their classroom instruction. Extensive word lists accompany each activity. Group-administered assessments are provided as well as suggested grade-level sequences and resources for materials and rhyming stories.

Blachman, B. A., Ball, E. W., Black, R., & Tangel, D. M. (2000). *Road to the code: A phonological awareness program for young children.* Baltimore: Paul H. Brookes.

This activity-based program is designed for kindergarten students as well as 1st graders struggling to learn to read. The program includes an introduction with information about phonological awareness and guidelines for getting started with the lessons. The remainder of the book contains scripted lessons in phonological awareness. Teacher guidelines for instructing each lesson are also provided. Each lesson includes say-it-and-move-it activities involving segmenting words with manipulatives, letter name and sound instruction with activities teaching letter names and sounds, and phonological awareness practice for reinforcement of various phonological awareness skills. Reproducible pictures and cards needed to complete the activities are also included.

Kress, J. (1993). *The ESL book of lists.* Upper Saddle River, NJ: Prentice-Hall.

This book provides useful lists for teachers on a number of topics, including the identification of difficult English sounds for specific language groups and word lists for a variety of objectives.

McCormick, C. E., Throneburg, R., & Smitley, J. (2002). *A sound start: Phonemic awareness lessons for reading success.* New York: Guilford Press.

This is a resource for teachers who want to include explicit phonemic awareness instruction in an early reading program. One volume provides three separate sets of phonemic awareness lessons, complete with scripted directions and reproducible learning materials and assessment tools. Each set is field-tested and research based, and the lessons may be used independently or in conjunction with other early literacy programs.

O'Connor, R. E., Notari-Syverson, A., & Vadasy, P. F. (2005). *Ladders to literacy.* Baltimore: Paul H. Brookes.

This activity book is intended for kindergarten students. Lessons for instructing students on print awareness, phonological awareness, and oral language are included. Activities that are appropriate for the beginning, middle, and end of the year are identified. Teachers are encouraged to use activities that fit their classroom routines and units studied. Each lesson contains a written objective for the teacher and an outline of targeted skills. After each activity, specific instructions for providing further teacher support or scaffolding at three different levels are given: high demand/low support, medium demand/medium support, and low demand/high support. It is intended to assist teachers in adjusting the amount and type of support as needed.

Torgesen, J. K., & Mathes, P. G. (2000). *A basic guide to understanding, assessing, and teaching phonological awareness.* Austin, TX: Pro-Ed.

Phonological awareness and its importance as well as specifics related to assessment and instruction are described. The book is organized into three sections. The first section describes phonological awareness and gives teachers benchmarks of the normal development of phonological awareness in conjunction with general information regarding the role of instruction in the development of phonological awareness. The second section provides information on assessing phonological awareness and gives detailed descriptions of eight published assessments available for teacher use. The third section provides information regarding instruction in phonological awareness and presents detailed descriptions of 12 published programs in phonological awareness available for teacher use.

◆ ◆ ◆

Web Sites That Teach

www.ldresources.com/readwrite/readingtolearn.html
This Web site provides an overview of learning to read with an emphasis on phonological awareness and word identification.

www.ldonline.org/ld_indepth/reading/teaching_children_to_read.html
This Web site provides specific information on phonemic awareness, alphabetic principles, and phonics.

www.ldonline.org/ld_indepth/teaching_techniques/cld_hownow.html
This Web site provides activities on phonemic awareness for collaborative classrooms.

www.texasreading.org
This Web site from the University of Texas Center for Reading and Language Arts, University of Texas at Austin, provides numerous resources and links for reading instruction, including phonological awareness.

www.Ericec.org/digests/3540.htm
The Web site provides information on phonological awareness.

www.pbskids.org/lions
This is the PBS Web site for the television show *Between the Lions*, which contains information and activities for beginning reading with emphasis on phonological awareness and phonics.

◆ ◆ ◆

3 Phonics and Word Study

IN A RECENT CONVERSATION, TEACHERS OF ENGLISH LANGUAGE LEARNERS (ELLs) voiced concerns about the teaching of phonics to students in their classes who have several levels of English proficiency.

"English is so irregular, it doesn't make sense to teach students all the rules because there are so many exceptions."

"True," continued another teacher, "but students have to learn the relationship between letters and sounds to learn to read and spell."

"But does it make sense," wondered another teacher, "to teach students the rules if they don't know what many of the words mean? What concerns me is that one of the principles of English as a second language instruction is that we should teach in context to support student learning, but phonics is often taught in isolation and is very decontextualized."

"How can we make instruction more meaningful?" asked the fourth teacher.

The above points are valid and worthy of consideration in planning phonics instruction for ELLs. In this chapter we discuss what we know about teaching phonics to English language learners and provide some activities that have been effective in schools. We describe a phonics approach to instruction that includes a range of skills from alphabetic knowledge to reading in decodable books—everything you need to know for word study.

What Is Phonics and Word Study Instruction?

Gough and Tumner (1986) identified two basic processes necessary to learn to read: learning to convert letters into recognizable words and comprehending the meaning of print. Learning to convert letters to recognizable words requires knowledge of the relationship between sounds and the letters or other symbols that represent them, then remembering the exact patterns and sequences that may represent various speech sounds (Goswami, 2006; Moats, 2000). The orthographic system of a language consists of the relationship among the visual symbols used in the writing system, the mapping of these symbols onto speech, and meaning (Seymour, 2006). As children map sounds to print, they are also accessing the words in their vocabularies. They use this knowledge to support them in identifying the word they are reading. Although there are similarities in learning to read across languages, differences in the orthography of the language lead to differences in how long it takes to learn to read and how much difficulty some children may have. In some languages, like Finnish, Italian, and Spanish, the relationship between letters or symbols and sounds is fairly consistent—that is, there are few exceptions and fewer relationships to learn. Other languages, like Kanji, English, and Danish, are not as consistent. There are many inconsistencies in English that puzzle English language learners.

Children have to learn which letters have consistent relationships and which do not, and when to apply the rules that govern them. For children learning English as a second language, understanding the relationship between letters and sounds is critical, since some of the sounds will be new to them—sounds they have not heard or spoken as meaningful units of speech. They may be applying a phoneme (sound) from their home language to a different grapheme (letter) or using letters alone or in combinations that do not exist in their home language. In addition, they lose the advantage provided by accessing their knowledge of words, since their English vocabularies may be limited.

Converting letters to recognizable print can be taught through phonics instruction and can lead to students comprehending the meaning of text. Phonics is an approach in which children are taught to decode words by using and applying their knowledge of the relationship between letters and individual sounds to read. In planning phonics instruction for ELLs, you will have to decide among several forms of phonics instruction. All the approaches include instruction in letter-sound relationships but vary in the explicitness of the instruction and how systematic the process is in determining the sequence of instruction. In synthetic approaches to instruction, students are taught the individual letter-sound relationships and then taught explicitly to blend the letters into words. Teachers who use embedded phonics teach letter-sound relationships during the reading of connected text. Embedded phonics is less explicit than synthetic phonics instruction.

An effective phonics program for English language learners uses a synthetic approach that follows a defined sequence and includes direct teaching of a set of letter-sound relationships.

Each instructional set includes major sound-spelling relationships of both consonants and vowels. This sequencing arrangement provides students opportunities not only to begin to learn the relationship between letters and sounds but also to use that knowledge to begin blending these sounds to read words and to segregate the sounds to write words even before they have learned all the letter-sound correspondences. For ELLs, who are learning to read in an inconsistent orthography like English, instruction using analogy-based phonics provides children an additional strategy for reading a larger number of words as they are building their English oral language skills. In addition, the program should include books and stories that contain a large number of words that children can decode by using the letter-sound relationships they have learned and are learning. Finally, programs should provide ELLs opportunities to spell words and write their own stories with the letter-sound relationships they are learning (Blevins, 1998; Center for the Improvement of Early Reading Achievement [CIERA], 2001; NRP, 2000; Texas Education Agency [TEA], 2000). English language learners struggling with reading acquisition who receive explicit phonics instruction as part of comprehensive literacy instruction tend to develop stronger foundational reading skills (Denton, Anthony, & Parker, 2004; Linan-Thompson & Hickman-Davis, 2002; Vaughn et al., 2006). Even students with limited English proficiency made gains in reading skills, indicating that a wide range of ELLs benefit from explicit instruction.

Good readers rely primarily on letter-sound correspondences in words rather than context or pictures to identify words; use reliable strategies to decode words; and read words enough times so that they become automatic. Phonics instruction provides ELLs the knowledge needed to develop those same skills effectively and efficiently by providing a road map for making sense of how English works as well as effective decoding strategies. However, phonics instruction should not be the entire reading program, but rather it should be integrated into other elements of reading instruction, such as language activities, story time, and small-group tutoring to create a balanced reading program. Learning to read in languages with less-consistent orthographies like English takes longer than learning to read in languages with more consistent orthographies (Seymour, 2006). For most students, two years of phonics is sufficient; other students may require more instruction. English language learners whose initial reading instruction is in English may require more time, since they are learning both a new language and a new process. Older ELLs or those who learned to read in their home language will still need phonics instruction to learn the structure of English but may acquire the knowledge more quickly. Use assessment information to adapt phonics programs to meet the needs of individual students (NRP, 2000). Most important, starting early is key: "Early and systematic instruction in phonics seems to lead to better achievement in reading than later and less systematic instruction" (Stahl, 2001, p. 333).

Why Should I Teach Phonics and Word Study?

Imagine trying to put together a 1,000-piece puzzle without a picture for reference. You might begin using strategies such as finding all the pieces that have a straight edge to form the perimeter and then grouping pieces by color. Through trial and error, you would begin to form the picture. Children learning to read in English are faced with the same situation when they are given bits and pieces of information about English orthography, but not a systematic way of learning, applying, and practicing the spelling patterns and rules they are learning.

Children learning to read in English have to learn the letter-sound relationships among 44 speech sounds and more than 100 spellings used to represent them (Blevins, 1998; Bos & Vaughn, 2006). In addition, students have to apply this knowledge to read both known and unknown words in isolation and in context, and they need to be able to read irregular words. Although it might seem that English is too irregular to teach systematically, there are enough regularities to make a systematic approach to phonics instruction appropriate. For example, the teaching of vowels is often identified as an area for concern in teaching English language learners, but we can see from the table that the exceptions account for fewer than one-third of the words (see Figure 3.1).

Phonics and word study instruction provide an opportunity to teach children that there are systematic relationships between letters and sounds, that written words are composed of letter patterns that represent the sounds of spoken words, and that recognizing words quickly and accurately is a way of obtaining meaning from what is read. In addition, children learn that they can blend the sounds to read words and segment words into sounds to spell (Adams, 1990; Chard & Osborn, 1999; NRP, 2000).

What Elements Should I Include in My Phonics and Word Study Instruction?

We know that ELLs can learn to read in English even when their oral skills in English are not fully developed (Gunn et al., 2000; Hudelson, 1984), but this instruction is more effective if it is accompanied by development of their oral language skills (Gersten & Baker, 2003). Most important, given that it takes longer to learn to read in English than it does in most languages, reading instruction should not be withheld until children have attained oral language proficiency in English (Quiroga et al., 2002). Because the development of reading processes for ELLs is essentially the same as that for native English speakers, you can use the same instructional sequence (Edelsky, 1981a, 1981b; Hudelson, 1984). Therefore, provide instruction that includes print awareness, alphabetic knowledge, phonological and phonemic awareness, the alphabetic principle, decoding, irregular/high-frequency words, reading practice with decodable text, and reading fluency when children enter school. The exception would be for children who speak no English at all. Two of these elements, phonological and phonemic awareness and reading fluency, are covered in depth in Chapters 3 and 5, respectively.

FIGURE 3.1 ➤ **Phonics Rules and the Percentage of Exceptions to Them**

Principles	Percentage of Exceptions
When the letter c precedes the letters e, i, or y in a syllable, the c has the /s/ sound.	0%
When the letter g precedes the letters e, i, or y in a syllable, the g has the /j/ sound.	23%
When a stressed syllable ends in e, the long sound of the vowel is used and the final e is silent.	32%
When a stressed syllable contains only one vowel and ends with a vowel, the long sound of the vowel is used.	17%
When there is only one vowel in a stressed syllable and the vowel is followed by a consonant, the short vowel sound is used.	32%
When a word of more than one syllable ends with the letter y, the final y has the /short i/ sound. When a word of more than one syllable ends with the letters ey, the e is silent and the y is pronounced /short i/.	0%
When a syllable contains only the one vowel a, followed by the letters l or w, the sound for a rhymes with the vowel in saw.	7%
When there are two adjacent vowels in a syllable, the first vowel is pronounced using the long sound and the second vowel is silent.	50%

Sources: From *Vowel Situations in a Primary Reading Vocabulary,* by R. Oaks, 1950, master's thesis, Teacher's College, Temple University, Philadelphia.
From "A study of the consonant situations in a primary reading vocabulary," by E.B. Black, 1952, *Education, 72*(9), p. 618–623.

How much time you spend on each of these elements will depend on the age, level, English proficiency, and previous reading experience of your students. As children participate in phonics and word study activities, their understanding of the conventions that govern spoken and written language will increase. These elements do not have to be taught sequentially, and the rate at which students acquire these skills will vary. In general, however, kindergarten students benefit from instruction that teaches prerequisite skills for strong word recognition, the communicative function of print, alphabetic knowledge, phonemic awareness, and the alphabetic principle (Chard, Simmons, and Kame'enui, 1998). Most students who have had effective phonics instruction can read quickly and easily and have an effective decoding strategy for reading unknown words. English language learners will also need to develop their oral language skills as they are acquiring reading skills.

For each of the crucial elements, a brief description and characteristics of effective programs are provided.

Print Awareness

Students who understand that written language is related to oral language and that printed language carries messages have print awareness. They also know that the structures of written language are different from spoken language and know the difference between words and nonwords (Blevins, 1998; Reutzel & Cooter, 1999; TEA, 2000). This awareness of the forms and functions of printed language is a reliable predictor of future reading achievement.

Children develop print awareness when they have opportunities to hear books and participate in read-aloud activities. To help students develop print awareness, you can reinforce the forms and functions of print found in classroom signs, labels, posters, calendars, etc.; teach and reinforce print conventions, such as print directionality, word boundaries, capital letters, and end punctuation; and teach and reinforce book awareness and book handling. These activities will be critical for students who come from home languages that use right-to-left or up-and-down directionality in reading, such as Hebrew or some Asian languages. You can also allow children to practice what they are learning by listening to and participating in the reading of predictable and patterned stories and books, and you can provide opportunities to practice with predictable and patterned

books (Reutzel & Cooter, 1999; TEA, 2000). These activities help ELLs not only develop print awareness but also gain knowledge of English vocabulary. However, students will be less likely to be able to use context and picture clues if they are in the beginning stages of English development. Use books and stories that have illustrations that are highly correlated to the story to explicitly build vocabulary.

Alphabetic Knowledge

The goal of instruction that develops alphabet knowledge is to get children to recognize and name letters quickly and accurately (Adams, 1990). Knowledge of letter names is strongly related to children's ability to remember the forms of written words, to treat words as sequences of letters, and to develop the alphabetic principle: the association of letters with their corresponding sounds. Alphabetic knowledge progresses from letter names to letter shapes (the form) to letter sounds. Learning letter names and sounds seems straightforward; however, children whose home language is logographic will also be learning a new alphabet system, while children from other alphabetic languages may only be learning new names and sounds for letters they have seen before. You may need to provide more explicit instruction and more opportunities to practice those sounds and letters that have no equivalent in children's home language, since they may have difficulty hearing and pronouncing them. Their inability to pronounce some sounds does not necessarily indicate lack of knowledge. While you want to support children in pronouncing the sounds correctly by demonstrating how to position the mouth, teeth, and tongue, be careful not to turn the lesson into a speech lesson or to stop instruction of new letters until they master one that is difficult to pronounce. Figure 3.2 provides an example of some of the sounds that may be difficult for children from some language groups.

FIGURE 3.2 ➤ Sounds That Are Difficult for ELLs

Spanish: b, d, dg, h, j, m, n, ng, r, sh, t, th, v, w, y, z, s-clusters, end clusters

Chinese: b, ch, d, dg, f, j, l, m, n, ng, long o, sh, th, v, z, l-clusters, r-clusters

Vietnamese: long a, long e, k, l, ng, p, r, sh, s, y, l-clusters, r-clusters

Korean: b, l, long o, ow, p, r, sh, t, th, l-clusters, r-clusters

Source: From *The ESL Book of Lists*, by J. Kress, 1993, Upper Saddle River, NJ: Prentice-Hall.

Children who do not know letter names and sounds, whether due to lack of instruction or because they are just learning English, need planned instruction that provides many opportunities to see, play with, and compare letters. Some children can learn several letters each week, while others may only learn one. Include games, songs, and other activities that help children identify and name letters, provide activities in which children learn uppercase and lowercase forms of letters, and point out differences and similarities among the letters. In addition, plan writing activities that encourage children to practice making the letters they are learning and

provide them opportunities to experiment with and manipulate letters to make words and messages (Blevins, 1998; TEA, 2000).

Alphabetic Understanding

Alphabetic principle refers to the systematic relationship between phonemes (sounds) and graphemes (letters). In particular, English language learners need to know that in English

- Some letters represent more than one sound
- Different letters can represent the same sound
- Sounds can be represented by a single letter or combinations of letters

To help children understand the alphabetic principle, include the following practices in your teaching:

1. Teach letter-sound correspondences explicitly and in isolation initially; then provide multiple opportunities daily to practice using this new knowledge to read and write.

2. Provide practice opportunities with new letter-sound relationships as well as previously taught relationships.

3. Give your ELLs opportunities to apply their knowledge of letter-sound relationships to the reading of phonetically spelled words that are familiar in meaning (TEA, 2000).

4. Provide additional practice in the sounds that are not part of a student's home language.

Remember, effective instruction in the alphabetic principle requires that teachers plan and sequence instruction to avoid teaching words that have a similar look or sound, since they might be confusing for ELLs. Once you start phonics and word study instruction, some students will begin to make connections between letters and sounds on their own. However, many of your students will need even more explicit instruction to learn all the letter-sounds correspondences they will need to know.

Decoding and Reading Practice with Decodable Text

Decoding is the understanding of how to read letter or letter patterns in a word to determine the word and its meaning. English language learners who can decode words have a strategy for reading unknown words. Furthermore, once children have developed this understanding and can apply it to read words, they can begin to read words rapidly, automatically, and effortlessly. This will allow them to focus on getting meaning from what they are reading (NRP, 2000; TEA, 2000). For ELLs, the level of their knowledge of English will impact meaning. Many children will learn to decode but will not be able to gain meaning from text until they have sufficient vocabulary. Chapters 5 and 6 provide many activities for building children's vocabulary and comprehension.

Initially, provide opportunities to work with word families, spelling patterns, and onsets and rimes. The use of analogy-based phonics will be useful at this point. Once students are familiar with letter-sound correspondences, teach students to use that knowledge to read unknown words. In analogy-based phonics, students use their knowledge of a word they know—for example, night—to read similar words, such as light or plight.

As students become more sophisticated readers, they will need more advanced decoding strategies that focus on the structure of words. This knowledge provides ELLs a strategy for segmenting multisyllable words into decodable parts and for determining the meaning of the word (Henry, 1997). In particular, teaching affixes shows children that there are word parts that are common across words. This will help them with reading, spelling, and accessing meaning because it highlights the regularities in the language. Learning to analyze the structure of words provides students knowledge of letter combinations, derivatives. and affixes.

Instruction should include the meaning of word parts, such as the following:

- Inflectional ending—a meaningful word part (morpheme), such as *-ed* or *-es*, that indicates tense, number, person, or gender when added to a base word
- Prefix—a word part, such as *pre-*, *in-*, or *un-*, at the beginning of a base word
- Suffix—a word part, such as -ful or -ly, at the end of a base word

When teaching structural analysis, teach the meanings along with recognition and model how to look for word parts. Teaching students to use structural analysis will increase the number of words they can decode easily. Consider the following. The most common affixes in the primary grades are *re-*, *un-*, *con-*, *-ness*, *-ful*, and *-ion*. The prefixes *un-*, *re-*, *in-*, *im-*, *ir-*, *il-*, and *dis-* are used in 58 percent of all prefixed words. Three inflectional endings, *-s/-es*, *-ed*, and *-ing* are found in

65 percent of words that have inflectional endings and suffixes (White, Sowell, & Yanagihara, 1989). In addition, many prefixes and inflectional endings are common across languages.

Effective programs provide students opportunities to use their knowledge of letter-sound correspondences to practice decoding words in isolation and in text and teach students the meaning of unknown words to provide context for their reading. Instruction in the meaning of words should not be time-consuming when the focus of instruction is phonics, but should rather be a quick introduction with a picture or other visual or easy definitions—just enough to give the students context. More in-depth vocabulary instruction can take place in a preview or review session. The use of decodable text lets teachers model how to blend and segment sounds, sound out words when unknown, and use onset-rimes or word chunks to decode words.

Reading decodable text should include discussions about the text to promote comprehension and reinforce the idea that the purpose of reading is to get meaning (TEA, 2000). While decodable books offer students opportunities to expand their new skills in decoding, gradually introduce them to books and stories that are less controlled to extend both their reading skills and exposure to new vocabulary.

Irregular Words

Not all words can be read completely using a decoding strategy. Irregular words are less phonetically regular, that is, some or all the letters in the word do not represent their most commonly used sound. Irregular words may be the most difficult for English language learners, because students have to learn these words by sight and in many cases the words will not be a part of either their receptive or expressive vocabularies.

These elements are important components in beginning reading instruction, whether students are just learning to read or have just immigrated to the United States and are learning to read in English. Systematically teaching children the structure of English beginning with letter-sound correspondences through the reading of connected text gives students a framework for making sense of English orthography. Daily, integrated lessons that include explicit introduction of letter-sound relationships and provide opportunities to blend the sounds to read words, to build words, to read decodable texts, and to practice spelling words will enhance students' beginning reading experience (Blevins, 1998).

The rate at which children move through the stages described above will depend on their age, knowledge of the reading process, and level of English proficiency. Older students with limited English proficiency may need only minimal instruction in the elements that are different from those in their home language. Younger students will need instruction similar to that which is provided to English monolingual children.

How Can I Teach Phonics and Word Study?

By emphasizing all of the processes that contribute to growth in reading, teachers will have the best chance of making every child a reader. (NRP, 2000, p. 2–92)

In this section, we focus on the sequence of instruction and provide guidelines for integrating the four subprocesses essential in teaching phonics and word study to beginning readers: letter-sound knowledge or alphabetic understanding; regular word reading; irregular word reading; and reading in decodable text.

Instructional Factors

Letter-sound knowledge helps English language learners understand that individual letters or clusters of letters that make up words represent the separate sounds of spoken language. Students who have alphabetic understanding know that to read a word they must first identify the most common sound of each letter and then blend the sounds together to form the word. Figure 3.3 provides the most frequent spellings of the 44 sounds of English and a key word to guide pronunciation. Remember, teach the most common sound for each letter first, and highlight to the extent possible the similarities or differences between students' home language and English when appropriate.

In introducing letters, a combination of a vowel and a few consonants allows ELLs to form a number of words. These combinations might include /m/, /s/, /a/, and /t/, so students can form words even if they only know a few letter-sound correspondences. In addition, teach new learners sounds that are easier to articulate first. Continuous sounds such as /m/ and /s/ are easy to articulate and hear because the sound can be held without distortion. Stop sounds such as /p/ and /b/ are easily distorted when the sound is held. Use your judgment and knowledge of students' ability. If a student is experiencing great difficulty remembering the letter-sound associations, limit the number of letter-sound relationships taught and focus on correspondences that are easier to pronounce. However, if the difficulty is in pronunciation, give the student more explicit instruction on how to pronounce the word, focusing on how to form the sound, but keep the instruction moving.

In addition, separate confusing letter-sound associations during initial instruction and be sure your students are comfortable with the first one before teaching the second. Characteristics that might cause confusion are visual similarity and auditory similarity. Visually similar letters can differ in the vertical direction of their extension (b/p, d/q), their left-right orientation (b/d, p/q), or their top-bottom orientation (w/m, u/n) (Blevins, 1998). Auditorily similar sounds can also cause some student difficulty. For example, some students may have difficulty hearing the differences among /b/, /p/, and /d/. In addition, students may confuse the sound of letters if the sound of a letter in English is similar to the sound of a different letter in another language. For example, the /long e/ sound in English is the same as the sound for i in Spanish. While it would be difficult to know all the letter-sound correspondences for all the language groups represented in your class, if you notice that students from the same language group are having similar problems with particular letter-sound correspondences, it would be worth investigating the source of confusion by asking an adult speaker of the language.

A basic lesson to introduce letter-sound correspondences to ELLs once they are familiar with the names and forms follows:

FIGURE 3.3 ➤ **Guide to Pronunciation of English Sounds**

Sound	Key Word	Most Frequent Spelling	Other Spellings
/i/	it	i (66%)	y
/t/	tip	t (97%)	tt, ed
/p/	pig	p (96%)	pp
/n/	nose	n (97%)	nn, kn, gn
/s/	see	s (73%)	c, ss
/a/	at	a (96%)	
/l/	lip	l (91%)	ll
/d/	did	d (98%)	dd, ed
/f/	fly	f (78%)	ff, ph, lf
/h/	him	h (98%)	wh
/g/	get	g (88%)	gg, gh
/o/	on	o (79%)	
/k/	kit	c (73%)	cc, k, ck, lk, q
/m/	man	m (94%)	mm
/r/	rat	r (97%)	rr, wr
/b/	bin	b (97%)	bb
/e/	elm	e (91%)	ea, e_e
/y/	yet	y (44%)	i
/j/	jar	g (88%)	j, dg
/u/	us	u (86%)	o, ou
/w/	wet	w (92%)	
/v/	vet	v (99.5%)	f (of)
/z/	zoom	z (23%)	zz, s
/th/	thorn	th (100%)	
/ch/	chill	ch (55%)	t
/sh/	shop	sh (26%)	ti, ssi, s, si, sci
/zh/	azure	si (49%)	s, ss, z
/hw/	wheel	wh (100%)	
/ng/	song	n (41%)	ng
/oi/	boil	oi (62%)	oy
/ou/	house	ou (56%)	ow
/ōō/	soon	oo (38%)	u, o, ou, u_e, ew, ue
/ŏŏ/	book	oo (31%)	u, ou, o, ould
/ā/	aim	a (45%)	a_e, ai, ay, ea
/ē/	ear	e (70%)	y, ea, ee, ie, e_e, ey, i, ei
/ī/	ice	i_e (37%)	i, igh, y, ie, y_e
/ō/	oat	o (73%)	o_e, ow, oa, oe
/yōō/	use	u (69%)	u_e, ew, ue
/ŧħ/	the	th (100%)	
/û/	bird	er (40%)	ir, ur
/ä/	car	a (89%)	
/ /	alarm	a (24%)	e, i, o, u
/ə/	chair	a (29%)	are, air

Source: Adapted from *Phonics from A to Z: A Practical Guide*, by W. Blevins, 1998, New York: Scholastic Professional Books.

1. Present the letter and tell students the sound. Hold up a letter card. Say, "This letter is *m*. The sound for *m* is /mmm/."
2. Ask students to tell you the name and then the sound. Be sure they know the difference between the name and the sound.
3. Ask students to write the letter as they say the sound.

If students at the beginning of 1st grade still do not know any letter names or only know a few, or if you are teaching older students who are new to English, teach letter names and letter sounds simultaneously. In particular, with older ELLs, move the introduction of letter-sound correspondences at a quicker pace so students can apply them to the texts they are reading.

Once children know three or four letter-sound associations, begin regular word-reading and word-building activities. For example, if students have learned the letter-sound correspondences for *i*, *t*, *p*, *n*, and *s*, they can begin to apply this knowledge to read words such as *it*, *in*, *pit*, *pin*, *sit*, *sip*, and *tip*. Teaching them the short sound for *a* can more than double the number of words they can read and write. Older students who know how to read in their home language may not need explicit instruction in word reading. It is more likely that they will need opportunities to apply the letter-sound correspondences they are learning in context.

After students have learned enough letter-sound correspondences to form words, integrate regular word reading into the lesson. A basic regular word-reading lesson to teach students to blend the sounds follows:

1. Sound out words without stopping between sounds. If you use words with letters that have continuous sounds at the beginning of the word, like *sit*, this step will be easier.
2. After students have sounded out the word, ask them to read it quickly. For example, present the word *sit*. Students say each sound without stopping, *sssiiit*, then say the whole word quickly: *sit*.
3. Transition students from sounding out words aloud to sounding out words silently before saying them quickly.

General guidelines for planning and teaching regular word reading follow:

- During initial instruction, first choose words that are short vowel–consonant words and consonant–short vowel–consonant words: *it* to *sit* and *pit*; *in* to *pin* and *tin*; *at* to *sat* and *pat*. Then go on to patterns that include blends and digraphs: CCVC (*stop*), CVCC (*mast*), CVC silent *e* (*bike*), CCVCC (*truck*).
- Progress from simple to more complex sound spellings.
  - Teach consonant sounds (/b/, /m/, /s/) before blends (*br*, *cl*, *sn*) or digraphs (*sh*, *ch*).
  - Teach short vowel sounds, then long vowel sounds followed by variant vowels (*ea*, *oa*) and diphthongs (*oi*, *oy*).
- Select words that have stop sounds at the end of the word.
- Select words that represent vocabulary familiar to the children and that they are likely to encounter in their reading (Blevins, 1998; Chard & Osborn, 1999).

- Clarify or review the meanings of all words used in the lesson.

Students who are taught to apply their letter-sound knowledge and are given opportunities to practice using them will be able to read and write sentences even before they learn all the letter-sound correspondences. This procedure not only allows ELLs to practice the skills they are learning in isolation and in context, but it also introduces the elements of English gradually and systematically so they can internalize the structure of English.

As not all words can be completely sounded out, include instruction in irregular word reading, because about a fourth of the most frequently used words in children's writing and texts are irregular (Moats, 2000). The list includes words such as *the*, *to*, *was*, *do*, *they*, *you*, and *is*. Since students cannot apply their knowledge of letter-sound relationships to these words, they will have to learn them as whole words. Guidelines for selecting and teaching irregular words follow:

- Select and teach words that appear frequently in stories and informational texts.
- Teach students the meanings of the words, as they are not likely to encounter them in either their receptive or expressive vocabularies.
- Determine the number of words taught in each lesson based on the abilities of the student.
- Teach new irregular words before they appear in a story. Discuss the word and any special features and point out parts of the word that are regular.

- Review previously taught words on a daily basis.
- Provide students with opportunities to use these words in their reading and writing activities (Blevins, 1998; Chard & Osborn, 1999).

Learning letter-sound relationships in isolation is necessary but not enough for English language learners. They also need to apply their knowledge to reading text. Provide students with opportunities to practice reading connected text. Begin with decodable text and gradually move to less-controlled text as students' ability and confidence grow. Because most decodable texts contain irregular words, be sure to teach those in advance if students do not know them. After reading as a group, give students opportunities to reread the text.

Several activities to teach these elements are provided in the instructional activities section of this chapter.

Progress Monitoring

Monitoring student progress will help you plan instruction and alert you if a student is falling behind. You can then use the information to group students for instruction and to modify the pace of instruction based on the level of students in each group. You can monitor student progress in each area informally. To assess the acquisition of letter-sound relationships, you can maintain a list of letter-sound associations that have been taught and mastered. About every two weeks, ask your ELLs to identify the sounds of letters or to give the letter name of the sound provided. You can also give students a letter dictation. You provide a letter name or sound, and they write the corresponding letter.

Monitor regular and irregular words separately, but use the same process for each type of word. Monitor word reading in isolation by asking students to read a set of words that have been taught. The goal is for students to read the words automatically. In most instances, that will be within three seconds. You can also keep a record of the words students miss repeatedly while reading connected text. Progress monitoring will also help you get a sense of how students are doing in terms of learning and applying the structure of English orthography in their reading and writing. Research with English language learners representing various language groups demonstrates that progress-monitoring measures in basic phonics skills such as letter naming and regular and irregular word reading are valid predictors of later reading ability. These measures let you know what students know and do not know but do not necessarily indicate that the student will have trouble learning. How they respond to well-thought-out instruction will be a better indicator of how well they are able to learn.

What Are Some Useful Phonics and Word Study Activities?

Basic Lesson in Letter-Sound Knowledge: Fish for Letters

Objective. Given a letter, students will identify the letter name and sound.

Materials. Multiple copies of letters students have learned on cards, fishbowl

Sequence. Introduce one vowel and three to four consonants initially. As students master letters, add new letters.

1. After reviewing letters learned, tell students that they will pick a card from the fish bowl and say the name and sound.
2. Model for the students. Pick a card, show it to the students, and say the letter name and then the sound.
3. Ask students to take a turn.
4. If students give the incorrect name or sound, provide it. Ask all students to repeat and have student return card to the bowl.
5. If the student gives the correct name and sound, he or she keeps the card.
6. Continue until all cards are gone.

Scaffold. Give only letter names or sounds.

Regular Word Reading: Read the Word (Phoneme Level)

Objective. Given a regular word, students will read the word.

Materials. Word cards

Sequence.

- VC: *in, at, am, it, up, ox*
- CVC: *mat, hop, cut, sit, pin, can, ten, get, not, cup, cut, tap, red, him, cob, run, gum, ham, mad, hid, dip, box, bug, big*
- CCVC: *stop, flap, snap, trip*
- CVCC: *mast, jump, bunk, fall, hand, will, bend, rock, told, dash, back, duck*
- CVC silent *e*: *bike, take, joke, made, time, more, cape, kite, five, name*

- CCVCC: *truck*, *sport*, *blast*, *small*

1. Tell students they will be reading new words.
2. Tell students that when shown a word card, they will first sound out each letter-sound correspondence and then read the word quickly.
3. Show students a word card. Model saying each sound continuously as you point to each letter, for example, *iiiinnnn*.
4. After sounding out the word, read the word fast: *in*.
5. Show a word and ask the students to say each sound. Make sure each sound is correct. If a student makes an error, review the correct letter-sound correspondence and repeat.
6. After students have sounded out the word, ask them to read the word fast. If a student reads the word incorrectly, ask him or her to sound it out and then read the word fast.
7. Review the meaning of the word. Ask if anyone knows what the word means. If no one gives a definition, give a quick definition using a picture, gesture, synonym, or short description.
8. Continue with the remaining word cards.

Scaffolds. (1) Review the individual letter-sound correspondences for the letters used to form the words. (2) Students point to each sound as it is pronounced and sweep their fingers under the word when they read it fast. (3) Students use letter tiles and pull down each letter tile as they say the sound and then sweep their finger under the tiles when they say the word fast.

Regular Word Reading: Read the Word (Onset-Rime Level)

Objective. The student will identify a particular word pattern given a group of words (see Figure 3.4).

Materials. Blank index cards, marker

Sequence.

- VC: *in*, *at*, *am*, *it*, *up*, *ox*
- CVC: *mat*, *hop*, *cut*, *sit*, *pin*, *can*, *ten*, *get*, *not*, *cup*, *cut*, *tap*, *red*, *him*, *cob*, *run*, *gum*, *ham*, *mad*, *hid*, *dip*, *box*, *bug*, *big*
- CCVC: *stop*, *flap*, *snap*, *trip*
- CVCC: *mast*, *jump*, *bunk*, *fall*, *hand*, *will*, *bend*, *rock*, *told*, *dash*, *back*, *duck*
- CVC silent *e*: *bike*, *take*, *joke*, *made*, *time*, *more*, *cape*, *kite*, *five*, *name*
- CCVCC: *truck*, *sport*, *blast*, *small*

1. Tell students that many English words contain a group of letters that look and sound the same. Explain that learning to read this group of letters or the pattern of the word will help them read other words.
2. Introduce the pattern for the lesson. "Today we will learn the ending pattern *-ap*. The sounds are /a/ /p/. When you blend them together, they say /ap/."
3. Ask students to tell you other words with the ending pattern /ap/.
4. Write student contributions on the index cards, one word per card.
5. If students give a nonsense word, acknowledge that the pattern is correct but that it is not a real word in English. Write the word.
6. When students cannot provide any more words, ask students to read the word cards.

FIGURE 3.4 ➤ **Most Common Rimes**

-ack	back/sack/stack/black	-ide	side/ride/wide/slide
-an	an/can/man/ran/plan/than	-ight	right/light/night/bright
-aw	saw/paw/draw/straw	-ill	fill/hill/bill/will/still
-ain	main/rain/train/plain/strain	-in	in/pin/fin/bin
-ake	make/take/bake/cake	-ine	fine/line/mine/nine/pine
-ale	pale/tale/scale	-ing	sing/king/ring/bring/thing
-all	all/ball/fall/wall/small	-ink	sink/rink/think
-ame	name/same/came/game	-ip	dip/lip/sip/ship/trip/strip
-ank	tank/bank/rank/plank	-ir	fir/stir
-ap	map/tap/cap/clap/snap	-it	it/sit/hit/fit
-ash	cash/bash/dash/trash	-ob	job/cob/sob/knob
-at	at/bat/sat/hat/rat/that	-ock	rock/sock/knock
-ate	date/late/gate/state	-oke	woke/poke/joke/broke
-ay	day/way/say/stay/play	-op	cop/hop/chop/stop/shop
-eat	eat/beat/heat/meat	-ore	more/store/shore
-ell	well/tell/spell	-uck	duck/luck/truck
-est	rest/test/west/pest	-ug	bug/hug/rug/drug
-ice	ice/nice/rice/mice	-ump	jump/bump/dump/stump
-ick	pick/kick/sick/stick	-unk	punk/chunk/trunk

Source: From *Essential Reading Strategies for the Struggling Reader: Activities for an Accelerated Reading Program—Expanded Edition* by the University of Texas Center for Reading and Language Arts, 2001, Austin, TX: Texas Education Agency.

Have them segment the word at the onset-rime level. Then blend them together to read the word.

7. Review all the cards again; this time ask student to read the entire word when it is shown.

8. Review the meaning of all the words.

Source. Adapted from *Essential Reading Strategies for the Struggling Reader: Activities for an Accelerated Reading Program–Expanded Edition*, by University of Texas Center for Reading and Language Arts, 2001, Austin, TX: Author.

Regular Word Reading: Building Words

Objective. Students will practice reading words containing rime patterns.

Materials. A set of cards of previously studied onsets and a set of cards with previously studied rime patterns

Sequence. Onsets: single letter, blends (*bl, fl, sn, st*), digraphs (*gr, br*)

Rimes:

- VC: *-an, -ap, -at, -aw, -in, -ip, -ir, -op, -or, -ug, -it, -et, -ot, -up, -ut*
- VCV: *-ake, -ale, -ame, -ate, -ice, -ide, -ine, -ore, -oke, -ade, -ike, -ime*
- VVC: *-ail, -ain, -eat, -eek, -een, -oot, -eed, -eep, -ait, -eet, -eem, -oop*
- VCC: *-ack, -ank, -ash, -ell, -est, -ick, -ill, -ing, -ink, -ock, -unk, -ump, -uck*

1. Review the onset and rime cards.

2. Place the two sets of cards face down in the middle of the table.

3. Explain to the students that they will pick the top card from each pile, put them together, and read the word.

4. Model the activity.

5. Ask each student to take a turn. If all students can do the activity, have students take turns picking cards and reading the words. After the word is read, the student identifies it as a real or made-up word.

Scaffolds. (1) Limit the number of rimes used—either rimes with the same vowels or the set of rimes. (2) Limit the number of onsets used. (3) Ask all students to read each word formed.

Regular Word Reading: Changing Word

Objective. Students will practice reading previously taught regular words.

Materials. Chart paper or chalkboard with a ladder drawn on it, marker or chalk

Sequence. Change only the onset, change only letters in the rime, change letters in both the onset and rime

1. Tell students they will be making new words by changing one letter at a time.

2. On the bottom rung, write a word with a pattern they have learned.

3. Model how you will change one letter to form a new word. Ask students to read the word.

4. Ask a student to change one letter to make a new word. Move up the ladder.

5. Students will continue providing new words until they reach the top rung.

6. Ask students to review the meanings of the words on their board.

Variation. Accept both real and nonsense words.

Challenge. Impose a time limit to read the word.

Irregular Word Reading: What's the Word?

Objective. Students will learn irregular words
Materials. Word cards (three to five per lesson), pocket chart, notebook with each page marked with one letter of the alphabet, pencils
Sequence. Begin with most common irregular words

1. Tell students they will be learning some words that do not follow the letter-sound correspondences they have been learning, so they have to learn these words as a whole.
2. Show students the first word card and read the word. Ask students to repeat the word in unison.
3. Spell the word as you point to each letter and then ask the students to spell the word in unison.
4. Ask the students to read the word again. Then students write it in their notebooks on the appropriate page. Monitor to make sure they spell the words correctly.
5. Ask students if anyone knows the meaning of the word. If no one knows the meaning of the word, provide a quick definition.
6. Ask students to make a quick note in their notebooks to help them remember

the meaning. Students may want to write the meaning in their home language.
7. Place the word card in the pocket chart.
8. Follow steps 2–7 with the other words.
9. Review the words taught. Point to each word in the pocket chart and ask the students to read it in unison. Then ask individual students to read the word and provide the meaning.

Variation. Use words that will appear in text that students will be reading.

Analogy-Based Phonics: What Do I Already Know?

Objective. Students will use analogy to sound out unknown words.
Materials. Words with patterns students know written on cards (three to four per student)
Sequence. CVC words with rime patterns that are decodable (*bat*), CCVC words with rime patterns that are decodable (*stop*), CVCC words with rime patterns that are decodable (*bump*), words with irregular rimes (*night*)

1. Tell students they will be reading new words using what they know about spelling patterns to help them sound out the words.
2. Review the clue word (*night*) by showing the students the word card and asking, "What is our clue word?"
3. After students respond, ask, "What are the letters in night?"
4. After students respond, underline the *-ight* and tell students that the new words they will be reading also end in *-ight*.

5. Ask students to repeat the ending.

6. Ask students to read the words as you present them one at a time. Remind them to sound out the initial sound or sounds and then use what they know about the ending to read the word.

7. Ask students to tell you the strategy they used to read the new words.

8. Review the meanings of the new words in the lesson.

Scaffolds. (1) Begin with simple rimes and syllable patterns such as -VC and new words that have a one-letter onset. (2) Use new words with onsets that are blends or digraphs. (3) Use rimes and word-spelling patterns that are irregular.

Analogy-Based Phonics: Strategy Use in Context

Objective. Students will use analogy to sound out unknown words they encounter in texts.

Materials. Texts that have several words with a rime or spelling pattern students know

Sequence. Texts that have only one or two patterns; texts with more patterns for which students will have to use their knowledge of various rimes and patterns

1. Tell students they will be reading a book that has words they have not read before.

2. Remind them to look for the part of the word they can already read.

3. Tell students to sound out the first part of the word and add the part they know to read the word.

4. Remind them that you will review the meaning of the words after you read the story.

Irregular Word Reading: Irregular Word Road Race

Objective. Students will practice reading irregular words that have been previously taught.

Materials. For each student: a game board, word cards matched to game board, a chip or game piece (see Figure 3.5)

1. Explain the game to students. Tell them: "You will place a chip in the start box, read the word in the first box, then read each word card aloud until you find the card with the word that matches the word in the first box. Now, you move the chip into the box containing the first word." Explain that they then go on to read the word in the second box, and read the word cards again until they find its matching word card. Continue to the end of the game board. Note that cards are not discarded but are placed in the back of the pile.

2. Model the procedures in step 1 for students.

3. Review the meanings of the words.

4. Give each student a game board, a set of cards, and a chip. Remind students to read each card in the set aloud.

5. Monitor students.

Variations. Fill the squares with regular words or specific onset-rime patterns; for kindergarten students and struggling 1st

FIGURE 3.5 ➤ Road Race Game Board

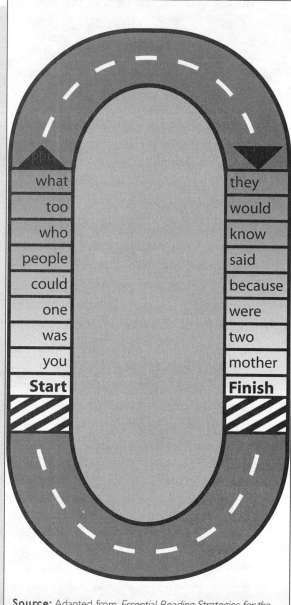

what	they
too	would
who	know
people	said
could	because
one	were
was	two
you	mother
Start	**Finish**

Source: Adapted from *Essential Reading Strategies for the Struggling Reader: Activities for an Accelerated Reading Program—Expanded Edition*, by University of Texas Center for Reading and Language Arts, 2001, Austin, TX: Texas Education Agency.

graders, fill each square with a letter (students provide either the name or sound as directed).

Scaffolds. (1) Pair a more able reader with a struggling reader. Students take turns so the more able student reads the word cards until finding the first word. Then the second student reads the word cards for the second word. (2) Limit the number of words.

Challenge. Impose a time limit to read the word.

Lesson for Learning the Doubling Rule (*-ing* and *-ed*)

Objective. Students will learn the doubling rule for adding *-ing* or *-ed* to CVC verbs and will practice writing CVC + *-ing* or *-ed* words independently.

Materials. Flip chart, blackboard, or dry-erase board; writing notebooks and pencils; marker

1. Tell students they will learn the doubling rule for adding endings to CVC words. Explain that in English, when we add *-ing* or *-ed* to a CVC word, we double the last consonant then add the ending. Model the process using only one of the endings and a pattern that students know well.
2. Give students a word. Ask them to write the word in their notebooks. Then ask them to add the ending.
3. Ask a student to write the word on the chart.
4. Ask students to check their work.
5. Give students several more words.
6. Review the meanings of all the words.

Review Lesson for the Doubling Rule

Objective. Review the doubling rule for adding *-ing* or *-ed* to a CVC verb.

Materials. Flip chart, blackboard, or dry-erase board; writing notebooks and pencils; marker

Sequence. Complete the activity as a group, complete activity in pairs, add CVCC words

1. Review the doubling rule with students. Remind them that in English when they add an ending to a CVC word they must double the last letter.
2. Write a CVC verb on board. Ask students what they must do to add an ending. Rewrite the word with the ending.
3. Tell students that they will have a tick-tack-toe tournament.
4. Draw a tick-tack-toe board, and write a CVC verb in each square.
5. Tell students that to gain a square, they have to change the verb by adding either *-ing* or *-ed* correctly. If the new word is written correctly, the student may draw an X or O. If the student does not add the ending correctly, the square remains open. In the first round, students play against the teacher.
6. Have students determine whether an answer is correct or not by showing thumbs up or thumbs down. Continue until someone wins the game by getting three in a row.

Variation. Students play in pairs.

Scaffold. Use only one type of ending.

Structural Analysis: Let's Add Word Parts

Objective. Students learn that affixes (prefixes and suffixes) change the word meaning.

Materials. Chart paper, marker, a list of root words students can read and give the meaning for each

Sequence. Most-common prefixes, most-common suffixes, less-common prefixes, less-common suffixes

1. Tell students that adding word parts to a word will change the meaning of the word. Tell students that prefixes appear at the beginning of the word and that they will learn the meaning of the prefix and then add it to root words.
2. Write a prefix on the chart paper. Read the prefix and tell students its meaning.
3. Ask students to read the prefix and tell its meaning.
4. Write a root word on the chart paper. Ask students to read the word and give its meaning. If students do not know the meaning, provide it.
5. Write the root word with the prefix. Ask students to read the word.
6. Model how to determine the meaning of the new word. For example, *un-* means "not"; *happy* means "with joy"; so *unhappy* means "not happy" or "without joy."
7. Provide additional root words and ask students to read and define the prefix, read the root word, read the word with prefix added, and define the new word.
8. Repeat steps 2–7 with the second prefix.

Variation. Use suffixes.

Scaffold. Limit the number of prefixes introduced.

Advanced Word Analysis: Make a New Word

Objective. Students will add previously taught prefixes or suffixes to a root word and will give the meaning of the new word.

Materials. Root words written on cards (three to four per student), small sticky notes with a prefix or suffix written on them

Sequence. Most-common prefixes, most-common suffixes, less-common prefixes, less-common suffixes

1. Tell students they will be reviewing the meaning of prefixes and suffixes they have learned and will practice reading words with prefixes and suffixes.

2. Review the prefixes and suffixes written on the sticky notes. Ask students to read them in unison and provide the meaning.

3. Ask students to read the root words in unison. Then give each student three to four root word cards.

4. Tell students you will pick an affix from the pile; each one in turn will add it to one of his or her root word cards, read the new word, and say its meaning.

5. If a student has difficulty providing the meaning, ask the student the meaning of the affix, then the meaning of the root word. If the student still cannot provide the meaning, model the process. For example, *un-* means "not" and *happy* means "with joy"; *unhappy* means "not happy" or "without joy."

6. Continue with the other affixes.

Scaffolds. (1) Limit the number of affixes used. (2) Use only prefixes or suffixes.

Advanced Word Analysis: Word Part *Jeopardy!*

Objective. Students will identify prefixes, suffixes, and roots in words and their meanings.

Materials. Category cards for each of the three categories: prefixes, suffixes, and root words; answer cards for each category; dollar amount cards (for sample Q&A see Figure 3.6)

1. Place game pieces on the board as you explain the game.

2. Tell students they will be playing *Jeopardy!* to test their knowledge of word parts and their meanings.

3. Divide students into teams.

4. Tell them that under each dollar amount there is an answer to a question related to its subject category card.

5. They will pick a category and dollar amount, expose and read the answer, then give the question to the answer.

6. If they get the answer correct, they get the dollar card. If they answer incorrectly, another team gets a chance to answer.

7. Game continues until all the cards are exposed.

FIGURE 3.6 ➤ **Sample Answers and Questions**

Sample Answers	Sample Questions
The suffix -er or -or means this.	What is "a person who does something"?
Narrator	Who is "someone who narrates"?
The prefix re- means this.	What is "again"?
The prefix in *bicycle* means this.	What is "two"?
Give an example of a word using the prefix *trans*.	What is "transport"?
A prefix is found in this part of the word.	What is the beginning?
This is the main base of a word.	What is the root?
The root in geography.	What is "graph"?
This root means "write."	What is "graph"?

Advanced Word Analysis: Is It Real?

Objective. Students will use the prefixes they have been studying to make words.

Materials. Word cards using prefixes from previous lessons; game board with words that combine with prefix cards to make real words, and some that combine to make nonsense words; dice or spinner; game pieces

1. Review what a prefix is. Review the prefixes from the previous lessons. Make sure that students can read, spell, and define each prefix.
2. Ask students to read the word cards in unison. Periodically ask a student to define the word or to use it in a sentence.
3. Introduce the game and explain the rules.
4. Distribute a prefix card to each student or pair of students. Tell students they will take turns rolling the dice or spinning and then moving their game piece the appropriate number of spaces. Then they combine the prefix on their card with the word on the space and read the new word. The students must decide if it is a real word or a nonsense word. If it is a real word, they must define it and use it in a sentence. If unable to complete all steps correctly, they can ask a peer for help. If it is not a real word, the student tells what it would mean if the prefix were used correctly.
5. Continue until one of the students reaches the end.

Scaffold. Pair students of high and low levels of English proficiency.

Annotated Bibliography

Bear, D. R., Templeton, S., Ivernizzi, M., & Johnston, F. (2008). *Words their way: Word study for phonics, vocabulary, and spelling instruction.* Upper Saddle River, NJ: Prentice-Hall.

This book gives information on how to provide word study instruction to students based on their spelling developmental stages. The text provides a description of the basis for this approach to instruction, instructions for assessing students prior to beginning instruction, and activities for students in each of the stages of development.

Blevins, W. (1998). *Phonics from A to Z: A practical guide.* New York: Scholastic Professional Books.

This guide provides a wealth of information for teachers in an easy-to-read and easy-to-use format. The book begins with a brief description of phonics and then provides activities, lists, and teaching guidelines for alphabet recognition, phonemic awareness, letter-sound correspondences, and regular and irregular word reading.

Cunningham, P. M. (2004). *Phonics they use: Words for reading and writing* (4th ed). Boston: Allyn and Bacon.

This research integrates the strategic approaches needed to help students develop reading and spelling skills using a coherent collection of practical, hands-on activities that provide a framework for teaching phonics. It emphasizes the importance of students using phonics for decoding, reading, and spelling a new word, and for writing. Rather than subscribe to a single theory, the book stresses a balanced reading program—incorporating a variety of strategic approaches—tied to the individual needs of children.

Diaz-Rico, L. T. (2004). *Teaching English learners: Methods and strategies, my lab school edition.* Boston: Allyn and Bacon.

Chapter 8 provides activities for teaching grammar through integrated language skills and gives a history of English to help explain the peculiarities of the language.

Donat, D. J. (2003). *Reading their way: A balance of phonics and whole language.* Lanham, MD: Rowman & Littlefield Publishers.

This book fulfills the goal of increasing reading achievement with a balanced literacy program for kindergarten and beyond, using the best of phonics and whole-language approaches. Donat presents reading-instruction strategies, scheduling and grouping options, assessments, evaluations, and sound and spelling patterns for each grade level. Teachers will find an abundance of ideas for immediate implementation in their classrooms, and school administrators will appreciate the guidance in developing quality literacy programs. Supplemented by an appendix of suggested resources and a reference section.

Henry, M. K. (2003). *Unlocking literacy: Effective decoding and spelling instruction.* Baltimore: Paul H. Brookes.

Designed for general and special educators of students from prekindergarten to middle school, this book offers a range of creative strategies for helping students learn and a refresher course on language skills. The text is filled with classroom activities; lesson plans incorporating multisensory, language-based instruction; samples of student work; explanations of current research; and extensive word lists.

Kress, J. (1993). *The ESL book of lists.* Upper Saddle River, NJ: Prentice-Hall.

This book provides useful lists for teachers on a number of topics, including the identification of difficult English sounds for specific language groups and word lists for a variety of objectives.

McCormick, C. E., Throneburg, R., & Smitley, J. (2002). *A sound start: Phonemic awareness lessons for reading success.* New York: Guilford Press.

One volume provides three separate sets of phonemic awareness lessons, complete with scripted directions and reproducible learning materials and assessment tools. Incorporating a variety of activities, each set is field-tested and research based and the lessons may be used independently or in conjunction with one another.

Moats, L. C. (2000). *Speech to print: Language essentials for teachers.* Baltimore: Brookes Publishing Co.

This comprehensive book on the English language will help you understand the organization of written and spoken language, make the connection between language structure and how children learn to read, and provide sample lesson plans and adaptations. This information is essential for teachers of English language learners.

Web Sites That Teach

www.starfall.com

This Web site provides reading instruction and reading games for students in preK–1.

www.gigglepotz.com/eslreading.htm

Offers other links for enhancing reading, such as teaching grammar and phonics.

http://reading.uoregon.edu/big_ideas/au.php

This Web site presents the definition of alphabetic principle, research findings on phonics, the importance of phonics, and how to sequence phonics skills in grades K–3.

http://reading.uoregon.edu/instruction/instruc_ap.php

This Web site provides information on critical phonics skills and critical features of phonics instruction.

www.texasreading.org/tcrla/publications/primary/
    primary_phonics.htm

This Web site allows readers to download the professional development guide on phonics and decoding instruction. This guide provides a variety of phonics and decoding

strategies and instructional materials, including information on English language learners.

www.ed.gov/offices/OESE/SASA/rb/slide009.html

This Web site provides research findings on phonics instruction (e.g., approaches to phonics instruction, cautions about phonics instruction).

www.nrrf.org/aboutphonics.htm

This Web site introduces science-based phonics instruction and contains links to several papers on phonics instruction and a list of phonics product companies.

www.ldonline.org/ld_indepth/reading/ldrp_chard_
    guidelines.html

This Web site presents articles on effective phonics and word recognition instruction for students with reading disabilities.

http://doe.state.in.us/publications/phonics
    .html#anchor3978700

This Web site allows readers to download the Phonics Tool Kit booklet and to watch the videoclips that explain the Phonics Tool Kit. The Phonics Tool Kit booklet introduces a variety of reading strategies (including phonics strategies) and provides practical tips for teachers.

◆　　　◆　　　◆

4 | Fluency

HOW MANY OF YOUR STUDENTS RECOGNIZE LETTERS, READ WORDS, OR READ connected text with less accuracy or more slowly than needed to promote reading? Problems in fluency are not specific to English language learners (ELLs), but they may be more prevalent with these learners. Why? Because both decoding and understanding affect fluency. English language learners are more likely to have difficulty with word meaning—thus, they are more likely to be slow readers.

We think of problems with accuracy and speed of key reading tasks as difficulties with automaticity or fluency. Fluency problems can occur at the very early grades with letters and sounds or in the upper grades with word and text reading. What are some examples of reading fluency difficulties?

Lupina is a kindergarten student who has been working on learning the names of letters. In April of her kindergarten year, all of Lupina's classmates know the names of at least 20 letters. Lupina knows the names of letters, but sometimes she needs to look up at the alphabet and say the alphabet in order to remember the name of the letter. She knows the names of about 12 letters, but it often takes her several seconds to name the letter. Lupina has difficulties with fluency. She knows the names of letters but she does not know them quickly enough to name them automatically. She has this same difficulty with naming sounds. Sometimes it takes Lupina a second or more to think of the sound and say it.

Juin, a 2nd grader, reads words on a list provided by her teacher this way:

/f/ /r/ friendly

/b/ /i/ bicycle

/m/ /a/ manage

Rather than reading each word quickly, Juin sounds out the beginning letters and then blends them with the remaining sounds to read the word. She reads the word correctly, but it takes her much longer than other 2nd grade students. She reads very few words automatically or as sight words. Juin's teacher is concerned that if she does not learn to read words as sight words and improve her speed of reading, she will lose her motivation to read and her reading comprehension will be affected.

Juin is unable to read words quickly enough to be a mature reader who interacts with text. Fluent readers are able to read words quickly and accurately. They can perform fluent reading whether they are reading word lists, sentences, or passages. Juin would benefit from fluency instruction.

Do you have students who read the words correctly and as sight words, but very slowly and with little expression? Jose reads each word accurately to his teacher but his voice has no inflection, almost as though each word is a separate unit unconnected to the other words. The teacher asks Jose to read as though he were reading to a young child, but there is very little change in his voice.

Jose also has difficulty with fluency. He may need assistance in thinking about text while he reads, so the meaning of the text is reflected in his oral reading. He may also benefit from hearing good oral readers "model" reading the text fluently so he can practice reading the way they read.

You can see from the above examples that fluency is an essential element of reading for students in kindergarten through 4th grade. Fluency challenges are problematic for many English language learners—regardless of their native language. Also, fluency is not just a worry for 2nd and 3rd grade teachers. Fluency develops from the beginning stages of reading. Fluent readers read automatically, with little effort, so they can focus their attention on the meaning of text.

What Is Fluency Instruction?

There are three components to fluency: Fluent reading should involve accurate and automatic word recognition, with appropriate prosody or inflection. Each component affects comprehension in its own way. (McKenna & Stahl, 2003, p. 72)

Fluency instruction addresses the rapid and accurate reading of words in connected text. Prosody, an aspect of fluency, refers to the extent to which students read this text as though they understand what it means. Fluency in very early grades may also refer to the rapid and accurate naming of letters, sounds, words, and sentences. When students can perform reading and reading-related tasks quickly and accurately, they are on the path to fluent reading, an essential element of comprehension and mature reading.

English language learners benefit from fluency activities that address effortless decoding of words in isolation and within text. They need opportunities for oral repeated reading that includes support and feedback from teachers, peers, and parents, and time to read a wide range of interesting texts with teacher guidance and instruction. Monitoring students' progress in fluency also helps guide instruction and motivates English language learners.

You may wonder how fluency differs with English language learners. These students may have slower rates of reading in English related to their lack of knowledge about word meanings. Determining whether slow reading rates are related to decoding (word reading) versus word meaning is an important first step.

Why Should I Provide Fluency Instruction to English Language Learners?

[Reading aloud] is especially valuable for use with English language learners because it incorporates the modeling of fluent, expressive reading of English text with techniques for clarifying vocabulary, periodic checking for understanding, and the providing and activating of knowledge that helps students make connections between text and personal experience. (Herrell & Jordan, 2004, p. 199)

A recent National Assessment of Educational Progress [NAEP] report on our nation's reading ability (Institute for Education Sciences, 2005) revealed that nonwhite Hispanic students in 4th grade performed, on average, 21 points lower than white 4th graders. Though these differences are very concerning, the good news is that in 1975 the performance difference between white 4th graders and nonwhite Hispanic 4th graders was 34 points. One of the critical elements of

reading associated with improved performance on the NAEP is fluency.

Why do many English language learners struggle with fluency? There is no one answer to this question, but there are several issues for teachers to consider, as these issues influence their instruction. ELLs may struggle with fluency because they are unable to read the words accurately. Poor decoding is common with English language learners because English is one of the most challenging alphabetic languages to decode. Students may also struggle with fluency because they do not know what many of the words mean. Fluent readers focus their attention on understanding what they are reading. Readers who struggle with fluency focus their attention on decoding, leaving less attention for understanding what they read.

Perfetti (1977, 1985) suggests that slow speed of reading words interferes with automaticity and thus impairs reading comprehension. Memory is "clogged" with decoding tasks and is not available to assist with understanding reading.

Most of us learned to teach reading with a focus on accurate word reading and comprehension. Few of us received explicit instruction in how to teach students to read fluently. Research indicates that students who have reading difficulties demonstrate significant problems with fluency and continue to be slow readers into adolescence and adulthood (Shaywitz & Shaywitz, 1996; Stanovich, 1986; Torgesen, Wagner, & Rashotte, 1994).

Accurate word reading is only the first step with English language learners. We need to assure that word meaning and fluency are essential elements that bridge an important gap between word recognition and comprehension. Some students will learn to read accurately, quickly, and with prosody (good expression) with little direct instruction from teachers. However, many students require practice and support from peers and teachers to improve their fluency.

As English language learners transition to English or learn English reading initially, it is natural for reading to be slow and labored and then to become more rapid and automatic over time. Fluency instruction provides students with the practice they need to read smoothly, at a rapid pace, and with prosody.

How Can I Teach Fluency to English Language Learners?

Understanding the source of the oral reading errors that English language learners make while reading in English may help teachers to determine whether these students need help with fluency. (Garcia, 2003, p. 37)

There is more research on fluency instruction with monolingual students than with ELLs, but recent research suggests that students who are provided explicit and systematic interventions do improve their rate and accuracy of reading connected texts (Gunn et al., 2005). This section presents several practices associated with improved outcomes in reading fluency.

What Instructional Factors Contribute to Fluency for English Language Learners?

There is evidence from a number of sources that educators can re-engineer instruction, both in remedial environments and in whole-class environments, to improve children's fluency. (Stahl, 2004, p. 207)

One question that teachers might have is whether *practice in reading silently* during school or other times improves fluency. "No research evidence is available currently to confirm that instructional time spent on silent, independent reading with minimal guidance and feedback improves reading fluency and overall reading achievement" (No Child Left Behind Act of 2001, p. 13). However, this should not be interpreted to mean that extensive opportunities to read, including before and after school, during free time, at home, and whenever else possible, are not excellent strategies for promoting wide reading and improving knowledge, vocabulary, and interest in reading. This is particularly true for English language learners.

Another question teachers may have is *what texts students should read when practicing activities related to fluency*. One thing teachers should consider is the level of text that students read during fluency activities. *Independent-level* text is that which students can read easily and with few errors (fewer than 5 mistakes in every 100 words, or 95 percent correctly). *Instructional-level* text is slightly more challenging, and students typically read about 90 percent correctly, or 90 in 100 words. *Frustration-level* text is that in which the student is reading fewer than 89 percent of the words correctly, or more than 10 errors in 100 words.

When students are engaged in fluency activities alone or with a peer, teachers may want to be sure that students can read the selected text with relatively few errors. When students are working with a tutor or other knowledgeable adult, the instructional level may be somewhat more challenging. English language learners should not be engaged in fluency activities at their frustration level, particularly when they are reading alone or with a peer. While students are reading, be sure they have an opportunity to identify words they do not understand and to reflect on text so they are reading with meaning in mind.

What about the text type (information, expository, poetry, narrative) that students read for fluency? The most important thing is that the passage is interesting and at an appropriate level. Teachers may want to use poetry representing the cultural backgrounds of students for fluency practice. When selecting text, students benefit when teachers consider whether the text is a "cold" read (first time the student has read the text) or whether the student has read it before. For the purpose of improving fluency, English language learners benefit from reading and rereading text with a proficient model. When engaging in fluency activities with English language learners, it is also beneficial to provide support for word meaning. Remember, the goal in fluency is to have students improve accuracy and speed so they read effortlessly.

How much time each day should be devoted to supporting fluency? Teachers may consider dedicating approximately 20 minutes each day

to fluency-related activities. This includes such activities as model reading and rereading, model reading and choral reading, paired reading with another adult or student, readers' theater, and tape-recorded readings. Providing students with time to monitor their progress in reading fluency is also valuable. If English language learners are struggling with fluency, teachers may want to monitor their progress more frequently, such as every two weeks. If English language learners are demonstrating few problems with fluency, progress can be monitored less often.

> Regardless of how book difficulty is determined, it is critical that all children in a classroom, including the least able readers, have easy "fingertip" access to books that they can read accurately, fluently, with good comprehension.... Easy reading material develops fluency and provides practice in using good reading strategies. (Allington & Cunningham, 2002, p. 57)

What Practices Can Teachers Use to Directly Teach Fluency to English Language Learners?

Here are several practices that will benefit ELLs.

- *Provide explicit instruction.* When we teach explicitly, we fully and clearly explain what is being taught and use such practices as (1) making our thinking processes visible through well-structured think-alouds; (2) organizing lessons so we introduce a few new strategies or skills but always build on previously learned material; (3) pacing instruction in a way that interests students and maintains their attention but that is not so fast that they fall behind; (4) providing background knowledge and new vocabulary to assure meaning is part of every lesson; (5) using visual support, including pictures, gestures, graphs, and other materials, so that key ideas, words, and concepts are made real; and (6) applying feedback and correction.

- *Maintain and generalize skills.* Provide students with multiple opportunities to read passages they know well and can read with confidence to other students, family members, other adults in the school, and to you!
- *Scaffold the fluency practices of your students.* Increasing and decreasing support and guidance for your students as they progress with fluency activities is a valuable part of their learning. Dickson, Simmons, and Kame'enui (1995) suggest using four types of scaffolding: (1) teacher/peer scaffolding with extra support for new material, (2) content scaffolding that provides background knowledge and information prior to the task, (3) task scaffolding, where the difficulty of the task determines teacher support, and (4) material scaffolding, whereby cue cards and think sheets are used to support students' use of the strategy.
- *Provide adequate time to practice.* Fluency activities require adequate time to practice to assure success. Students who spend more time reading and practicing fluency activities are more likely to be more fluent readers.

- *Preteach unfamiliar words.* Teaching words students do not know is an essential element of effective fluency instruction.
- *Engage students and provide choices.* All of us benefit in our learning when we are highly engaged in what we are doing and have options and choices about what we read and how we practice. Though there are clearly activities and strategies that provide less flexibility, whenever possible, provide for student choice.
- *Use cooperative learning strategies.* It may be useful to have students work in teams of four, where they are also able to quickly break into pairs. When in cooperative groups, students learn to help each other, encourage each other, solve problems, give and accept feedback from others, and stay on task (Calderon, 1998).

What Fluency Practices Are Associated with Improved Reading Outcomes?

Reading and rereading passages with feedback and guidance is a practice associated with improved fluency outcomes. Fluency instruction for English language learners includes the following:

- Encouraging students to reread previously read passages (Lenters, 2004).
- Promoting multiple rereadings as well as listening to audiotapes of texts read by native English speakers (Koskinen et al., 1999).
- Supporting rereading of texts both orally and silently (Gersten & Jimenez, 1994).

- Reading familiar and predictable texts (Hudson & Smith, 2001).
- Using sentence strips from a previously read story to read and sequence (Kreuger & Townshend, 1997).

Following are several practices that provide good opportunities for students to reread passages, since nearly all fluency studies indicate gains for students when rereading is involved (Kuhn & Stahl, 2003):

- *Reading with a model reader.* The model reader can be the teacher, the teacher's assistant, a volunteer adult with training, or an older student. The most important thing about the model reader is that he or she is capable of reading the passage with automaticity and accuracy. The model reader reads the passage first. Then the student reads the passage. Next, the student reads the passage again as quickly and accurately as he or she can (without speed-reading). The model reader and the student can ask each other questions about what they have read, or they can summarize the key points they have read. The amount of time the model reader reads before providing the student with turns to read depends upon the age of the student. For students in grades K–1, the amount of time should be relatively short (45 seconds to 1 minute). For students in grades 2–4, the amount of time can be longer (1–3 minutes). This process can be repeated. With English language learners, it is valuable to discuss key words that students may not know prior to reading.

- *Choral reading.* In choral reading, students read a designated passage aloud. The leader is usually the teacher or another model reader. First, the teacher and the students preview the passage and make predictions about what the passage will be about. Second, the teacher reads the passage aloud. Third, the students and the teacher read aloud together. Fourth, the teacher fades his or her voice and allows the students to take the lead in reading the passage aloud. During this reading, the ELLs read as quickly as possible as a group without speed-reading. If there is time available, the teacher selects pairs of students to read the passage again. Again, it is important that teachers ensure that English language learners have adequate background knowledge and vocabulary knowledge for the passages they are reading. Also, many English language learners are sensitive about reading aloud because of their pronunciation and difficulties with English.

- *Tape-recorded readings.* These can be books on tape or books on CD-ROM accessed through the computer. In either case, the books are available to students and read aloud by a model. The main role of the teacher is to make sure students are following along and reading the text while the story is read aloud. Vocabulary and key concepts can be reviewed with students prior to the use of recorded readings. Work with students to select books or poems that they find engaging and interesting, especially books and materials that represent the cultural backgrounds of the students in the class.

- *Readers' theater or reading performances.* With readers' theater or reading performances, students rehearse the script from a book, play, short story, or poem until they are highly fluent. Consider selecting plays and performances that are related to the cultural backgrounds of students in your class. The critical aspect of readers' theater or reading performances is that students repeatedly read a text until they can recite it fluently and with expression. When using readers' theater or reading performances with English language learners, be sure they master the oral language necessary to present in front of others with success.

- *Partner reading.* When students read and reread passages with a classmate, we refer to it as partner reading. Teachers can use partner reading by pairing a more proficient reader in the class (reader A) with a less proficient reader (reader B). With English language learners, also consider that the student partner is able to assist them in word meaning, if needed. Reader A reads the passage first. Reader B rereads the same passage. Students continue taking turns reading the same passage until they complete the text. Figure 4.1 provides an overview of the guidelines for partner reading.

In summary, there are several critical elements that have been documented to improve the reading fluency of English language learners. These include the following:

- Providing an explicit model of fluent reading.
- Giving students multiple opportunities to read the same text.
- Establishing performance criteria for the speed and accuracy of reading text. This includes establishing baselines for the number of words read correctly per minute in a specified text level and then systematically monitoring progress to improve the rate and accuracy of reading as well as increasing the level of text.
- Assisting English language learners in obtaining word meaning and background for the passage before and during oral reading.
- Being mindful about engaging English language learners in oral reading practices that are too challenging or embarrassing.

Two research studies suggest that three or four rounds of repeated reading may be an effective number for many students (O'Shea, Sindelar, & O'Shea, 1987; Sindelar, Monda, & O'Shea, 1990). Students who read the same passage multiple times outperformed, in both reading fluency and story retelling, those students who had read the passage only one time.

There are some practices that teachers may use with good intentions that are *not* associated with improvements in fluency. One practice is turn taking in reading, or round-robin reading. During this practice, teachers work with a small group of students. Each student takes a turn reading aloud for a brief period, and then another student takes a turn. This is not a fluency practice. A second activity is sustained silent reading without teacher guidance or support. This may be referred to as sustained silent read-

FIGURE 4.1 ➤ Guidelines for Partner Repeated Reading

Partner Reading Procedures
- First reader reads.
- Second reader reads.
- Students discuss reading, with one student asking questions and other student answering.
- Repeat until story is complete.

Tutoring Rules
- Talk only to your partner.
- Talk only about partner reading.
- Be cooperative.

Kinds of Errors
- Saying the word wrong
- Leaving out a word
- Adding a word
- Waiting longer than four seconds

Feedback about Words
- Partner points to the word not read correctly. "Do you know this word?"
- "Yes, that word is ____." Now read the sentence again.

Considerations for English language learners: Be sure partners understand that correction should not occur for words that may be pronounced differently by a partner who is an English language learner. Determine that passages selected are meaningful and appropriate. Provide word meanings when needed.

Source: Adapted from *Strategies for Teaching Students with Learning and Behavior Problems* (6th ed., p. 181), by C. S. Bos and S. Vaughn, 2006, Boston: Allyn and Bacon.

ing (SSR) or drop everything and read (DEAR). These are not effective substitutes for the reading practices described above that are associated with improved outcomes in reading.

Providing ongoing assessment of students' progress in reading is one of the most valuable things you can do as a teacher. Students who monitor their progress with fluency improve in reading rate and accuracy. Perhaps it is a bit like monitoring our progress in weight lifting or counting calories when we are on a diet.

The most valuable way to monitor English language learners' progress in fluency is to take timed measures of the number of words they read correctly in a minute. This is very important in grades 2–4 and in grade 1 after students are able to read connected text. For English language learners, it is important that texts selected for progress monitoring have content that makes sense to them. Fluency can be reduced when students are asked to read about topics they simply do not understand or with which they have little or no experience.

When students are making good progress in reading fluently (averaging gains of more than 1.5 words per week, over several weeks), you may increase the level of text incrementally and continue to monitor progress by documenting words correct per minute (WCPM). When students meet goals (e.g., increasing from 50 to 60 words correct in a leveled passage), the difficulty of the text is increased or the goal for the number of words correct is raised (e.g., from 60 correct words per minute to 70 correct words per minute).

Norms for reading fluency (see Figure 4.2) are based on a large population of students but have not been normed separately for English language learners. Having high goals for English language learners is important; however, it should be noted that the norms provided are based largely on monolingual students and may be challenging for many English language learners to achieve. If English language learners are significantly below the norms provided in Figure 4.2, their reading progress should be monitored every two weeks. Once per month is simply crucial in slightly below average readers. The following procedures should be implemented for progress monitoring of oral reading fluency passages:

1. Select two to three passages that are unfamiliar to the student but that are on the student's level. All passages should be at the same level. You can use passages that are described in the activities section of this chapter.

2. Make two copies of each of the passages.

3. Give one copy of the first passage to the student and keep the second copy to mark errors.

4. Tell the student, "When I say 'begin,' start reading aloud at the top of the page. Do your best reading. Read as quickly as you can but do not race."

5. Use a stopwatch to time the student's reading for one minute.

6. While the student reads, mark errors on your copy of the passage.

7. If the student does not read the word in three seconds, tell the student the word and then mark it as an error. Typically, with monolingual English students, mispronunciations, substitutions, omissions, and reversals are all considered errors. Consider students' accents and error types based on their knowledge of English and be sensitive to over-marking errors that are related to lack of familiarity with word meanings or English pronunciation. Do not count as errors when students self-correct or repeat.

8. If the student is in the middle of the sentence when the time is up, let him or her finish the sentence, but only count the words correct up to when time was over.

9. Count the number of words read correctly during the one-minute period. Repeat the above procedure with one or two more passages. Average the number of words read correctly.

10. Chart the average number of words read correctly per minute for each student. For students who are below average, monitor their progress every two weeks and implement additional fluency activities. Figure 4.3 presents a sample chart that documents a student's fluency progress over time.

11. It is particularly important with English language learners that words pronounced

FIGURE 4.2 ➤ **Sample Reading Fluency Chart**

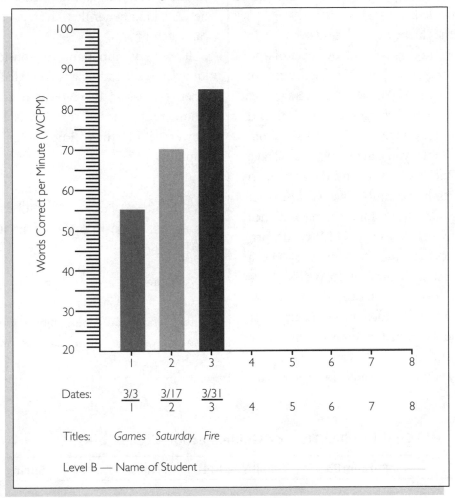

differently in the student's dialect are not considered reading errors.

Note: In the next section of this chapter on assessment, a number of ways to obtain passages that have been leveled for monitoring oral reading fluency are provided.

One way to determine if rate and accuracy are within the norm for the students' grade level is to compare their WCPM to the national norms available. The national norms grades 1–4 are provided in Figure 4.3. Unfortunately, these norms are for all students and are not disaggregated for English language learners.

As you can see in the table, the number of words read correctly per minute varies by time of year (fall, winter, spring) and by grade (grades 2–4). There are no norms for 1st grade, since many 1st graders are not reading connected text fluently that early. The reading norms for the

25th percentile, 50th percentile, and 75th percentile are provided.

Let us use the fluency guidelines table to help our teacher, Ms. Rodriguez. In November of 2nd grade, she is concerned about the fluency rate of three of her students: Maria, who averages 44 WCPM; Omar, who averages 26 WCPM; and Gustavo, whose average is 51 WCPM. From examining the table, you can see that the average in the fall of 2nd grade is 55 and the average in the winter is 78. In November, we would expect average 2nd graders to be approaching 53. Since Maria is slightly below average (44 WCPM), prioritizing fluency activities for her would be a good strategy. Since Omar is at 26 WCPM, he is considered quite low (just over the 25th percentile), and additional activities and time for fluency should be initiated immediately. Since Gustavo is close to average, he can continue with the fluency activities already in place with careful monitoring and guidance to ensure that he is making better-than-average progress so he can catch up.

It is very important to consider students' knowledge of reading and knowledge of English when evaluating the rate of reading. Students whose proficiency in English is low will read slower until their knowledge of English improves.

What Measures Can Teachers Use to Assist with Progress Monitoring of Fluency?

Accurate, fast, and even prosodic reading that does not result in the reader's understanding the text is not good enough, though in some cases such word-level fluency may be necessary for attaining comprehension. (Pressley, 2006, p. 195)

FIGURE 4.3 ➤ Oral Reading Fluency Guidelines for Grades 2–4

Grade	Percentile	Fall WCPM	Winter WCPM	Spring WCPM
2	75	82	106	124
	50	53	78	94
	25	23	46	65
3	75	107	123	142
	50	79	93	114
	25	65	70	87
4	75	125	133	143
	50	99	112	118
	25	72	89	92

Source: Data compiled from *Oral Reading Fluency: 90 Years of Assessment* (BRT Technical Report No. 33), Behavioral Research & Teaching, January 2005, Eugene, OR: Author.

- *AIMSweb Assessment System (AIMSweb Progress Monitoring and Improvement System)*. This system informs instruction through ongoing progress-monitoring data. It provides curriculum-based measurement on oral reading fluency for all grade levels. The system also provides assessments and progress monitoring for fluency with curriculum-based measures in Spanish, including letter-naming fluency, letter-sound fluency, syllable segmentation and reading fluency, syllable and word spelling, and oral reading fluency. Web site: http://aimsweb.com

- *DIBELS Oral Reading Fluency (DORF) and Retell Fluency, 6th ed.* (Good et al., 2003). The one-minute oral reading fluency measure is part of the Dynamic Indicators of Basic Early Literacy Skills (DIBELS). It is a standardized, individually administered test designed to monitor students' accuracy and fluency reading of connected text. The oral reading fluency test is followed by a retell fluency comprehension check. Both measures are for children from mid-1st grade through 3rd grade. The tests are given in the winter and spring of 1st grade and the fall, winter, and spring of 2nd and 3rd grades. Materials include student and examiner copies of grade-level passages. Students read a grade-level passage aloud for one minute. Teachers mark errors such as words omitted and substituted as well as hesitations of more than three seconds. The student's oral reading fluency rate is the number of words correct per minute (WCPM). Measures in Spanish are forthcoming. Web site: http://dibels.uoregon.edu

- *Texas Primary Reading Inventory Fluency Probes* (University of Texas Systems and Texas Education Agency, 2005b). Fluency measures that serve as probes and are at reading levels appropriate for 1st grade, 2nd grade, and 3rd grade can be used to monitor progress of ELLs in fluency. The fluency kit includes a teacher's guide, story booklet, and grade-specific student record booklets. Web site: http://webmaster@tpri.org

- *Monitoring Basic Skills Progress: Basic Reading* (Fuchs, Hamlett, & Fuchs, 1997). This computer program conducts curriculum-based measurements and monitors student progress in reading. Students receive immediate feedback and teachers and schools receive complete reports. Published by Pro-Ed, Austin, Texas. Web site: www.proedinc.com

- *Peabody CBM Reading Passages* (Peabody College of Vanderbilt University). Curriculum-based measures in reading fluency are available for letter-sound fluency, with students saying as many sounds as they can in one minute; word identification fluency, in which students read words in one minute; oral reading fluency, in which students read passages; and maze fluency, in which students read for meaning through a maze procedure. Measures are available through flora.murray@vanderbilt.edu

- *Gray Oral Reading Tests, 4th ed. (GORT-4)* (Wiederholt & Bryant, 2001). This is a widely used test that assesses oral reading progress and reading comprehension. Using rate and accuracy, the GORT-4 provides an oral reading fluency score. Published by Pro-ED. Web site: www.proedinc.com

In addition to assessing fluency, teachers may want to assess the expressive reading of their English language learners. Expressive reading is provided when students alter the pitch, stress, intonation, and phrasing when they read. You can ask students to read aloud a passage that they have had a chance to read previously, either aloud or silently. You can score them based on their expressive reading (see Figure 4.4). Web site: www.colorincolorado.org/placement/fluency.php

What Are Some Useful Classroom Fluency Activities for English Language Learners?

Beat the Clock

Objective. When shown words on word cards, students will read the words fluently.

Materials. 30–35 sight words (familiar irregular and high-frequency words and regular words with sounds students have mastered) written on index cards

1. Explain that the goal is to read as many words as possible in 30 seconds.
2. Show students the word cards one at a time.
3. Determine that students know what the words mean—you can do this quickly by using the words in a sentence or asking students to do so.
4. Show the word cards again, this time asking students individually or as a group to read the word. Place correctly read words in one stack and missed words in another stack. If the student hesitates or has difficulty for more than three seconds, say the word and place it in the stack of missed words.
5. After 30 seconds, count the words the student read correctly. Review any missed words with the student.

FIGURE 4.4 ➤ **Expressive Reading Scores**

Score	Criteria
4	Uses meaningful phrase groups when reading aloud. Story is read with interpretation. Rate and accuracy are appropriate.
3	Phrases in three- or four-word units. Much of the phrasing is appropriate and is related to author syntax. Expressive interpretation is limited. Generally uses an appropriate rate.
2	Phrases in two-word units. Some of the reading is word by word. Some of the word groupings are awkward and unrelated to context. Reads large amounts of text slowly.
1	Does little or no phrasing while reading and reads primarily word by word. Reading is slow with little attention to punctuation. No expression while reading.

6. Have the student practice reading the word cards while you work with another student.

7. Give students a second turn to read the word cards in 30 seconds.

8. Explain that the goal is to read more words than the first time.

9. Follow the same procedure. Compare the second reading to the number of words the student read the first time. Provide feedback on accuracy and student progress.

Adaptations

- Ask students to read the words silently and to organize the words into piles based on their meaning. For example, put all the action words in one pile.

- Ask students to read a word card to themselves and then turn it over. Using a whiteboard, students can then write the word. Turning the card over again, they can check to see if it is written correctly. Repeat.

- Working in pairs, one student can read the word; the other student can use the word in a sentence. Then students can switch roles.

Fast Start

Objective. To engage parents and other key family members in fluency work with the student.

Materials. Poems printed on paper with plenty of white space for writing

1. Parents or other key members of the family sit next to the child and read the poem several times with expression. Be sure the

child can see the poem and can follow along with them.

2. If there are any words the child does not understand, explain their meaning.

3. Read the poem again together and point to the words as they are reading.

4. After reading the poem several times together, let the child read it aloud.

5. If the child makes errors when reading, identify the words and read them aloud together. Be sure the child knows the meaning of the word.

6. Be sure to give lots of positive feedback and support during the reading.

7. Select two to four interesting words from the poem and write them with the child. Be sure all participate in the selection of the words.

Adaptations

If students are reading text in a language other than the one used at home, be sure to consider whether parents can participate. Any adult or older student, with parents' approval, can do this.

Reading Outlaw Words Fluently

Note: This activity is adapted from Rasinski (2003, p. 135).

Objective. Students will increase their rate and accuracy reading irregular words or "outlaw" words.

Materials. Reading passage, tape recording of irregular words; tape player; headphones; copies of a grid with irregular words from the tape recording (see Figure 4.5)

1. From a reading passage identify the "outlaw" words or irregular words you want students to read automatically. Construct a grid and make a recording of the words. Be sure students know the meaning of the words before they participate in the activity.

2. Model how to use the tape player and the headphones. Show students how to point to the words while reading quietly.

3. Explain that students will listen to the tape three times. The first time students listen and point to the words. The second and third times, students read quietly along with the tape.

4. As students listen to the tape, ensure that students are pointing to the words, are correctly pronouncing them, and are not skipping words or lines. Provide assistance if needed.

5. Provide corrective feedback if students are having difficulty pronouncing words.
   • For example, for inaccurate word reading, point to the word and say, "This word is _____. What is this word?" (Student responds.) Then, have the student go back and read the words from the beginning of the grid.

6. Monitor students' progress. For example, determine the following:
   • Were the students able to track the words as they were read?
   • Were there any words that students had difficulty reading? If yes, do the students require additional response time to read these words?
   • Will any specific words require more instructional time? If yes, then how will this time be scheduled?
   • Can students work in pairs and both read the word and use it in a sentence?
   • How was students' speed of reading related to their background knowledge of the passage?

Source. Adapted from *Reading Strategies and Activities: A Resource Book for Students at Risk for Reading Difficulties, Including Dyslexia*, by the University of Texas Center for Reading and

FIGURE 4.5 ➤ **Sample Irregular Word Grid**

the	to	of	you	was
of	the	was	to	you
to	was	you	the	of
you	of	to	was	the
was	you	the	of	to

Language Arts, 2002, Austin, TX: Texas Education Agency.

Echo Reading

Objective. Students will read text fluently and with prosody after practicing with a model.

Materials. Copies of instructional-level texts of interest to students. Be sure to use both narrative and expository texts over time.

1. Preview the text with students to be sure they are familiar with the key concepts and vocabulary.
2. Give students a copy of the text.
3. Explain that you will read part of the text while students follow along. Then students read (echo read) the same text, trying to repeat your rate and expression. With English language learners, you may want to chunk the text in smaller units and then increase the amount of text over time as students become more fluent.
4. Read fluently two to four sentences of the text.
5. Have students read the same section of text trying to copy (echo) your rate and expression.
6. Read the next two to four sentences, modeling fluent reading. Again, have students read the same sentences trying to echo your rate and expression.
7. Continue the procedure by reading the passage in two- to four-sentence sections.

Adaptations

- Tape-record two- to four-sentence sections of a reading passage. Pause between sections to allow time for students to echo read. Have students listen to the tape while following along in the text. At the pauses, they echo read.
- If English learners are comfortable doing so, ask that one student be the model reader. The class echoes the student's reading.
- Read each section of text using different character voices; do not sacrifice fluency or proper expression. Students echo fluent reading using the character voices.
- Use a self-developed "microphone" (a pencil with a ball of aluminum foil at the top to appear to be a microphone). Allow students to read into the microphone as though they were reading on the radio.

Source. Adapted from *Effective Fluency Instruction and Progress Monitoring*, by the University of Texas Center for Reading and Language Arts, 2002, Austin, TX: Texas Education Agency.

Choral Reading

Objective. Given a reading passage and a model of fluent reading, students will read the text fluently and with expression.

Materials. Copies of instructional-level texts

1. Give students copies of texts.
2. Review the text to be sure students know the meanings of words and to check that the topic makes sense to them.

3. Model reading aloud the first part of the text. Set the pace and read with proper phrasing, rate, and expression.

4. Read the same part of text again with students reading along with you.

5. Give students a chance to read it again without your lead.

6. Give students a chance to pick a partner and read the passage aloud with their partners.

7. Ask students to volunteer to come up to the front of the room and to "direct" the reading of the class chorus while they read.

Adaptations

• Use choral reading with the whole class, in small groups, or with student pairs.

• Allow students to read interesting and fun passages alone, in pairs, or in small groups to younger students in other classes.

Source. Adapted from *Effective Fluency Instruction and Progress Monitoring*, by the University of Texas Center for Reading and Language Arts, 2002, Austin, TX: Texas Education Agency.

Repeated Readings: Using a Tape as a Model

Objective. Given a taped read-aloud of a passage and the corresponding text, students will read the text fluently and with expression.

Materials. Copies of independent or instructional-level passages or books. For younger readers, use decodable texts, pattern language books, or poems. For older readers, select high-interest texts. Also needed: tape recorder, headphones, assisted reading logs (see Figure 4.6).

Preparation.

1. Before reading the poem, passage, or book, preview the text and identify key words and ideas and discuss them so students know the meaning of words prior to hearing the story read aloud. This preview can be done with the whole class or can be part of the tape-recorded reading.

2. Audiotape a poem, passage, or book using a conversational rate and good expression. Use appropriate phrasing.

3. Provide students with cues to assist them as they read along, such as the following:
   • Before you start reading, allow 10 seconds of blank tape.
   • Remind students to use strategies that you have taught them, such as pointing a finger to each word as they read.
   • Use a signal or cue for turning the page. Say each page number.
   • Direct students to place a finger on the first word of the page.
   • Provide students with paper and pencil, so they can write down unfamiliar words for later discussion.

4. On each side of the tape, include approximately 10 minutes of text. Label each side of the tape with the title and the corresponding page numbers.

Procedures

1. Model how to insert cassettes into tape recorders and how to start, stop, and rewind tapes. Show students how to handle and wear the headphones.
2. Model the procedures for reading along, such as pointing to words and reading quietly.
3. Have students read the book with the audiotape.
4. Monitor students to ensure that they are following along with their fingers and reading quietly. Provide individual assistance if needed.
5. Have students read the passage three times: with the tape, with another student, and with the teacher.
6. Encourage students to document their readings using the assisted reading log.

Adaptations

- Have students follow the above procedures as they listen to computer-based books and commercial software reading programs. Many software programs are available in both English and Spanish with built-in record-keeping systems to monitor students' progress.
- After reading along with a tape or computer, have students record part of the passage or book and then listen to it. Help students evaluate their reading, with the following questions and tips:

  "When you read orally, what do you do well?"

FIGURE 4.6 ➤ Assisted Reading Log

Date	Title	Read With			
		Tape/ Computer	Self	Student	Teacher
	1.				
	2.				
	3.				
	4.				
	5.				
	6.				
	7.				
	8.				

"What is one thing you can work on to improve your reading?"

- Provide additional opportunities for students, especially struggling English language learners, to repeatedly read taped passages and books at home. Send home notes explaining procedures for listening to tapes and reading along to improve students' fluency.

Source. Adapted from *Strategies for Teaching Students with Learning and Behavior Problems* (6th ed.), by C. S. Bos and S. Vaughn, 2006, Boston: Allyn & Bacon.

Reading with a Partner

Objective. Given a reading partner and selected text, the student will increase accuracy and rate by rereading the text.

Materials. Copies of short and interesting texts at the lower-performing reader's instructional level for each pair of students (a selected list of publishers of high-interest and low-vocabulary texts is provided in Figure 4.7)

1. Typically, for reading partners, a high-performing reader is paired with a lower-performing reader for fluency practice. Try the following:
   - Rank the class based on reading proficiency as follows:
   - Pair the higher-performing (HP) half with the lower-performing (LP) half, the top-ranked HP student is paired with the top-ranked LP student. The same pairing is done for the remaining students.

Partner A Higher-Performing (HP)	Partner B Lower-Performing (LP)	Pairs
Top-ranked HP	Top-ranked LP	Pair 1
2nd-ranked HP	2nd-ranked LP	Pair 2
3rd-ranked HP	3rd-ranked LP	Pair 3

However, when partnering English language learners, be sure that the partner is appropriate and, if needed, can assist with word and text meaning. In all cases, be sure partners understand that they provide feedback for errors, not pronunciation variations due to second-language acquisition.

2. Provide reading texts or passages at the lower-performing student's instructional-reading level. One easy way to match books to students' reading levels is to give the students a list of words from the text. If students have difficulty with no more than approximately 1 in 10 words, the text is considered to be at their instructional level. Note: Independent-level text can also be used.

3. Model and explain partner-reading procedures before students begin the process of reading together.

4. Give each student a copy of the reading text. (The text matches the reading level of partner B.)

5. Have students take turns reading. Partner A reads the text aloud (modeling fluent reading) for one minute. Partner B follows along. Partner B reads aloud the same text for one minute.

FIGURE 4.7 ➤ **Selected List of Publishers of High-Interest Texts with Controlled Reading Levels**

Publishers	Contact Information
Academic Communication Associates	www.acadcom.com 1-888-758-9558
Capstone Press	www.capstone-press.com 1-888-747-4992
Curriculum Associates	1-800-225-0248
Globe Fearon	1-800-872-8893
High Noon Books	www.academictherapy.com 1-800-422-7249
Incentives for Learning	www.incentivesforlearning.com 1-888-444-1773
Modern Curriculum Press	www.pearsonlearning.com 1-800-321-3106
National Geographic	www.nationalgeographic.com 1-800-647-5463
National Reading Styles Institute	www.nrsi.com 1-800-331-3117
National Wildlife Federation	www.nwf.com 1-800-822-9919
New Readers Press	www.newreaderspress.com 1-800-448-8878
Perfection Learning	www.perfectionlearning.com 1-800-831-4190
Phoenix Learning Resources	www.phoenixlr.com 1-800-526-6581
Remedia	www.rempub.com 1-800-826-4740
Rigby	www.rigby.com 1-800-822-8661
Saddleback Educational	www.sdlback.com 1-888-735-2225
Scholastic (includes book clubs and software club)	www.scholastic.com 1-888-246-2986
Smithsonian Institute	www.siedu.com 1-800-766-2149
Steck-Vaughn	www.steck-vaughn.com 1-800-531-5015
Sundance	www.sundancepub.com 1-800-343-8204
Wright Group	www.wrightgroup.com 1-800-523-2371

Source: Adapted from *Strategies for Teaching Students with Learning and Behavior Problems* (6th ed.), by C. S. Bos and S. Vaughn, 2006, Boston: Allyn and Bacon.

6. When using this procedure, the whole class can participate while you time the readings.

Adaptations

- Be sure students know not to make corrections because another student says a word differently.
- Ask students to identify unknown words so you can discuss them.
- Have students read one page at a time, rather than reading for a specific time. Use this procedure to allow time for you to work with other students or teach a small reading group.
- Incorporate content area texts and other reading materials, such as children's magazines and newspaper articles.

Source. Adapted from *Second Grade Teacher Reading Academy*, by the University of Texas Center for Reading and Language Arts, 2001, Austin, TX: Texas Education Agency.

Previewing and Fluency

Objective. Given a reading passage or text, students will increase rate and accuracy by previewing the text before reading.

Materials. Copies of independent- or instructional-level passages or texts. Be sure to select texts that are appropriate for the background knowledge and understanding of students.

1. Give students copies of the passage or text.
2. Ask students to work with a partner. Be sure English language learners have suitable partners who will give them opportunities to interact.
3. Explain that previewing before reading can help them understand texts as well as improve their fluency.
4. Introduce the passage or text using the title and looking through the text or section. (For longer texts, preview only one section of the text or book at a time.)
5. Introduce new or difficult words. Include words that may be difficult for English language learners to recognize automatically and concepts or words with unfamiliar meanings. Have students write words in learning logs or on word cards.
6. Read a section of the text aloud at a slow conversational rate (approximately 130 words per minute). Have students follow along.
7. Have students take turns reading aloud the previewed section. Ask the more proficient readers to read first.
8. Monitor students' reading. Encourage students to review difficult vocabulary and periodically check and confirm predictions.

Adaptation

- Use big books to enhance previewing and to spark students' interest.

Source. Adapted from *Strategies for Teaching Students with Learning and Behavior Problems* (6th ed.), by C. S. Bos and S. Vaughn, 2006, Boston: Allyn and Bacon.

Partner Reading: Fluency Plus Comprehension

Objective. Given a selected text, the student will increase accuracy and rate and improve comprehension by rereading the text.

Materials. Copies of instructional-level texts; comprehension check cards (see Figure 4.8)

1. Explain that during partner reading, students can stop and check their understanding of stories as they read.
2. Model how to ask questions about the story, as shown in the figure.

FIGURE 4.8 ➤ **Comprehension Check Card**

1. WHO was the main character in the story?
2. WHEN did _____ happen?
3. WHERE did _____ live? (work, eat, sleep)
4. WHAT is the meaning of the word _____?
5. WHY do you think _____?

3. Give students copies of the text and comprehension cue cards.
4. During partner reading, have students take turns reading the same passage and checking each other's understanding using the comprehension cue cards. Following is an example:
   - Partner A reads a page of text. Partner B reads the same text.
   - Partner A asks partner B the questions on the comprehension cue card.
   - Partner B reads the next page of text. Partner A reads the same page of text. Partner B asks Partner A the questions on the comprehension cue card.
   - Partners continue reading the text following the above procedure.
5. Monitor pairs. Provide assistance as needed.

Adaptations

- If the reading passage is expository text, have students ask questions about the main idea and supporting details.
- Be sure to preview any unfamiliar vocabulary.

Sources. Adapted from "Peer-Assisted Learning Strategies: Making Classrooms More Responsive to Diversity," by D. Fuchs, L. S. Fuchs, P. G. Mathes, and D. C. Simmons, 1997, *American Educational Research Journal, 34*(1), 174–206.

Adapted from *Second Grade Teacher Reading Academy*, by the University of Texas Center for Reading and Language Arts, 2001, Austin, TX: Texas Education Agency.

Partner Reading with Retell

Objective. Given a selected text, the student will increase accuracy and rate and improve comprehension by rereading the text.

Materials. Copies of instructional-level texts; retell cue cards (see Figure 4.9)

1. Pair students for partner reading.
2. Give students copies of the text and retell cue cards.

3. Have the higher-performing partner read aloud first.

4. Have the lower-performing partner read the same text.

5. The higher-performing reader asks the following:

   - "What did you learn first?" (This question is only asked once at the beginning of each section.)

   - "What did you learn next?" (This question is asked as many times as needed to cover all the information that the student learned while reading.)

6. Have pairs continue the above procedure, with the lower-performing reader retelling each section after reading it.

Adaptations

- Have students take turns retelling sections of text.

- Read the text aloud to students prior to their practicing with partners. Discuss words and ideas they do not understand.

Sources. Adapted from "Peer-Assisted Learning Strategies: Making Classrooms More Responsive to Diversity," by D. Fuchs, L. S. Fuchs, P. G. Mathes, and D. C. Simmons, 1997, *American Educational Research Journal*, 34(1), 174–206.

FIGURE 4.9 ➤ Retell Cue Card

1. What did you learn first?

2. What did you learn next?

Adapted from *Second Grade Teacher Reading Academy*, by the University of Texas Center for Reading and Language Arts, 2001, Austin, TX: Texas Education Agency.

Spotlight Readers

Objective. Given a previously read passage, students will read the passage fluently and with expression.

Materials. Copies of previously read stories, books, or passages

1. Select three students to be spotlight readers.

2. With their assistance, select a passage or poem for them to practice to read aloud to the class or a small group.

3. Identify the day they will read their passage.

4. Ask students to practice the passage at home and with other students in the class.

5. Prior to the day they are to be the spotlight reader, ask them to read aloud to you. Provide support and feedback.

6. Provide the spotlight reader with a special place to stand, in front of a small podium or table.

7. Remind the student to read in a loud, clear voice so that everyone can hear. Offer assistance with difficult words.

8. After the reading, have the class applaud.

9. Repeat with a second and third student.

10. Use this activity a couple of times each week so that all of the students get an opportunity to be spotlight readers during the month.

Show Time

Objective. Students will work with a partner or team to read a script, text, poem, or play with expression.

Materials. Copies of texts converted into a play format (a list of books adaptable for reading performances is provided at the end of the lesson); cards with characters' names written on them; or poems that can be read by two or more students

1. Select instructional-level texts that consist of dialogue for several characters.
2. Highlight individual characters' parts on each script.
3. Explain that students will perform a play and that they will practice rereading their part to rehearse for the reading performance of the play. Clarify that reading performance is not a big production with costumes and props. It does not require students to memorize their parts.
4. Set a day and time for the reading performance.
5. Model by reading aloud the text at an appropriate rate with proper phrasing and expression to convey each character's feelings.
6. Group students. Assign students their individual roles.
7. During class, have students practice reading and rereading their assigned roles both independently and with their group.
8. Encourage students to practice at home.

9. Have students perform their readings in front of the class or for another audience, such as family, friends, and other classes.

Adaptations

- Write a class play or group play that is based on family stories.
- If poems are used for a reading performance, have students read alternating lines or stanzas.
- Have students perform their reading within their small group with you as the audience.
- Have the audience sit in the center of the room with the readers surrounding them.
- Select plays and scripts that represent the cultural backgrounds of the students.

Source. Adapted from *Second Grade Teacher Reading Academy*, by the University of Texas Center for Reading and Language Arts, 2001, Austin, TX: Texas Education Agency.

Reading Words and Phrases Fluently

Objective. To assure that students can read high-frequency words singly and in phrases.

Materials. Write high-frequency words on word cards. Write phrases or sentences with these high-frequency words in them. For example, *was* is a high-frequency word; *was there to help* is a phrase.

1. Take a small group of students, and ask them to read aloud the high-frequency words on the word cards. Sort the cards into words read correctly and words missed.

2. Review words missed, providing multiple opportunities for students to read and remember the words.

3. Ask students to read aloud the phrases with the high-frequency words in them. Sort the phrases into two groups— phrases read correctly and phrases missed.

4. Provide multiple opportunities for students to read and reread phrases until they are read accurately and with reasonable speed.

Adaptations

• Provide frequent checks to be sure students know what the words and phrases mean.

• Initially, use relatively few word cards and phrases and then increase the number as students become more proficient.

Reading Difficult Text

Objective. Students will gradually increase the difficulty of the text that they can read with accuracy, speed, and expression.

Materials. Working with students, select texts that interest and challenge them. Provide copies of the reading material to each student participating.

1. Read a passage to the students aloud while they follow along.

2. Reread the first two sentences of the text aloud, asking students to follow along.

3. Ask the students to follow your reading, in unison, with expression as well as speed and accuracy.

4. Continue by reading two sentences and have students follow the same two sentences.

5. Follow this procedure until multiple paragraphs have been read.

6. After reading several paragraphs, give selected students a chance to reread aloud.

Adaptations

• Pair students with older, more proficient readers from another class who have been taught how to read with a partner.

• Use with the entire class.

Reading 'Round the Clock

Objective. Students will read throughout the day to varied persons and document their reading time.

Materials. Whom I Read To Chart (see Figure 4.10); copies of texts to practice reading—texts can be previously read stories, books, or passages

1. List the names of people to whom students can read aloud across the top of the chart. For older students, brainstorm five or six different people to whom they can read and have students complete their own charts. Examples of people to whom students can read include their parents, older siblings, other teachers, paraprofessionals, peers, grandparents, neighbors, and parent volunteers.

2. Ask students to select a story, book, or reading passage (previously read in class) for their Whom I Read To Chart.

3. In the chart's left-hand column, write the title beside the number.

4. Explain that students will read their passage to each person on the chart. The person they read to will sign and date the chart. When the chart is completed for one selection, they will read the passage to the principal (or some other designated person).

5. Allow students to complete the chart over time. Periodically, check on their progress and provide feedback.

6. After one passage is completed, the chart can be used again for additional reading.

◆   ◆   ◆

FIGURE 4.10 ➤ Whom I Read To Chart

Title						
1.						
2.						
3.						
4.						
5.						
6.						
7.						
8.						
9.						
10.						

Annotated Bibliography

Blevins, W. (2001). *Building fluency: Lessons and strategies for reading success*. New York: Scholastic.

This resource presents lessons, activities, fluency charts, oral reading passages, and word lists for helping students fluently read words and connected texts. The author explains how to measure fluency, calculate students' fluency scores, and set fluency goals based on fluency norms. Twelve "quick-and-easy" lessons for building fluency address a variety of fluency-building techniques, such as echo reading, audiobook modeling, phrasing, repeated reading, and speed drills.

Great Leaps Reading.

This program has three levels of fluency: (1) phonics—students participate in activities in which they identify sounds and decode simple word patterns quickly and accurately; (2) sight phrases—students participate in activities in which they read phrases with sight words quickly and accurately; and (3) text fluency—students read stories and graph progress in accuracy and speed. Contact: Diarmuid, Inc., Box 35780, Gainesville, FL 32635; 1-877-GRL-EAPS; www.greatleaps.com; e-mail: info@greatleaps.com

Hiebert, E. H. (2002). *Quick Reads: A research-based fluency program*. Parsippany, NJ: Modern Curriculum Press.

The Quick Reads program features short, high-interest, nonfiction texts at 2nd through 4th grade levels. The program focuses on improving students' fluency, comprehension, and background knowledge. Each grade level sequentially builds across the three books and includes increasingly more difficult high-frequency words and phonics elements. The program includes a pre- and post-test for placement, 12 copies each of the three leveled student books per grade level, a teacher's resource manual, and three read-along audio CDs per grade level. Additional comprehension strategies and extension lessons can be used to support ESL/ELL students. Contact: Modern Curriculum Press, 299 Jefferson Road, Parsippany, NJ 07054; 1-800-321-3106; www.pearsonlearning.com

Peer-Assisted Learning Strategies–Reading (PALS and K-PALS). Students work with a partner using peer-tutoring methods. First Grade PALS incorporates lessons designed to improve reading skills as students actively participate. The 35-minute sessions (performed three times weekly) consist of two segments: (1) sounds and words—a code-based activity in which students practice phonological awareness and recoding and the application of both in connected text; and (2) storytelling—a partner reading activity in which students read, reread, and summarize stories with their partners. K-PALS includes 20-minute, gamelike sessions. During the first 5 minutes of each session, the teacher demonstrates activities with the class as a group. In the remaining 15 minutes, students perform the same activities with a partner. Sessions focus on developing pronunciation, letter knowledge, and phonological/phonemic awareness. Contact: Sopris West, 4093 Specialty Place, Longmont, CO 80504; 1-303-651-2829; www.sopriswest.com; e-mail: customerservice@sopriswest.com

Practices for Developing Accuracy and Fluency.

This manual presents a set of decodable grade-level passages and a set of rapid-word-recognition charts. Passages range from 1.0 to 4.5. The word-recognition charts can be used with the whole class to help students automatically read words. Students are timed as they read aloud the first 100 words of a passage. Record forms are included for students to document each story read, the date and time, their fluency rate, and any errors. Contact: Neuhaus Education Center, 4433 Bissonnet, Bellaire, TX 77401; 1-713-664-7676; www.neuhaus.org

Read Naturally.

Students improve fluency while reading along with a tape in which a model reader is reading the passage. Text is leveled so students can gradually increase both their rate of reading and the level of text they read. Students graph the number of words they read correctly prior to and after practicing. Vocabulary and comprehension questions are also provided to reinforce and build students' knowledge of words and concepts and to determine if students understand what they read. Each sequenced level includes 24 high-interest nonfiction stories, 12 cassette tapes (one story per side), and a teacher's manual. Software programs and computer-based progress-monitoring tools are also available. Contact: Read Naturally, 2329 Kressin Avenue, Saint Paul, MN 55120; 1-800-788-4085; www.readnaturally.com; e-mail: info@readnaturally.com

Web Sites That Teach

www.colorincolorado.org/educators

This Web site is a collaboration of Reading Rockets and the American Federation of Teachers and is designed to provide information, strategies, and resources to teachers of English language learners. There is also a section for bilingual parents. A specific section of the Web site addresses reading fluency for English language learners.

www.earlyreading.info

This Web site represents the Regional Education Laboratory at Pacific Resources for Education and Learning to help provide information on fluency based on research and then adapted for instruction. A focus on fluency summarizes research on fluency and is available as a PDF format online.

www.ldonline.org/ld_indepth/reading/
   reading_fluency.html

This Web site provides information on how to determine and adjust a student's reading rate and introduces a variety of fluency activities, such as repeated reading, choral reading, and commercial fluency programs.

www.nifl.gov/partnershipforreading/publications/k-3.html

This Web site is cosponsored by the National Institute of Child Health and Human Development, U.S. Department of Education, and National Institute for Literacy; it includes documents and materials related to early reading and fluency for parents, teachers, and school leaders. Most documents can be downloaded free.

http://ecot.rice.edu/conferences/acpweb/UST/EDUC5325/
   fluency.html

This Web site provides a video clip of the fluency technique, partner reading. The video clip explains partner reading in detail by explaining how to set up partner reading and implement it in a classroom.

www.sil.org/lingualinks/literacy/referencematerials/
   glossaryofliteracyterms/
   whatistheneurologicalimpressme.htm

This Web site introduces the neurological impress method, an approach to improving reading fluency. Various reading activities that incorporate some form of the neurological impress method are presented (echo reading, repeated reading, shared reading).

http://texasreading.org

This Web site provides information on teaching reading to English language learners and how and when to teach fluency, how to sequence fluency skills, and what effective, research-based fluency programs are available.

www.usu.edu/teach/text/fluency/FluencySynthesis.pdf

This Web site presents a review of fluency practices. The review provides stages of reading development, findings from research on fluency instruction, and implications for classroom approaches.

http://aimsweb.com

This Web site provides curriculum-based measures for reading fluency in English and Spanish as well as writing and spelling measures.

http://readingserver.edb.utexas.edu/downloads/
1998_enhance_read_1.pdf

This Web site provides a downloadable professional development guide for enhancing reading fluency. Specifically, the guide introduces partner reading as a fluency-building technique.

www.fcrr.org

This Web site at Florida State University provides considerable information on programs, assessments, and practices related to reading across the grade levels but with special emphasis on early reading in kindergarten through 3rd grade.

◆   ◆   ◆

5 Vocabulary Instruction

KNOWING WHAT, HOW, AND WHEN TO TEACH VOCABULARY IS PERHAPS THE MOST difficult task facing a teacher of English language learners (ELLs). We are often told that English-speaking children must learn approximately 3,000 new words each year (Honig, 1999). That number increases with ELLs, because they not only need to learn the specific vocabulary associated with a lesson but also need to build their oral vocabulary as they learn English as a second or perhaps a third language. We also know that we need oral vocabulary to make the transition from the oral to the written form of a language because to understand words we decode, the word read orally has to be part of our oral vocabulary (Kamil, 2004). In addition, if words that appear in print are not part of our oral vocabulary, they cannot be part of our reading vocabulary, and reading vocabulary is essential for comprehension. No one understands this relationship better than the teachers of English language learners who witness the great effort their students put forth as they build both their reading and oral vocabulary during instruction.

The role of vocabulary in reading is clearly understood: vocabulary knowledge, the understanding of word meanings and their use, contributes to reading comprehension and knowledge building. In the past few years, great strides have been made in the identification of practices that support ELLs' acquisition of foundational reading skills; however, improvement in vocabulary and reading comprehension often lag behind. This is not surprising, given the complexity of the skills associated with comprehension and vocabulary development, particularly when combined with language acquisition. It is nonetheless a challenge teachers must address if they want to improve student outcomes. Teachers can help students build their vocabulary and expand their understanding of word meanings by providing them opportunities to encounter new words in texts, by presenting repeated exposure to words that expand understanding, and by explicitly teaching word meanings.

Though we know that English language learners need to acquire basic vocabulary to understand directions during lessons or even communications like, "It's almost time for lunch," in this chapter we will focus primarily on vocabulary instruction in the context of reading instruction. However, the activities and principles presented can be applied to vocabulary instruction in content areas as well.

What Is Vocabulary Instruction?

There is evidence that language can be substantially affected by experiences in which children are exposed to a wider range of meaningful vocabulary and the meanings of unfamiliar words are explained. (Biemiller, 1999, p. 29)

Before we address what vocabulary instruction is, we must first determine what type of vocabulary we are talking about and what it means to know a word. Particularly with ELLs, we often hear references to different types of vocabulary, such as speaking or reading vocabularies. Other times we hear references to a student's expressive or receptive vocabulary. Receptive vocabulary is the vocabulary you understand from listening to others or from reading. Expressive vocabulary is the vocabulary you use either in speaking or writing—the words you use to express yourself.

You may recall from your own experiences learning a second language that you can often understand more than you can express. This is true whether or not you were already literate in your first language when you learned a second language. If you were older when you learned the second language, you may also recall that reading the new language was easier than writing it, because it is easier to construct meaning when the information is provided than it is to produce meaning ourselves.

So what are we referring to when we talk about these different vocabularies? Our reading vocabulary consists of the words in print that we can recognize or can figure out as we read. We refer to the words we can use appropriately in our writing as our writing vocabulary. Our oral vocabulary represents our listening and speaking vocabularies: the words we hear and understand from listening to the language of others, and the words we use in ordinary speech.

Our listening vocabulary is larger than our speaking vocabulary. Likewise, our reading vocabulary is larger than our writing vocabulary. There are many words we know when we read them, but do not use when we write. Although all of these are important to language and literacy development, we do not know, nor are we expected to know, the meanings of all words equally.

When we come across words, they usually fall into one of the following four stages: (1) never heard of the word before; (2) heard of it but have no idea what it means; (3) recognize generally what it means but cannot provide a specific description; and (4) know the word well and can use it and understand meaning when the word is used orally or in writing (Dale, 1965).

Although the goal should be to move as many words in students' vocabulary from stage 1 to stage 4, you will have to consider when to provide instruction that will result in deep understanding of the word, and when you just want to make sure ELLs know a word well enough so that they are not just repeating sounds. For example, when you have a list of words you will be using for a phonemic awareness or phonics activity and you know that the students may not know the meaning of all of those words, you can quickly provide the meaning with a picture, gesture, or object—achieving stage 2 knowledge. However, before reading a story to them or asking them to read a story, teach them the three to five words that are critical to understanding the story more completely. Following is a three-step example of how you might do that.

First, say: "We are going to learn some words before we read our story. The first word is *deteriorate*. Raise your hand if you have ever even heard the word *deteriorate*. Some of you have heard of the word and some of you have not." Have students brainstorm the meaning and use.

Then ask, "Who can tell me something about the word *deteriorate*? Now, I'm going to show you a sentence that we will read today with the word *deteriorate* in it. Let's see if we can add to our understanding of the word *deteriorate*."

Finally, give students a definition that matches the context in which this word is used in the story.

Teachers of ELLs can use these four stages as a means for determining the word knowledge of their students. Understanding what your students know about a word will help you determine not only which words to teach but also how to teach the word. We can think of words as representing two dimensions: a label and a concept. The extent of students' knowledge of a word on these two dimensions, combined with the learning goals, will impact the instructional focus. Depending on their age, English proficiency, and home language proficiency, English language learners will have varying levels of knowledge of the label and concept represented by words in one or both languages. In many cases, older, literate students will only be learning a new label for a known concept. Though it may seem to be a stage 1 word, in reality all these students need to learn is the English label. Other times, students will be learning an actual stage 1 word that is not in either their oral or reading vocabulary and for which they have neither a label nor a concept. Multiple-meaning words will require that students learn a new meaning for a word they already know in one context, but now need to learn in a new context. An example would be the difference between *cool water* and a *cool guy*. Understanding the shades of meaning and usage of closely related words will help them clarify and enhance the meaning of known words (Graves, Juel, & Graves, 1998; Graves & Slater, 1996).

Now that we have established what we mean by vocabulary and what it means to know a word, what is vocabulary instruction? Vocabulary instruction supports students in building both their receptive and expressive vocabularies, so they can comprehend what they read and hear and can express themselves clearly orally and in writing. As a teacher, you can provide comprehensive and systematic vocabulary instruction that teaches words and their extended meanings, provides multiple opportunities to use and practice key vocabulary, and assures that knowledge of words is an ongoing part of the instructional day. As often as possible, you should provide students opportunities to use oral language and to read and listen to texts.

Why Should I Teach Vocabulary?

The easy answer to this question is that for ELLs, more so than for English monolingual students, it is critical for all other learning. Vocabulary instruction provides the foundation for making sense of a new language. Beyond that, we know that vocabulary knowledge is one of the critical skills needed for reading comprehension (Davis, 1942). We also know that the more limited a student's vocabulary, the more likely the student is to experience difficulty comprehending text. To develop adequate levels of vocabulary, English language learners need instruction to learn specific words, skills that promote independent learning of words, and many opportunities to learn new words.

Even among English monolingual students, the difference in the number of words that students know can be as high as 30,000 (Hart & Risley, 2003; Nagy & Anderson, 1984). Though we know we cannot teach all the words students need to know directly, we do have to teach some words. How do you decide which words to teach directly? By now many of us are familiar with the three tiers of words as defined by Beck, McKeown, and Kucan (2002). In their classification system, the most basic words in our lan-

guage, words like *car, water, man,* and *candy,* are tier I words. These tier I words are usually not taught directly because when English-speaking children start school they already know these words. They are in their listening and speaking vocabularies. Tier II words are those words that are used often and carry high impact for learning and language use, such as *considerate, altitude, mobilize, concentrate,* and *industry.* Words that are infrequently used, such as *bellicose* and *exacerbate,* or that are associated with learning in a specific domain, like *isosceles, algorithm,* and *sedentary,* are tier III words.

For instruction, teachers have been told to focus on tier II words, but teachers of ELLs know that many of their students do not know many tier I words. Does it make sense to teach them tier II words when they do not even know most tier I words? The answer is yes. We want ELLs to learn basic vocabulary but understand that they must also develop a large and rich vocabulary. After working with English language learners, Calderon and Minaya-Rowe (2003) added a tier and modified the criteria for categorizing words. Tier I included words that required little or no instruction, such as clear cognates—*number* and *número* or *plate* and *plato*—or words students were likely to learn during everyday instruction. Tier II included multiple-meaning words, like *bank, play,* and *take,* that would otherwise be considered tier I words. Some tier II words were moved to tier III and expanded to include cognates that are not as obvious, such as *tend* and *atender.* Content-specific and infrequently used words were reclassified as tier IV words.

To determine which words to teach, ask yourself the following:

- What is the likelihood that the majority of the class already knows this word? If most students know the word, preteach it to ELLs if they will need to know it to benefit from instruction.
- Do students know other related words that are simpler or less sophisticated or a cognate? If so, instruct them to relate other words to this word and use them when appropriate to help them with the meaning.
- Will this word help students understand text and be useful in their own experiences?

Because we cannot teach all words directly, we must help students develop skills that promote independent learning of words, such as structural analysis. In the phonics chapter, we provided activities to help students use the structure of the word to decode it; students can also use that knowledge to determine the meanings of words. For example, we can teach students to identify and use morphological cues that indicate meaning, such as -s, -es, or -ies to indicate plurals, or a word part like -ly to determine the meaning of unknown words. Teaching students to use prefixes, suffixes, and roots gives them a tool for determining the meanings of words independently.

Teaching the use of cognates is another helpful skill for learning word meanings independently. However, many students will not use or even recognize cognates without some instruction (Nagy et al., 1993). Keep in mind that cognates are only helpful if the words are already part of the students' vocabulary and they have at least a stage 3 level of knowledge about the word in their home language.

Finally, we can help students learn new words by giving them many opportunities to read independently, or by reading to them if they have not yet learned to read or do not know enough English to read books with "rich" language. Reading is essential to building vocabulary. In fact, the more we read, the more words we encounter. Students who read just over an hour a day will encounter 4,358,000 words in a year, and students who only read 21 minutes each day will be exposed to 1,823,000 words; however, students who read about 10 minutes a day will only encounter 622,000 words, about a third as many as students that read twice as much (Cunningham & Stanovich, 1998).

If we agree with Beck and her colleagues (2002, p. 810) that "The goal for vocabulary development is to ensure that students are able to apply their knowledge of words to appropriate situations and are able to increase and enrich their knowledge through independent encounters with words," then the importance of providing vocabulary instruction is undeniable.

What Elements Should I Include in Vocabulary Instruction?

We can use the three principles for teaching vocabulary described by Stahl (1985) as a framework for instruction: teach both the context and definition of words, encourage deep processing, and provide multiple exposures.

When teaching a new word, teach both the definition and the context. Instruction that includes both definitional information and context with multiple and varied activities using the word in context is most effective for improving comprehension. If ELLs know the dictionary definition of a word, we say that they have definitional knowledge of the word. They can demonstrate definitional knowledge of words by providing the definitions, synonyms, antonyms, prefixes, suffixes, roots, or classifications of words.

If, in addition, students have "knowledge of the core concept the word represents and how that core concept is changed in different contexts" (Stahl, 1986, p. 663), then they also have true contextual knowledge of the word. A student who has contextual knowledge of a multiple-meaning word will understand the difference between homonyms—words that are spelled and pronounced the same but that have different meanings depending on the context or part of speech. Students learn to use contextual information through exposure to a word in context, but the context of some concrete words can be provided with a picture or demonstration. To know a word, students have to know the definition of a word and must be able to interpret its meaning in a particular context.

The second principle of effective vocabulary instruction, encouraging deep processing, requires teachers to use practices that engage students in thinking about words and in making links to other words to better understand the connections between new and known information. There are three levels for processing words with the goal of having students internalize the word so it becomes a word they know well (stage 4).

At the first level, association, a student learns an association between a word and a synonym or between a word and a single context. The second level, comprehension processing, requires that the student demonstrate an understanding of the word by providing an antonym or nonexample, completing a sentence with a blank, or classifying the word with other words. Generation processing is the third level. At this level, the student extends the comprehended association by exhibiting either orally or in writing that he or she has a clear understanding of a word and can differentiate its use in multiple contexts. A critical element at this level—whether students restate the definition in their own words, compare the definition to one's own experiences, or create a sentence to demonstrate the word's meaning—is that the product include elements that make it clear that the ELL has processed the word. For example, if the word is *drizzling*, an appropriate sentence would be "I didn't get very wet when I walked home yesterday because it was only drizzling." On the other hand, the sentence "It was drizzling yesterday" does not indicate whether or not the student really understands that *drizzle* refers to a light rain.

The third principle of vocabulary instruction is to provide students multiple exposures to the target words. Both the number of times a student is exposed to a word and the type of information given each time have an impact on comprehension. You can provide multiple exposures using the same information and context, or provide the student with multiple exposures to the word in different contexts or settings.

An approach that integrates these three principles, balanced instruction of both definitional and contextual information about words, opportunities for deep processing of words, and multiple and varied exposures to words, will serve teachers of English language learners well.

How Do I Teach Vocabulary?

The task of teaching ELLs all the language and vocabulary they need to know may seem overwhelming, but it is important to remember that a systematic and comprehensive approach to language and vocabulary learning will make the task manageable. An effective vocabulary program should include both explicit and implicit learning opportunities. The National Reading Panel (2000) organized effective practices for teaching vocabulary into the following categories:

- *Explicit instruction:* Students are given definitions or other attributes of words to be learned. Practices include preteaching of vocabulary prior to reading a selection, and analyzing word roots or affixes. Pre-instruction of vocabulary is important for ELLs because it helps to reduce the number of unknown concepts and introduces the words to the students' receptive vocabulary. During pre-instruction, you can provide the label for known concepts, introduce proper nouns, and teach words for which ELLs know neither the label nor the concept.
- *Implicit instruction:* Students are expected to infer the definition of words they do not know through exposure to words in lists, oral language, read-alouds, or from engaging in wide reading.
- *Multimedia methods:* Students learn vocabulary that is drawn from media other than text. Examples of practices are semantic mapping and graphic representations of word attributes.
- *Capacity building:* Students concentrate on meaning of words rather than their orthographic or oral representations.
- *Association methods:* Learners are encouraged to draw semantic or contextual connections between known and unknown words.

In addition, students need multiple exposures to words in a variety of contexts; therefore, plan for multiple exposures of the target vocabulary. This can be accomplished by providing various activities for encountering the word orally or in print in other contexts, by providing texts on the same topic, and embedding systematic reviews of target words.

Finally, active student engagement and deep processing of words is critical to vocabulary learning. To engage students in actively processing new word meanings, teach them to use word-learning strategies, including using context, using word parts to understand meanings of unknown words, and developing word consciousness. Word consciousness refers to the knowledge and disposition to learn, appreciate, and understand the power of words. It combines metalinguistic awareness—the ability to reflect on units of language—with motivation for learning words (Scott & Nagy, 2004). Students who are conscious of words enjoy words and want to hear and learn new words (Honig, Diamond, & Gutlohn, 2000). Fostering this type of awareness and interest in words is critical for English language learners, given the large number of words they have to learn to be proficient in English.

In summary, focus on a small number of critical words and use a variety of teaching methods, such as visually presenting words, defining them, and using gestures and realia (objects from real life) to illustrate key features prior to reading. Teach individual words and word-learning strategies explicitly. Foster word consciousness to encourage students' interest in learning new words, and provide opportunities for wide reading or for storybook read-alouds in the case of young children to support implicit learning. The use of reciprocal teaching and direct instruction for teaching vocabulary is more beneficial for poor readers than average readers. Finally, abstract words and concepts, multiple-meaning words, and closely related words will be more difficult for ELLs, so pay particular attention to these.

What Are Several Useful Classroom Vocabulary Activities?

Dependence on a single vocabulary instruction method will not result in optimal learning. A variety of methods was used effectively with emphasis on multimedia aspect of learning, richness of context in which words are to be learned, and the number of exposures to words that learners receive." (*National Reading Panel, 2000*, p. 44)

In this section, we provide activities to enhance students' acquisition of vocabulary. All the activities provided require explicit instruction. Activities are divided to correspond to the levels of word processing presented in this chapter.

Association Processing: Say It Another Way

Objective. Students have to replace the target word with another word or phrase that means the same thing.

Materials. Previously taught vocabulary words on word cards

1. Tell students they will work in pairs.
2. Each pair will be given a word or phrase and they will replace it with another word that is a synonym, or means the same thing.
3. Model the process.
4. "My word is *solitary*. I know that solitary creatures live by themselves. Another word is *alone*."
5. Give students the next word and ask them to come up with a synonym.
6. As students provide their answers, ask them to provide their reasoning.
7. Repeat with other words.

Association Processing: Personal Vocabulary Books

Objective. Given a vocabulary word, students will define it and identify synonyms, pictures, and sentences related to the word.

Materials. Notebooks or blank books for each student; vocabulary words; assorted magazines and newspapers, trade books, and textbooks; tape or paste

1. As new vocabulary words are introduced, have students write the words, one word per page, in their vocabulary books.

2. Ask students to find the definition in a dictionary.

3. Encourage students to hunt for the words (or synonyms of the words) in old magazines or newspapers.

4. When students find the words (or synonyms of the words), have students cut out and paste them on that word's page in their vocabulary books.

5. When students encounter the words (or synonyms) in their reading (trade books and textbooks), have them copy the sentence and underline the word.

6. Occasionally, have students share pages in their vocabulary books with peers or the class.

Variations.

• Have students find antonyms for the words, if appropriate.

• Provide a template for their entries that includes the name of the source where they found the word, the date it was found, how the word was used (for instance, in a headline, a sentence, or a phrase in an ad), and the page number, if appropriate.

Association Processing: Synonym Web

Objective. Students will understand and explain common synonyms, use synonyms to determine word meaning, and distinguish words with multiple meanings.

Materials. List of multiple-meaning words with several synonyms

1. Explain that some words have different meanings depending on the context. Provide an example: *reduce*.

2. Print the target word on the board and review the various meanings for the word: "make smaller," "lower the price," or "make simpler."

3. Tell students they will be creating a web with synonyms for the word.

4. Ask students to brainstorm synonyms for the word and list responses: *decrease*, *shrink*, *cut*, *lessen*, *condense*.

5. Model categorizing synonyms based on the various meanings of the word.

6. Students work in their groups on the next word.

Scaffolds. (1) Begin with one or two different meanings. (2) Provide sentences with each of the meanings.

Variations.

• Use both synonyms and antonyms of the various meanings of the word.

• Ask students to create sentences to demonstrate the various meanings.

Association Processing: Concept Map

Objective. Students will develop definitions for concepts and words that include three elements: What is it? What is it like? What are some examples?

Materials. Concept maps on overhead projector or chart paper; concept maps for students

1. Tell students you will teach them a process for developing complete definitions for words and concepts by answering three questions: What is it? What is it like? What are some examples?

2. Tell them that you will complete one together with a concept they already

know: mammals. Write *mammals* in the center of the map.

3. Ask students to answer the first question: What is it? Write *animal* in the box under the question.

4. Ask students to answer the second question: What is it like? Tell them these can be words or phrases that describe the features of a mammal, such as *warm-blooded, has fur, gives birth to live young.*

5. Ask students to identify some examples of mammals: *cats, monkeys, lions, rabbits,* and *wolves.*

6. Ask students to work in pairs to come up with a definition for mammals using the information on the map. Remind students to include information from all three parts.

7. Ask students to share their definitions and discuss the accuracy of the definitions.

8. Ask students to modify their definitions as needed.

9. Ask students to complete a map for a second word, *reptiles,* on their own.

Association Processing: Elaborating Words

Objective. Students will provide at least one detail to describe a word in a sentence.

Materials. Familiar words (*dog, ocean, hat*); words that describe the familiar words (see below); overhead projector; overhead marker, transparency

Dog	Ocean	Hat
large	huge, gigantic	new
black	blue	red
white	salty	spotted

1. Explain that students can elaborate or tell more about words to make sentences more interesting.

2. On the transparency, write a sentence that uses a familiar word. Be sure to *underline* the word. For example: "The *dog* chased the cat."

3. Read the sentence, and have students read it aloud.

4. Model how to elaborate and add more words to describe the word. For example: "I will think of some words that tell more about the dog."

5. Add several describing words (e.g., *large, black, white*) to the sentence.

6. Rewrite the sentence. Add the describing words. For example: "The large, black and white dog chased the cat."

7. Read the sentence, and have students repeat the sentence.

8. Write another sentence on the transparency. Be sure to underline the familiar word. For example: "The shark lives in the *ocean.*"

9. Read the sentence, and have the students repeat it.

10. Ask students to think of words that tell more about the familiar word. For example: "What are some words that tell more about the ocean?"

11. Prompt students, if necessary. "Tell me about the size of the ocean."

12. Rewrite the sentence. Add the describing words. For example: "The shark lives in the huge, blue, and salty ocean."

13. Read the sentence, and have students repeat it.

14. Write another sentence on the transparency. Be sure to underline the familiar word. For example: "My sister bought a *hat*."

15. Read the sentence, and have students repeat it.

16. Ask students to think of at least three words to describe or tell more about the familiar word.

17. Have several students share their describing words. Rewrite the sentence, adding the words.

Variations.

• Use pictures of objects with specific details. Follow the above procedures.

Source. From *Reading Strategies and Activities: A Resource Book for Students at Risk for Reading Difficulties, Including Dyslexia*, by the University of Texas Center for Reading and Language Arts, 2002, Austin, TX: Texas Education Agency.

Association Processing: Definitional Knowledge

Objective. Students will demonstrate precise knowledge of the meanings of words.

Materials. A list of target words, 2–3 questions for each word

1. Introduce the first word, *hatchling*. Say the word and have students repeat it.

2. Tell students the meaning or definition of the word: "A hatchling is a baby animal that is born from an egg."

3. Ask students to repeat the definition.

4. Give students a number of examples to determine whether or not they understand the definition. Model for them, including the reason why or why not. For example, "Could a mother gorilla be a hatchling?" "No, because she is not a baby" or "No, because gorillas are not born from eggs." If students only answer yes or no, prompt them to give the reason by asking why or why not. If they are not able to provide an answer, scaffold with more specific questions: "Can a mother be a baby?" "Are gorillas born from eggs?"

5. Ask students to enter the word in a word bank or notebook.

Variation. Show students pictures and ask them whether or not they fit the criteria.

Comprehension Processing: Definitional Knowledge

Objective. Students will learn how to use a definition to increase their word knowledge.

Materials. Previously taught vocabulary words

1. Review previously learned words. Say the word and have students repeat it.

2. Ask students for the definition: "A hatchling is a baby animal that is born from an egg."

3. Ask students to restate the definition in their own words.

4. Scaffold students' responses by asking questions.

   For example:

   "Is a hatchling alive?"

   "Can a kitten be a hatchling?"

5. Provide sentences that include parts of the definition.

   For example: "Young Komodo dragons develop inside an egg. They are born with green bodies and yellow-and-black markings on their backs."

6. Ask questions to determine students' understanding of the word's meaning.

   For example:

   "Are Komodo dragon babies hatchlings?"

   "How do you know?"

7. Scaffold responses, if necessary.

   For example:

   "Komodo dragons are born from eggs."

8. Repeat the same procedure with other sentences.

Source. Adapted from *Direct Instruction Reading* (3rd ed.), by D. W. Carnine, J. Silbert, & E. J. Kame'enui, 1997, Upper Saddle River, NJ: Merrill.

Comprehension Processing: Vocabulary Word Sorts

Objective. Students will sort previously introduced vocabulary words into categories according to word meanings.

Materials. Index cards, marker, previously introduced vocabulary words

First, model and demonstrate steps 1–7. Next, have students work in pairs or in a small group. Provide support, as needed.

1. Identify two or more vocabulary words to use as the word sort categories. Write each word on an index card. These cards will be the heading cards for the two categories.

   For example:

   • *drowsy*

   • *amusing*

2. Identify several words or phrases related to the categories. Write each word on an index card.

   For example:

   • Related words for *drowsy* are *sleepy, tired, closing eyes*, and *snooze*.

   • Related words for *amusing* are *funny, laughing, comedy*, and *jokes*.

3. Place the heading cards on a table (or in a pocket chart).

4. Ask students to read aloud the words on the heading cards.

5. Review word meanings by asking students to describe or define each word.

6. Hold up each related word card. Ask students to read aloud each word.

7. Have students sort the related words into the two categories.

8. To check students' word sorts, have them read each heading card and the related words in that category.

Variations.

• For the word sort to be more challenging, have students complete an open sort. In an open sort, do not present the categories. Give students several index cards with vocabulary words written on them. Have students sort the words into two or more categories of their choice. After they have completed the sort, ask students to describe the categories they have chosen and how the words in each category are related.

- Include a few words that do not fit either category. You can create a "wild card" or "other" category for words that are not related to either category.
- Have students copy categories of related words in their personal vocabulary books.

Comprehension Processing: I Can Name It in Three Clues

Objective. Students identify a word based on clues to the meaning.

Materials. Previously taught vocabulary words

1. Tell students they will work in groups to identify words they have learned by using clues that you will give them.
2. Tell students that you will give them clues one at a time, and when they think they know the word, they will raise their hands.
3. Model the process using a think-aloud. For example, if the target word is *hatchling*, the first clue might be "It is a word for baby animals. I know several words for baby animals, but I need more information to know which is correct." The second clue is "This baby animal is born from an egg. I still need more information." The last clue is "This baby does not have feathers. The word I know for baby animals that are born from eggs and are not birds is *hatchling*."
4. Proceed with the next word.

5. Give the first clue and give the students one minute to identify the word.
6. Scaffold students as necessary.
7. Continue with other words.

Source. Adapted from "Promoting the Vocabulary Growth of English Learners," by D. August, M. Carlo, T. J. Lively, B. McLaughlin, and C. Snow, 2006. In *Supporting the Literacy Development of English Learners*, T. A. Young and N. L. Hadaway (Eds.), Newark, DE: International Reading Association, Inc.

Comprehension Processing: Relative Connections

Objective. Students will distinguish between closely related words.

Materials. List of antonyms and additional words on word cards, an elementary dictionary

1. Tell students that they will discuss the meaning of words in their groups and will then order them to show how they are related to each other.
2. Model the process. Begin with a pair of antonyms such as *hot* and *cold*.
3. Review the meaning of each word. "Something that is hot has a high temperature, and cold describes something that has a low temperature." Give age-appropriate definitions.
4. Introduce the remaining words in random order: *chilly, warm, tepid, cool, nippy, temperate*.
5. Set the antonym pair on the board with space between them.
6. Arrange the words in order from *hot* to *cold*. Model the process for arranging the

words. "I know that *warm* is like *hot* so it will be closer to *hot*, and *cool* and *chilly* have to do with *cold* so they will be closer to *cold*." Continue until all words are in place. Model how to determine between very similar words, such as *chilly* and *cool*.

7. Students will do the next set in their groups.
8. Ask students to discuss the meaning of each word to determine its position.
9. Tell students they will verify the order by checking the meaning of words in the dictionary.

Variation. Give students a set of words from a related topic, such as *prey, animals, predator, carnivore, omnivore, herbivore, plants*. Ask students to work in groups to create a map that shows the relationship between the words. After they have arranged the words, ask all but one student to move to another group. The remaining student explains to the new group the reasoning for the arrangement. The visiting group can ask clarifying questions, such as "Why did you put *predator* next to *carnivore*?" Continue moving through the groups. Then debrief as a class.

Source. Adapted from *CORE Teaching Reading*, by B. Honig, L. Diamond, and L. Gutlohn, 2000, Novato, CA: Arena Press.

Comprehension Processing: Can This Be Right?

Objective. Students determine whether a person with certain characteristics would act in a certain way.

Materials. List of previously taught vocabulary words and sentences for each; *Yes* and *No* cards for each student. Use words that students probably know, but occasionally use a word only some will know, and you can discuss as a class. That is another way to increase vocabulary.

1. Tell students that you will provide a word and then a sentence describing the word.
2. They will tell you whether or not the sentence can be true. If the sentence could be true, they will show the *Yes* card; if it cannot be true, they will show the *No* card.
3. Model the activity: "If the sentence is 'Does a miser give away money?' I answer *no* because I know that misers like to save."
4. Give students other sentences. After they answer *yes* or *no*, ask them to give their reasoning.
5. Continue with other words.

Variations. (1) You can also give students various options such as "What does an astronomer study: sea life, rocks, or space?" (2) Reverse the process. Give a characteristic and ask students who would be likely to behave in that way: "This person always looks for the best in a situation: Is he a pessimist or an optimist?"

Source. Adapted from "Promoting the Vocabulary Growth of English Learners," by D. August, M. Carlo, T. J. Lively, B. McLaughlin, and C. Snow, 2006. In *Supporting the Literacy Development of English Learners*, T. A. Young and N. L. Hadaway (Eds.), Newark, DE: International Reading Association, Inc.

Comprehension Processing: Is It or Isn't It?

Objective. Students will learn vocabulary words through examples and nonexamples.

Materials. Vocabulary words, pictures that provide examples and nonexamples of the words, overhead projector, transparency, marker.

Example pictures for the vocabulary word *gigantic*:

Dinosaur next to a small girl

Small dog next to a small boy

Tall building next to a small girl

Toy house next to a small boy

1. Write one of the vocabulary words on a transparency.
2. Say the word, and have students repeat it.
3. Ask "What does ___ mean?" Provide appropriate feedback.

   For example:
   - "What does *gigantic* mean?"
   - If response is correct, say "Yes, *gigantic* means 'huge.'"
   - If response is incorrect, immediately model the correct response: "*Gigantic* means 'huge.'"

4. Discuss pictures that represent examples and nonexamples of the word.

   For example:
   - Point to the first picture and say: "The dinosaur is gigantic."
   - Point to the second picture and say: "The dog is **not** gigantic."

5. Present the pictures one at a time. Have students determine if the picture is an example or nonexample of the word.

   For example:
   - "The tall building is gigantic."
   - "The toy house is **not** gigantic."

6. Provide opportunities for students to practice discriminating whether a picture represents an example or nonexample of a word.

   For example:
   - Have students sit in a circle.
   - Within reach of everyone, place the stack of pictures face down in the middle of the circle.
   - Have students take turns identifying whether the picture represents an example or nonexample of a word.

Source. From *Reading Strategies and Activities: A Resource Book for Students at Risk for Reading Difficulties, Including Dyslexia,* by University of Texas Center for Reading and Language Arts, 2002, Austin, TX: Texas Education Agency.

Generative Processing: Possible Sentences

Objective. Students will use sentence and word context to determine the meaning of unknown words.

Materials. Three to four key words from a lesson that may cause students difficulty

1. Tell students they will be learning some new words. Tell them that all the words are related to the topic they will be reading about: Komodo dragons.
2. List the target words on the board with four to six other words that students are likely to know:
   a. Target words: *inherited, generation, instinct*
   b. Known words: *behavior, learned, automatic, offspring*
3. Tell student that they will use the words to write sentences.
4. Model choosing two words and coming up with a sentence: "My *offspring* will be the next *generation* in the family."
5. Ask students to create sentences with at least two of the words.
6. Read the passage.
7. After reading, ask students to read the sentence and determine based on what they read whether or not the sentence could be true.

8. Discuss and rewrite as needed.
9. Ask students to include the new words in their vocabulary bank or notebook.

Structural Analysis: Roots Plus

Objective. Students create lists of words with a given root.

Materials. Target root word and student notebooks

1. Tell students that many related words have the same root. Words that have the same root also have related meanings (see Figure 5.1).
2. Tell students that you will give them a root and they will list all the words they can think of with that root. Tell them you will do the first one together.
3. Give students the root *bio,* and ask them to tell you the words they know.
4. List the words as they provide them.
5. If they give you a word that is not a real word, tell them.
6. Once the list is complete, ask students to write the words and to work with a partner to write a simple definition for each word.
7. Discuss as a class.
8. Ask students to include the words that were new to them in their personal vocabulary notebook.

Variations. (1) Reverse the procedure; ask students to determine the meaning of a root after examining several words that have the same root. (2) Give students a list of words with the root word underlined or highlighted. Ask them to work in a group to determine the meaning of the root word.

Source. Adapted from "Promoting the Vocabulary Growth of English Learners," by D. August, M. Carlo, T. J. Lively, B. McLaughlin, and C. Snow, 2006. In *Supporting the Literacy Development of English Learners*, T. A. Young and N. L. Hadaway (Eds.), Newark, DE: International Reading Association, Inc.

Structural Analysis: Number Morphemes

Objective. Students will use number morphemes to predict the meaning of unknown words.

Materials. Word cards with words that contain number morphemes (see Figure 5.2)

1. Tell students that words contain parts that indicate a number. Write

FIGURE 5.1 ➤ Latin Roots and Greek Combining Forms

Morpheme	Derived From	Meaning
scope	Greek	to see, a device used for measurement
phobia	Greek	fear or intense dislike
port	Latin	to carry
rupt	Latin	to break
therm	Greek	heat, warm
geo	Greek	earth
aqua	Latin	water
struct	Latin	to build, devise, or put together
hydro	Greek	water
bio	Greek	life
homo	Greek	same, man
script	Latin	to write
spect	Latin	to watch, see, observe
cred	Latin	to believe
auto	Greek	self
tele	Greek	distant, far
graph/gram	Greek	to write, written
phon/phone	Greek	sound, speech, voice
tract	Latin	to pull or drag

Source: Adapted from *Vocabulary Through Morphemes: Suffixes, Prefixes, and Roots for Intermediate Grades*, by S. M. Roberts, 2004, Longmont, CO: Sopris West.

FIGURE 5.2 ➤ Latin and Greek Word Parts

Number	Latin	Greek	Examples
1	uni	mono	unicycle, universal, unicorn, monoplane, monorail, unique, unison
2	bi, duo	di	bicycle, biped, bilateral, diameter, bilingual, binocular, dialogue, duo, duet, bisect, bifocals
3	tri	tri	triangle, tripod, trilingual, triad, triceratops, tricycle, trident, trilogy, triple, triplets
4	quad	tetra	quadruped, quadrangle, quadruple, tetrahedron
5	quint	penta	pentagon, pentameter, quintet, quintuplets
6	sex	hex	sextet, hexagon, hexameter
7	sept	hept	septet, heptahedron
8	oct	oct	octopus, octave, octagon, octogenarian
9	nove, nona	ennea	novena, nonagon, enneagram
10	deci	dec, deca, deka	decagon, decade, decapod, decimal, decathlon
100	cent	hect	century, centipede, centurion, centimeter, centennial, centenarian, centigrade, hectoliter, hectare
1,000	milli	khilo, kilo	kilometer, kilogram, millipede, kilohertz, kilowatts, milligram, milliliter

Source: Adapted from *CORE Teaching Reading*, by B. Honig, L. Diamond, and L. Gutlohn, 2000, Novato, CA: Arena Press.

monolingual, *bilingual*, and *trilingual* and underline *mono, bi,* and *tri.*

2. Tell students that a person who is monolingual only speaks one language. A person who is bilingual speaks two languages, and someone who is trilingual speaks three languages. Tell them that the word parts *mono, bi,* and *tri* give you information about the word; in this case, you know how many languages a person speaks.

3. Ask them to raise their hand if they are monolingual. Repeat, asking students to identify themselves as bilingual or trilingual.

4. Tell them that many words have word parts that indicate a number; if they learn to recognize those word parts, they can figure out the meaning of words on their own.

5. Ask students to look at the list and tell a partner what they would call a person

FIGURE 5.3 ➤ Common Prefixes

Prefix	Meaning/Function	Example Words
un-	not, opposite of	unable, unchangeable
re-	again	reread, redo
in-, im-, ir-, ill-	not	inactive, immature, irregular, illegal
dis-	not, opposite of	dishonest, disagree
en-, em-	cause to	enable, embrace
non-	not	nonfiction
in-	in or into	inside, interior
over-	too much	overdue, oversleep
mis-	wrongly	misbehave, mispronounce, misspell
sub-	under	submarine, subway
pre-	before	preheat, preschool
inter-	between	international, intersection
fore-	before	foreground
de-	opposite of	deactivate
trans-	across	transport
super-	above	supernatural
semi-	half	semicircle
anti-	against	antislavery, antisocial
mid-	middle	midnight
under-	too little	underpaid
ex-	out, out of	exterior, exhaust, expose

who speaks four languages. Ask them to share.

6. Review the chart with the students, clarifying the meaning of words.

7. Ask students a series of questions that will require them to use the chart, such as the following:

   "How many angles in a triangle?"

   "How many legs does a quadruped walk on?"

   "A decade has how many years?"

   "How old is a centenarian?"

Variations. Use this activity with math terms: quadrangle, triangle, quadratic, bisect, and so on.

FIGURE 5.4 ➤ Common Suffixes

Suffix	Meaning/Function	Example Words
-s, -es	plurals	cats, dishes
-ed	past-tense verbs	landed, smelled, wished
-ing	verb/present participle, noun/gerund	renting
-ly	characteristic of	gladly, happily
-er, -or	person connected with	painter, director
-ion, -tion, -ation, -ition, -sion	act, process	tension, attention, imagination
-ible, -able	can be done	comfortable, changeable
-al, -ial	having characteristics of	natural, remedial
-y	characterized by	rainy, tasty, salty
-ness	state of, condition of, having	kindness, happiness, illness
-ity, -ty	state of	necessity, honesty
-ment	action or process	government
-ic	having	poetic
-ous, -eous, -ious	having	joyous, gracious
-en	made of	wooden
-er	comparative	smarter
-ive, -ative, -itive	adjective form of a noun	active, affirmative
-ful	full of	fearful, beautiful, hopeful
-less	without	fearless, tireless, hopeless
-est	superlative	lightest, strongest
-ance, -ence	state of	importance

Scaffolds. (1) Limit the number of number morphemes. (2) Only use words students are familiar with in the examples.

Structural Analysis: Go Fish for Word Parts

Objective. Students will create words by combining root words with prefixes and suffixes.

Materials. Word cards with root words, prefixes, and suffixes (see Figure 5.3 and Figure 5.4)

1. Tell students they will be making words by combining word parts. They will work in groups and will play Go Fish with the students in their group.

2. Review the rules for Go Fish. Students will distribute the word cards face down. After reviewing their cards, they will take turns asking another person in their

FIGURE 5.5 ➤ **Word Map**

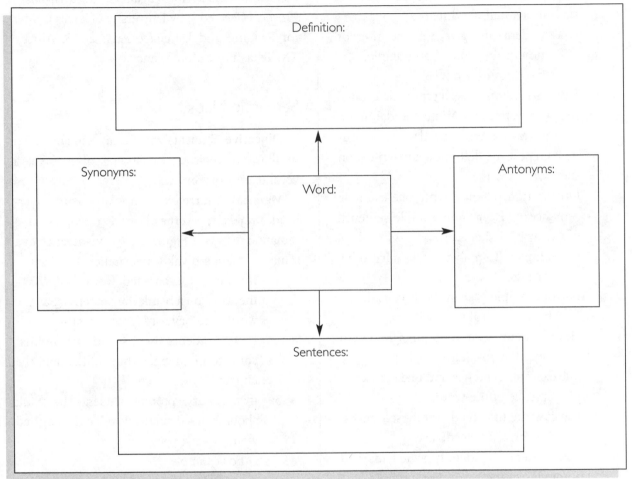

group for a prefix, a suffix, or root word card to form a word. If the person they ask does not have the card asked for, they draw one card from the pile. Tell students that the words have to be real words.

3. Continue playing until all cards are gone.

Scaffolds. (1) Provide a list of words for students to form. (2) Limit the number of prefixes, suffixes, and root words.

Creating Word Maps

Objective. Students will learn how to create a word map for a targeted vocabulary word in a text.

Materials. Targeted vocabulary word, overhead projector, overhead marker, copies of a word map for each student (see Figure 5.5), a transparency of a word map

1. Introduce the targeted word: *wicked*. On the transparency, write the word *wicked*.

Say the word, and have students repeat it. Then, have students write the word on their individual word maps.

2. Ask students to give the meaning or definition of the word. For example:

   "What does *wicked* mean?"

3. Discuss responses. As a group, determine the best definition. Write the definition on the transparency. Read it. Have students repeat the definition and write it on their word maps.

4. On the transparency, write one example sentence and one nonexample sentence of the word. Label each.

   Example: "Tom always tells a lie to his friends."

   Nonexample: "Diana is a considerate boss who is always willing to listen."

5. Have students turn to their neighbor. On their word maps, have each pair write one example sentence and one nonexample sentence of the word.

6. Have students read their sentences. Provide corrective feedback.

7. Ask students to identify synonyms and antonyms of the word. For example:

   "What is a synonym for *wicked*?"

   "What is an antonym for *wicked*?"

8. Ask students to record synonyms and antonyms on their word maps.

   For example:

   • Synonyms: *unkind, bad*

   • Antonyms: *good, considerate*

9. Encourage students to use the word in their conversations and to look for it in print.

Source. Adapted from *Effective Instruction for Elementary Struggling Readers: Research-Based Practices* (Rev. ed.), by University of Texas Center for Reading and Language Arts, 2003, Austin, TX: Texas Education Agency.

Semantic Maps

Objective. Students will create a semantic map to illustrate their understanding of a targeted vocabulary word in a text.

Materials. Targeted vocabulary word, overhead projector, overhead marker, copies of a semantic map (see Figure 5.6), transparency of a semantic map, a blank transparency

1. Introduce the targeted word: *owl*. Write the word on a blank transparency. Say the word, and have students repeat it.

2. Have students brainstorm words that come to mind when they think about the targeted word.

3. If necessary, prompt students to think about words that are related to the targeted word.

   For example:

   "Think about what owls look like, what they eat, and what they do."

4. Record words on the transparency.

   For example:

   feathers, talons, rodents, bugs, fly around, sleep, hoot

5. With students, group words into categories. Then, label each category.

   For example:

   "*Feathers* and *talons* can be placed in a category called *body parts*."

FIGURE 5.6 ➤ **Semantic Map**

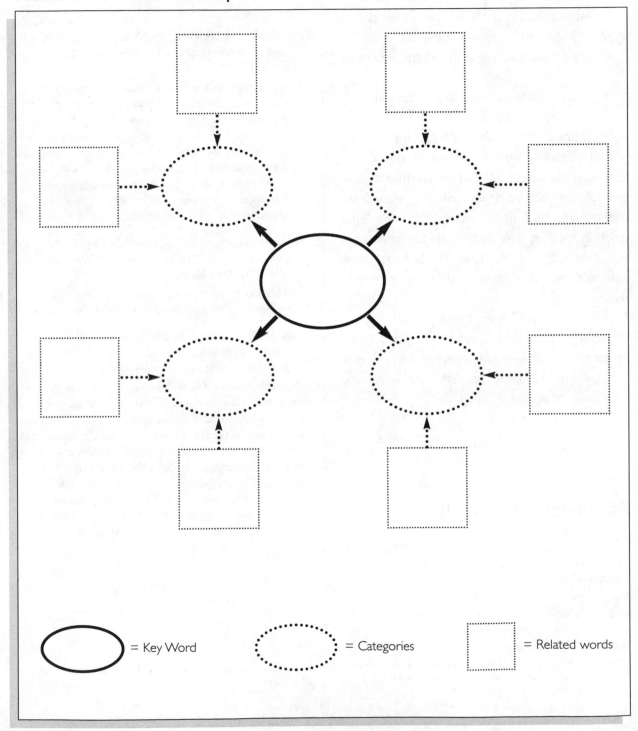

⬭ = Key Word   ⬭ = Categories   ☐ = Related words

6. Using the semantic map transparency, explain the different parts on the map using the key at the bottom of the page.

7. Model and explain how to create a semantic map using the words generated by your students.

8. Have students write the words on their semantic maps.

Variations. (1) With students, draw a simplified semantic web to represent the words that they generate. (2) Before reading a new passage, introduce a new vocabulary word from the passage and its meaning. Have students work in small groups or in pairs to construct a semantic map for the new word. Next, have students read the passage and add more words to their maps.

Source. Adapted from *Effective Instruction for Elementary Struggling Readers: Research-Based Practices* (Rev. ed.), by University of Texas Center for Reading and Language Arts, 2003, Austin, TX: Texas Education Agency.

◆   ◆   ◆

Annotated Bibliography

Beck, I. L., McKeown, M. G., & Kucan, L. (2002). *Bringing words to life: Robust vocabulary instruction*. New York: Guilford Press.

This book was written to provide teachers with practical ideas and activities for vocabulary instruction. Teachers are guided through the steps necessary to develop strong and powerful vocabulary lessons, from selecting vocabulary words to teach to getting students involved in thinking about and using new words. Vocabulary strategies and instructional examples for early grades (K–2) and later grades are included. Appendices list, by grade level, books that are rich with vocabulary resources.

Blackowicz, C. L., & Fisher, P. (2002). *Teaching vocabulary in all classrooms* (2nd ed). Upper Saddle River, NJ: Pearson.

This book presents practical instructional strategies and activities for developing vocabulary that can be applied across grade levels, from kindergarten through high school. Although the focus of the book is teaching vocabulary to enhance the acquisition of content knowledge, the ideas can be used with younger students, including students with special needs. The chapters include easy-to-read descriptions and examples for building vocabulary, from word play to using context and structural analysis.

Bowers, L., Huisingh, R., LoGiudice, C., Orman, J., & Johnson, P. F. (2000). *125 vocabulary builders*. East Moline, IL: LinguiSystems.

This book contains paper-and-pencil activities designed to provide practice with newly acquired vocabulary words.

Stahl, S. A., & Kapinus, B. (2001). *Word power: What every educator needs to know about teaching vocabulary*. Washington, DC: National Education Association.

This book provides detailed information about teaching vocabulary in the classroom. Its three chapters provide suggestions and guidelines for enhancing vocabulary through reading and instruction. Instructional activities for helping students learn words are also included. Provides practices for students to enhance their vocabulary and help them understand how words function in communication. Provides instructional strategies for teaching students not only the meaning of words, but also their appropriateness, value, and potential effects within our language.

◆   ◆   ◆

Web Sites That Teach

http://reading.uoregon.edu/big_ideas/voc.php

This Web site provides the definition of *vocabulary*, research findings on vocabulary, the importance of vocabulary, sequencing vocabulary skills in K–3, and vocabulary instruction.

http://reading.uoregon.edu/instruction/instruc_voc_q2.php

This Web site introduces types of vocabulary instruction, especially three vocabulary teaching strategies: (1) teaching vocabulary through modeling with examples, (2) teaching vocabulary by using synonyms, and (3) teaching vocabulary by using definitions.

www.mcps.k12.md.us/departments/dsd/70plus/VOCAB.pdf

This Web site allows readers to download resources for vocabulary instruction (e.g., principles of vocabulary instruction, semantic mapping, contextual analysis).

www.ed.gov/offices/OESE/SASA/rb/slide020.html

This Web site provides a summary of research-based vocabulary instruction and strategies.

www.allamericareads.org/lessonplan/vocab.htm

This Web site introduces strategies to promote vocabulary development (e.g., contextual clues, idiomatic expression, word mapping).

www.ldonline.org/ld_indepth/teaching_techniques/ellis_clarifying.html

This Web site introduces elaboration techniques for teaching new vocabulary words.

http://idea.uoregon.edu/~ncite/documents/techrep/tech13.html

This Web site presents findings from a synthesis on vocabulary acquisition.

http://idea.uoregon.edu/%7Encite/documents/techrep/tech14.html

This Web site presents converging evidences on vocabulary acquisition and provides curricular and instructional implications.

www.sd129.org/jpetzke/vocab_web/vocab_research.html

This Web site provides research findings on vocabulary instruction and acquisition.

6 | Comprehension

"ENGLISH LANGUAGE LEARNERS OFTEN HAVE LIMITED OPPORTUNITIES TO USE ORAL language during instruction and few opportunities to address challenging or higher-order questions. Because these students' language development may still be growing, teachers often ask them questions that allow for one- or two-word responses. ELLs may have difficulty providing the complex answer, but with structured conversation and opportunities to use academic language, their skills will improve" (Bos & Vaughn, 2006, p. 182).

Is there any more important goal in reading than comprehension? The whole purpose of learning to read is to understand and learn from text. While phonics and word reading are the beginning building blocks of reading, reading for pleasure and knowledge are the ultimate point.

Comprehension is particularly important with English language learners (ELLs). There is considerable research showing that the foundation skills in reading are acquired by English language learners, but there is often a breakdown with reading comprehension. This breakdown may be attributed to many reasons, including failure to understand word meanings; inadequate background knowledge; lack of interest in text; or disconnect between instruction, text, and learner. All of these can be considered when providing reading comprehension instruction for English language learners.

As you read about reading comprehension with English language learners, remember that books need readers who want to read them. Help English language learners enjoy reading more, and you will do much to improve their reading comprehension. Following are some guidelines for selecting reading materials for English language learners.

When selecting and using multicultural literature, you should do the following:

- Consider the linguistic and cultural backgrounds of your students, and select books and readings that reflect their experiences.
- Identify and read aloud writing from authors from various cultures.
- Select literature that incorporates dialects from other linguistic groups.
- Consider book lists, directories, Web sites, and textbooks that provide resources on multicultural books for young children.
- Display books, articles, and other written materials and photos that reflect a multicultural representation.

What Is Comprehension Instruction?

For children to become good comprehenders, they need to become fluent in word recognition processes, to acquire an extensive vocabulary, and to learn to be active in the ways that excellent, mature readers are active. (Block & Pressley, 2003, p. 188)

Comprehension instruction for English language learners is a complex, active process of constructing meaning from text and involves knowing how to read words accurately and automatically, accessing previous knowledge, understanding vocabulary and concepts, making inferences, and linking key ideas. Reading comprehension is not a skill that can be learned through rote instruction. Reading comprehension is a compilation of skills and strategies that require the following:

- Considering students' stages of development in their first and second language
- Using multiple ways for students to express their understanding other than through oral language—for example, young students enjoy drawing and illustrating stories and can even do story sequence through story boxes with pictures
- Applying the foundation skills of word reading and fluency with a series of strategies that influence understanding of text
- Interacting with the text in ways that blend knowledge and experience of the reader
- Setting purposes for reading and checking to see that these purposes and the text are aligned
- Using strategies and skills to construct meaning during and after reading
- Adapting the strategies used while reading to match the text and purpose for reading
- Recognizing the author's purpose
- Distinguishing between facts and opinions
- Drawing logical conclusions
- Making inferences and connections between and across texts
- Learning from and liking what you read

The starting point for teachers is to ensure that the student has adequate word and world knowledge to understand the text that he or she is reading. Of greatest importance is to assure students that reading comprehension is "sense making." Many English language learners have spent so much time reading words and text they do not understand that they lose sight of making sense and learning from text. Teachers can promote this understanding of reading for meaning by doing the following:

- Ensuring students understand the vocabulary in the passage
- Preteaching key ideas and background concepts central to understanding text
- Asking students to reflect on the author's intention, their own experiences, and the meanings derived from the text
- Welcoming questions about words and ideas and what they mean
- Using previous knowledge to understand text

Reading comprehension can be divided into three types: textually explicit, textually implicit, and implicit only.

Textually explicit suggests that information is in the text with little input from the readers' background knowledge. Questions that refer specifically to what a character did in the story, the meaning of a concept that is defined in expository text, or a summary of the most important events are examples of textually explicit comprehension questions.

Textually implicit information is derived from the text, but readers must use their own knowledge and experience to assemble the ideas. Textually implicit reading comprehension questions can be challenging for English language learners if their background knowledge and experiences are not aligned with the text. Readers are required to read between the lines and combine information from previous experience and reading to make inferences. Providing adequate background knowledge and key concepts prior to reading helps English language learners succeed with textually implicit questions.

Implicit only is information that is not stated in the text or is only vaguely suggested.

Over the last few decades, observations in teachers' classrooms have confirmed that the primary way teachers provide comprehension instruction is through question asking, but that is often not enough. For English language learners, it is critical to have opportunities to engage in and respond to text that involve scaffolding their responses to higher-order questions and responding to what they read.

Why Should I Teach Reading Comprehension?

Children are routinely asked questions after reading but are infrequently provided with demonstrations of the comprehension strategies needed to answer the questions posed. In short, too often assigning and asking are confused with teaching. (Cunningham, 1998, p. 47)

The current emphasis on passing high-stakes tests in reading at the district and state level is perhaps one of the biggest motivators for teachers to conduct comprehension instruction. Teachers who provide systematic and explicit instruction in comprehension will see real gains in their students' progress on these high-stakes assessments as well as enhance their students' joy in reading.

The following comprehension practices are associated with improved outcomes for ELLs (Gersten & Geva, 2003):

- Explicit teaching
- Promotion of English language learning
- Development of vocabulary and word knowledge

- Interactive teaching that maximizes student engagement
- Instruction that produces opportunities for accurate responses, with scaffolded feedback for struggling learners
- Making connections between the home language and the language in the school
- Connecting students' previous experiences with the learning in the text
- Planning discussions that promote and support use of academic language

Good readers use rapid and accurate word reading, set goals for reading, note the structure and organization of text, monitor their understanding while reading, and create mental notes and summaries. Good readers anticipate what will happen and revise and evaluate their thinking about text as they read. Good readers connect with what they are reading. In summary, they are active processors of text.

Poor readers lack the automatic word reading of good readers. They typically read more slowly and less accurately, understand the meaning of fewer words, and rarely monitor their understanding. Effective teachers of English language learners understand that the instruction needs to be as comprehensible as possible. Consider the backgrounds of students as a starting point to build and link new knowledge. Honor what students know and the homes and communities from which they come. Demonstrate new words and highlight them so students can recognize, hear, and practice them. Use text structures and make them visible to students. Expose the text to students by thinking aloud about the reading. Whenever possible, put "meaning" first!

How Can I Promote Reading Comprehension?

We do English language learners a disservice if we think of them as one-dimensional on the basis of their limited English proficiency. ELLs have diverse backgrounds, language, and education profiles. Some read and write above grade level in their own language; others have had limited schooling. (Short & Echevarria, 2005, p. 9)

Progress Monitoring

What measures should teachers use to determine the current reading comprehension of their English language learners and to monitor their progress in comprehension? Of all the elements of reading, the most challenging elements to assess and monitor are comprehension and vocabulary. This is particularly true for English language learners. The nature of their first language as well as their proficiency in their first language influences their success in reading comprehension in English.

There are a number of tests available to assess students' comprehension, but we have reservations about them—particularly with English language learners. See Figure 6.1 for a list of tests that may be used to make some beginning judgments, but teachers, again, need to combine these tests with their knowledge of students' language development in English.

Some considerations in choosing a test are (1) whether the test was normed with English language learners; (2) whether it is appropriate for English language learners; (3) the purpose of

FIGURE 6.1 ➤ Reading Comprehension Assessments Examples

Title Administration	Ages	Testing Time (est.)	Key Elements of Comprehension Assessment	Administration
Clay Observational Survey (Clay, 1993, 2002)	5–7 years	15 min.	• Oral reading • Reading vocabulary (words known in reading)	Individual
Comprehensive Reading Assessment Battery (Fuchs, Fuchs, & Hamlett, 1989)	Young readers	30–40 min.	• Fluency • Oral comprehension • Maze	Individual
Gates-MacGinitie Reading Tests (MacGinitie et al., 2000)	Grades K–12 and adult reading	55–75 min.	• Word meanings (levels 1 and 2) • Comprehension (levels 1 and 2—short passages of one to three sentences; levels 3 and up—paragraph reading)	Group
Gray Oral Reading Tests, 4th ed. (Wiederholt & Bryant, 2001)	6–18 years, 11 months	15–45 min.	Fourteen separate stories each followed by five multiple-choice comprehension questions	Individual
Gray Silent Reading Test (Wiederholt & Blalock, 2000)	7–25 years, 11 months	15–30 min.	Thirteen passages with five comprehension questions each	Individual, small groups, or entire class
Qualitative Reading Inventory (Leslie & Caldwell, 2001)	Emergent readers to high school	30–40 min.	• Oral reading and comprehension • Silent reading and comprehension • Listening comprehension	
Test of Early Reading Ability, 3rd ed. (Reid, Hresko, & Hammill, 2001)	Preschool–2nd grade	20 min.	Comprehension of words, sentences, and paragraphs (also tests relational vocabulary, sentence construction, and paraphrasing)	Individual
Test of Reading Comprehension (Brown et al., 1995)	7–17 years, 11 months	30–90 min.	• General vocabulary • Syntactic similarities (select two sentences conveying the same meaning) • Paragraph reading (six paragraphs with five questions each) • Sentence sequencing (five randomly ordered sentences for the student to put in the correct order)	Individual, small group, or entire class

(continued)

FIGURE 6.1 ➤ Reading Comprehension Assessments (cont.)

Title Administration	Ages	Testing Time (est.)	Key Elements of Comprehension Assessment	Administration
			Diagnostic Supplement: 5., 6., & 7. Content area vocabulary in math, social studies, and science 8. Reading the directions of schoolwork	
Standardized Reading Inventory, 2nd ed. (Newcomer, 1999)	6–14 years	30–90 min.	• Vocabulary in context • Passage comprehension	Individual
Woodcock Reading Mastery (Woodcock, 1998)	5–7+ years	10–30 min.	• Word comprehension (antonyms, synonyms, analogies) • Passage comprehension	Individual
Texas Primary Reading Inventory (TPRI) (University of Texas Systems and Texas Education Agency, 2005b)	K–3rd grade	20–40 min.	Assesses comprehension by asking students to read passages and then answer questions. Can be used as a diagnostic reading comprehension measure. Normed with a large sample of English language learners.	
Phonological Awareness Literacy Screening (PALS) (Invernizzi & Meier, 2002)	K–3rd grade	20–40 min.	Students read comprehension passages based on their word recognition score. Developed in conjunction with the Virginia State Department of Education.	
Fox in a Box (Adams, 2000)	Benchmarks marks for grades 1 & 2	10–20 min.	Students read stories aloud and then answer questions and retell the story.	

the testing (screening, monitoring, assessing level of reading, or assessing competence compared to peers); (4) the specific information needed about the student's reading comprehension (types of questions missed, level); (5) the number of students being tested (whether you can test individually, in small groups, or with the whole class); and (6) the experience or qualifications required to administer a particular test.

There are also informal ways to determine how much students understand about what they read.

• Listen to students talk about what they are reading. Ask questions to determine how well they are connecting with text and learning.

- Ask students questions that require implicit and explicit understanding of text. Listen carefully and probe to learn more.
- Confer with students before and after reading to determine how much they know about the text and what they have learned.
- Keep records of books students read and their responses to these books.
- Examine written work samples that reflect what students are reading.

Instructional Factors

This section of the chapter presents those powerful instructional strategies for reading comprehension that will yield the best outcomes in understanding text for your English language learners. For each of the questions below, ask yourself whether you implement the practice: (1) never; (2) some of the time, but not enough; or (3) whenever needed.

How often do you

- Ask students to make predictions about what they are going to read by using such features of the text as title, pictures, and key words?
- Provide students with opportunities to integrate their background knowledge with the critical concepts in the text?
- Identify the language demands of the text students are reading and preteach related vocabulary and concepts?
- Request that students monitor the words and concepts they do not understand

while they are reading, make note of them, and then follow up with them?

- Ask students questions they can answer and then scaffold responses to meet language needs?
- Model and provide opportunities for students to construct mental images that represent text, so they can better remember and understand what they read?
- Provide opportunities for students to seek clarification about confusing aspects of what they read?
- Plan language-related activities that link with comprehending text and then make these explicit to students?
- Give students adequate opportunities to develop questions about what they have read and pose these questions to fellow students?
- Give students adequate time and practice responding orally?
- Provide practice in summarizing and integrating information from text read?

Now, choose several instructional practices that you rated 1 or 2 and begin to implement them more frequently.

What Intervention Practices Facilitate Reading Comprehension for English Language Learners?

Now that you have some idea of the strategies that you are using and not using in your classroom, let us discuss several comprehension strategies in more detail.

Perhaps you might

- Provide students with guided practice and suggestions for how to monitor their comprehension and to adjust how they read when difficulties in understanding text arise.
- Select texts and topics that represent culturally relevant experiences and roles to draw upon prior knowledge and enhance retention of new concepts and vocabulary.
- Use cooperative learning practices as well as peer pairing within the context of reading and strategy application.
- Provide graphic and semantic organizers that provide a scaffold for drawing connections, relationships, and word meaning associated with story reading and writing.
- Use questioning practices such as (1) designing questions that address the story structure; (2) providing extended feedback and connections between students' responses; (3) giving students an opportunity to elaborate on each other's responses to questions; and (4) preparing students to ask and answer their own questions about what they read.
- Teach students to write down key information about what they have read while they are reading and to summarize these key points after they read longer passages.
- Provide small-group or paired cooperative-learning activities and encourage development of prior knowledge.
- Assist students in addressing higher-order questions by modeling more complex syntactic structures and fading support as students become more proficient in English.

Another way to consider instruction in comprehension is to plan the comprehension strategies you will teach before, during, and after reading.

Before-Reading Activities

For many English language learners, the before-reading plan is lots of text that is aligned with their interests and experiences. However, effective teachers are aware that the background knowledge of a few students prior to reading does not represent the experience and knowledge of all of their students. Teachers who assist students in making connections based on their varied backgrounds and experiences will reap dividends with respect to student interest and understanding.

How can these before-reading activities be initiated? Graves, Juel, and Graves (2001) make the following suggestions:

- Teach students to set a purpose for reading.
- Provide questions and connections that motivate students to be engaged when they read.
- Preteach key vocabulary and concepts.
- Link students' background knowledge and experiences with what they are going to read.
- Relate the reading to students' lives.
- Teach students text features and how to use them to understand what they read.

What are some additional practices teachers can use to engage students prior to reading? Text preview (Graves, Prenn, & Cooke, 1985; Graves et al., 2001) is one way to engage students prior to reading.

- . *Design the text previews.* Teachers design a preview of the text that includes four parts:

(1) an idea or question that "hooks" students into reading and piques their interest; (2) text that is connected to their own experiences; (3) a brief description of the theme or story organization; and (4) questions generated by teachers and students to guide reading.

- *Engage students in the text preview.* For 5 to 10 minutes, teachers can prep students about what they are going to read, discuss an interesting or important part of the story, connect students' experiences and knowledge to key ideas in the story, and present and generate questions to consider while reading.

During- and After-Reading Activities

Students need to monitor their understanding, use strategies to assist in understanding, and consider linkages between what they are reading and learning and previous knowledge and experiences. An engaged, active reader is the goal.

To help ELLs

- Teach students through demonstration and think-alouds how to monitor their understanding while they read and to recognize difficult concepts or words.
- Provide students with questions to consider while reading. These questions can be teacher- and student-generated.
- Assist students in considering inferences within text while reading and after reading.
- Identify selected paragraphs for students to summarize while reading.
- Ask students to consider predictions and questions generated prior to reading and to confirm, disconfirm, and extend these ideas.

- Ask questions that engage and extend learning and teach students to ask questions.

Figure 6.2 provides an organizer for how students might think about understanding text prior to, during, and after reading.

Questioning

Questions are the windows that can be used to see into the comprehension of students. Here are some examples of good question starters.

- "Why do you think the author. . . ?"
- "How would you have ended this story?"
- "What character was your favorite? Why?"
- "What information helped you decide **where** this story took place?"
- "How would you sequence the three most important findings?"
- "How would you compare the main character _____ in this story to the main character _____ from [a previous story]?"
- "What information is missing?"

See Figure 6.3 for a frame for answering questions.

Another effective way for teachers to assist students in asking and answering worthwhile questions about what they read is to "question the author" (see Figure 6.4). In questioning the author, the teacher has provided distinct goals and several queries that assist students in reaching those goals.

Using Students' Language and Experiences to Construct Text

Language experience practices demonstrate how experiences, written language, and reading connect. These practices can be particularly useful for English language learners who have good foundation skills (word reading) but struggle with making meaning from text. An example of how to use language experience to build and extend comprehension for English language learners follows:

1. Identify student(s) to participate who have shared a common learning experience, such as a field trip, informative video, cooking lesson, science lesson, or any other appropriate personal experience students want to discuss.

2. Ask students to sit so they can see the chart on which you are writing.

3. Identify a working title that defines the personal experience the class chose to discuss.

4. Ask students to engage in a conversation about it.

5. Select sentences from students and write them on the chart. If you want the story to be in a correct sequence, you can write students' comments on sentence strips and then put them in order later.

6. After the sentence strips are recorded, read each sentence strip aloud to the students, pointing to the words as you read.

7. Ask students to read the sentences aloud with you.

FIGURE 6.2 ➤ Organizer

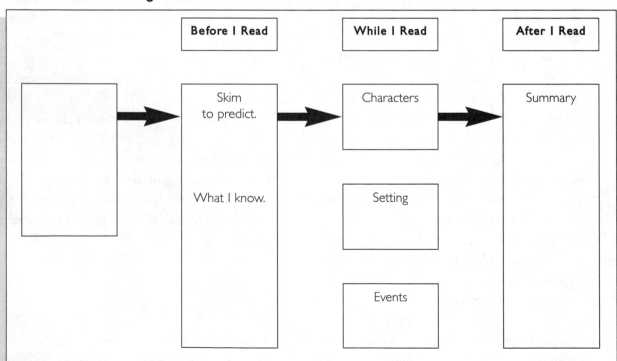

FIGURE 6.3 ➤ **Frame for Answering "5Ws" and "How" Questions**

Student Name: _____

Title: _____

Pages: _____

Date: _____

Who?	
What?	
Where?	
When?	
Why?	
How?	

Source: From *Strategies for Teaching Students with Learning and Behavior Problems* (6th ed., p. 201), by C. S. Bos & S. Vaughn, 2006, Boston: Allyn and Bacon.

8. Call on individual students to read sentences.
9. Ask students to work with you on the following:
   - Organizing sentence strips in the right order
   - Identifying questions a teacher might ask about the story
   - Selecting key words to teach others prior to reading the story
   - Illustrating the story and eventually making it into a class book

Main Idea and Summarization

Applying the main idea and summarizing are two crucial skills youngsters need to know in order to do well on high-stakes achievement tests. Explicit and systematic instruction in finding the main idea is associated with improved outcomes in reading comprehension (Graves, 1986; Jenkins et al., 1987; Jitendra, 1998; Jitendra et. al., 2000; Wong & Jones, 1982).

How can you improve understanding of the main idea with your students? Figure 6.5 offers examples of six basic questions that go to the main idea of many passages.

An example of a rule-based instructional strategy is given in Figure 6.6.

For narrative text, story retelling can be an effective practice for determining and ensuring reading comprehension. The teacher can first model retelling the story by identifying the key components: character, setting, problem, and resolution. For students who struggle with these components, teaching them separately and then combining them can be an effective

FIGURE 6.4 ➤ **Questioning the Author: Modified Procedures for English Language Learners**

Goal	Queries	Procedures
Initiate discussion.	"What is the author trying to say?" "What is the author's message?" "What is the author talking about?"	
Help students focus on the author's message.	"That's what the author says, but what does it mean?"	
Help students link information.	"How does that connect with what the author already told us?" "How does that fit in with what the author already told us?" "What information has the author added here that connects to or fits in with _____?"	Ask students to work in pairs.
Identify difficulties with the way the author has presented information or ideas.	"Does that make sense?" "Is that said in a clear way?" "Did the author explain that clearly? Why or why not?" "What's missing? What do we need to figure out or find out?"	Consider the language development of the students in the pairs so that students with better English oral language are paired with students with less well developed oral language skills.
Encourage students to refer to the text either because they have misinterpreted a text statement or to help them recognize that they have made an inference.	"Did the author tell us that?" "Did the author give us the answer to that?"	Give pairs several minutes to answer questions together before calling on students to respond.

Source: From "Questioning the Author: A Yearlong Classroom Implementation to Engage Students with Text," by I. L. Beck, M. G. McKeown, C. Sandora, and L. Kucan, 1996, *The Elementary School Journal, 96*(4), pp. 385–414.

tool. Be sure English language learners understand what is meant by character, setting, problem, and resolution. Using Figure 6.7 can help.

Simple retelling:
- Identify and retell the beginning, middle, and end of the story.
- Describe the setting.
- Identify the problem and resolution.

More complete retelling:
- Identify and retell events and facts in a sequence.
- Make inferences to fill in missing information.

- Identify and retell causes of actions or events and their effects.

Most complete retelling:

- Identify and retell a sequence of actions or events.
- Make inferences to account for events or actions.
- Offer an evaluation of the story.

Be sure to model each of these retelling elements so students see an expert practice them. Provide students an opportunity to work in very small groups to identify retell elements and practice retelling parts of the story.

Story Read-Aloud Practice

Reading comprehension instruction does not need to wait until students can read connected text independently. Even young children who are not yet readers can benefit from reading comprehension instruction that focuses on story read-aloud practice. English language learners benefit when this practice addresses vocabulary and oral language development. The basic elements of the story read-aloud practice in Figure 6.8 include the following steps:

1. Introduce the story and three or four new vocabulary words from the text. Remember, the goal here is to preview the text and to introduce new vocabulary using the meaning as it is used in context within the text. Be sure to use everyday meanings to make words "real."

FIGURE 6.5 ➤ **Finding the Main Idea**

Does the paragraph tell?
What or who is it about? (one or more)
What is happening?
Where—something is or happened?
When—something happened?
How—something looks or is done?
Why—something happened?
Note: Some paragraphs may contain a sentence or two that do not tell about the main idea!

Source: From "Enhancing Main Idea Comprehension for Students with Learning Problems: The Role of a Summarization Strategy and Self-Monitoring Instruction," by A. K. Jitendra, M. K. Hoppes, and Y. P. Xin, 2000, *Journal of Special Education, 34*(3), pp. 127–139. Reprinted with permission.

FIGURE 6.6 ➤ **Rule-Based Instructional Strategy: An Example**

Rule Statement

Teacher: "We are going to learn a rule about 'motive.' Motive is why a person in the story does something. For example, the police try to figure out the motive for a murder. They want to know why a person commits a murder. Why a person does something. That is the motive."

"What is a motive? Yes, a motive is why a person does something."
NOTE: Ask students to provide examples of a motive. If necessary, provide additional examples of a motive until students understand the meaning.

Example of Motive in a Story

Teacher: "We will find the character motive of a story together. First listen to the story, and then we will find the character motive. Here is the story:

'Victor was worried. He could not find it anywhere. It was in his room before he went to bed and now it was not there. He wondered who could have taken it. He knew that if he did not find it his mother would be very, very mad.'"

Multiple Procedure

Teacher: "Everybody. Who is this story about?"

Students: "*Victor*"

Teacher: "Everybody. What is Victor doing?"

Students: "*Looking for something important*"

Teacher: "Everybody. How does Victor feel?"

Students: "*Worried or upset*"

Teacher: "Everybody. Why was he worried or upset?"

Students: "*Because he was very worried that his mother would be mad if he did not find it.*"

Teacher: "Everybody. How do you know he was worried or upset?"

Students: "*He said his mother would be very, very mad if he did not find it.*"

Teacher: "What is 'motive'?"

Students: "*The reason a character does something.*"

Teacher: "Yes, motive is the reason a character does something. What is Victor's motive?"

Students: "*He wants to find it so his mother will not be mad.*"

NOTE: Read stories and determine the motive of the character of the story. Use the word "motive" throughout the day.

Source: From "The Differential Effects of Two Systematic Reading Comprehension Approaches with Students with Learning Disabilities," by K. Rabren, C. Darch, and R. C. Eaves, 1999, *Journal of Learning Disabilities, 32*(1), pp. 36–47.

2. Read the selected narrative or information passage aloud, addressing implicit and explicit comprehension. During the first read-aloud, comprehension is the goal; however, students are also asked to listen for the new vocabulary words.

3. After reading the passage through without stopping, reread the passage, drawing attention to the vocabulary words. On this reread, students are asked to hold up a finger, thumb, or hand when they hear the new vocabulary word. Encourage additional conversation about meaning within text.

4. Give students an opportunity to "own" the new vocabulary words by extending their use in talk and story comprehension. The teacher is the facilitator and students use oral language to retell the story and describe the key vocabulary. Promote oral language to express ideas and thoughts.

5. Initially model how to summarize what was read and key information learned.

FIGURE 6.7 ➤ My Story Retell

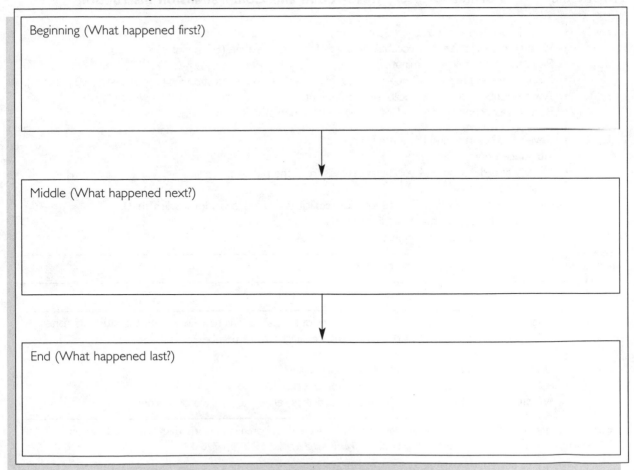

Beginning (What happened first?)

Middle (What happened next?)

End (What happened last?)

Slowly scaffold students as they summarize and identify key content. Encourage students to engage in meaningful dialogue about a topic related to the story or text, allowing students to connect the story or information text to their own experiences.

In summary, comprehension instruction is an essential element of an effective reading program for English language learners. Prioritizing instruction in listening comprehension for kindergarten and 1st grade students is vital. As students progress (2nd through 5th grade), it is essential to expand their text comprehension from listening comprehension to reading comprehension. Suggestions for specific lessons to enhance comprehension are provided in the following pages.

FIGURE 6.8 ➤ Format for Story Read-Aloud and Comprehension Instruction

Day 1	• Provide overview of passage (~2 minutes).
	• Identify and describe 3–4 vocabulary words from the passage (~3 minutes).
	• Read the story/text (~5 minutes).
	• Monitor comprehension (2 questions regarding explicit text, 1 question for implicit text (~10 minutes).
	• Ask students to use new vocabulary (~2 minutes).
	• Reread text, checking for understanding (~10 minutes).
Day 2	• Review vocabulary and key ideas from text.
	• Introduce new passage.
	• Identify and describe 3–4 vocabulary words from the passage.
	• Read the story/text.
	• Monitor comprehension (2 questions for explicit text, 1 question for implicit text).
	• Ask students to use new vocabulary words.
	• Reread text, checking for understanding.
Day 3	• Repeat steps from day 2 with new text.
Day 4	• Repeat steps from day 2 with new text.
Day 5	• Choose 4–5 vocabulary words from the previous days' lessons to review with the students (ones that may have been particularly challenging or difficult to remember).
	• Review the words.
	• Discuss and connect what students are learning.
	• Ask students to respond to comprehension questions.
	• Ask students to participate in vocabulary activities related to key words learned.

Source: Adapted from "Storybook Reading: Improving Vocabulary and Comprehension for English Language Learners," by P. Hickman, S. Pollard-Durodola, and S. Vaughn, 2004, *The Reading Teacher, 57*(8), pp. 720–730.

What Are Several Useful Classroom Activities?

Strategy instruction seems to consistently improve students' ability to see relationships in stories, answer comprehension questions, and retell what they have read in a more focused fashion. (Gersten et al., 2001, p. 296)

The following comprehension activities can be used at any level in a reading program and have been modified or are developed specifically for English language learners. As students become more proficient readers, the complexity of the texts increases and the students' abilities benefit from knowing multiple strategies.

Many English language learners are reluctant to speak because they are not yet confident about their language skills or the accuracy of their answers. Some people have called this "courteous silence." Make every effort with ELLs to get them to speak and to take risks in a protected environment.

Connecting with Text (During Reading)

Objective. Students will learn how to connect with text by identifying key sentences and ideas they relate to and indicating how those sentences and ideas connect with their life.

Materials. Student copies of narrative or information text, a student record sheet (see Figure 6.9), pencil for each student, a whiteboard with marker for the teacher

FIGURE 6.9 ➤ Connecting with Text: Student Form

What I liked from the text
How I connect
What I liked from the text
How I connect

1. Ask students to select text on their level to read.

2. Tell students that you are interested in what parts of the text they read that they connect to personally. Tell them to check with a pencil those parts: key idea, sentence, or picture from the text.

3. Ask students to write the page number of the text and a brief description of why they connect to the text or picture identified.

4. Ask students to share what they identified and their connections.

5. Summarize key responses on the whiteboard.

Making Predictions (Before Reading)

Objective. Students will learn how to make predictions about narrative and expository texts.

Materials. Student copies of narrative or expository text with previewing cues (title or pictures), overhead projector, marker, a blank transparency

1. Give a copy of the text to each student.

2. Introduce the topic of the text.

3. Explain that before reading, students will skim the pages of the story or take a "book walk."

4. With students, skim information presented on each page, such as the title, subheadings, pictures, graphs, and boldfaced or italicized words.

5. Encourage students to predict one thing they may learn by reading the text.

6. Have students share their predictions. Ask students to give reasons or evidence to support their predictions.
   For example:
   • "Why do you think you will learn about that?"

7. Ask other students to provide feedback.
   For example:
   • "Do you agree with the prediction?"
   • "Why?" or "Why not?"

8. Record students' predictions on a chart.

9. After reading, review predictions and discuss.

Reading with a Purpose: Information Text (Before and After Reading)

Objective. Given the title, pictures, and several key words from an information text, students will set a purpose for reading by generating questions they want answered in the text.

Materials. Instructional-level information text with pictures or subheadings (chapter titles or section headings), chart paper with the story graphic (see Figure 6.10)

1. Give a copy of the text to each student.

2. Read aloud the title to the students.

3. Begin a story graphic by writing the key words from the title in the square box on top.

4. Model how to generate a question about the story from the title.
   For example:
   • "I wonder why we are going to learn about forests all over the world. I

will write a question, 'Why do we have forests all over the world?'"

- Ask students if they have other questions. Scaffold responses for English language learners.

5. Write one of the questions in one of the boxes connected to the web's title square.

6. Provide students with two to three key words from the text. For example, "Today when we read about forests we are also going to read about *migrating birds*. What question might we have about *migrating birds*?"

7. Write each question in a separate box.

8. Continue to review key words from the text as well as preview the text (look at the pictures and read subheadings).

9. Have students generate questions they want answered in the story. Record their questions on the story graphic.

10. Before reading the story, review each question.

11. Encourage students to look for the answers to the questions as they read the story.

12. Have students read the story aloud.

13. When students find an answer to a question, stop and write the answer under the question on the web.

14. After reading, discuss any unanswered questions on the web.

Adaptations

(1) Begin with fewer questions so students are not overwhelmed by the number they have to answer. (2) Have students work in pairs or in groups of three to ask and answer questions.

Getting the Gist or Main Idea (During Reading)

Objective. Students will learn how to get the gist (or the main idea) of each paragraph in expository text.

Materials. Student copies of three short expository texts (two or three paragraphs initially; more paragraphs as ELLs become more proficient), overhead projector, marker, student copies of the gist log (see Figure 6.11), a transparency of the gist log

1. Give a copy of one of the expository texts to each student.

FIGURE 6.10 ➤ **Story Graphic**

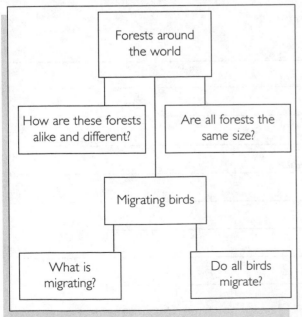

2. Explain that a gist statement represents the main idea of a paragraph. The main idea is the most important information in a paragraph.
3. To ensure that English language learners understand what a main idea is, use examples from everyday experiences (e.g., going to the store to get milk and finding the store is closed) to practice getting the main idea.
4. Explain the three steps of the "getting the gist" strategy:
   - First, name who or what the paragraph is mostly about.
   - Second, tell the most important information about "the who" or "the what."
   - Third, state the main idea in 10 words or fewer.
5. Read aloud a paragraph of the text.

6. Model how to identify who or what the paragraph is mostly about.
   For example:
   - "What is the paragraph mostly about?"
   - "Who is the paragraph mostly about?"
7. Record the who or what on the transparency.
8. Model how to identify the most important information about the who or what.
   For example:
   - "What is the most important information about _____ [insert who or what]?"
9. Record the most important information on the transparency.
10. Model how to combine the who or what with the most important information about the who or what. Limit the state-

FIGURE 6.11 ➤ Gist Log

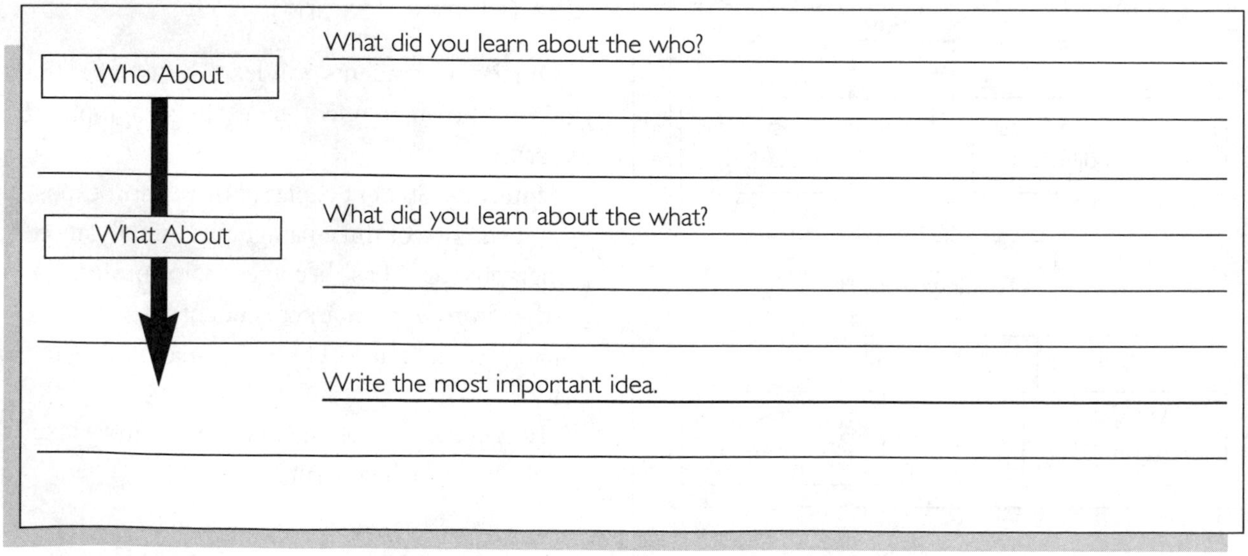

Who About — What did you learn about the who?

What About — What did you learn about the what?

Write the most important idea.

ment to 10 words or fewer. Ask students, if necessary, to count the words.

11. Record the gist statement on the transparency.

12. Provide opportunities for students to collaboratively practice the strategy. Provide corrective feedback, as needed.

    For example:
    - Give a copy of another expository text to each student.
    - Have one student read aloud the first paragraph.
    - Have several students tell who or what the paragraph is mostly about. Discuss responses, and record information on the transparency (the first box of the gist log).
    - Have several students tell the most important information about the who or what. Discuss responses, and record information on the transparency (the second box of the gist log).
    - Have several students read their gist statements of no more than 10 words using the information in the first and second boxes. Discuss responses, and record the main idea statement on the transparency (the third box of the gist log).
    - Continue the same procedure until the entire text has been read.

13. Provide opportunities for students to independently practice the strategy with a partner.

For example:
- Give a copy of another expository text and a gist log to each student.
- Review the three steps of the strategy.
- Pair students. Have them take turns reading aloud each paragraph.
- After reading each paragraph, have the pair use the strategy and record the gist of the paragraph on their gist logs.
- Monitor to ensure that students take turns reading and correctly follow the steps to determine the gist.
- As an activity with the whole group, have pairs read some of their gist statements.

Adaptations

(1) Use "get the gist" with narrative texts. (2) Ask students to read the same paragraph and then to work on the gist together. (3) Write students' "gists" on a transparency and use them to work with the class to write an improved gist.

Sources. Adapted from *Effective Instruction for Elementary Struggling Readers, Research-Based Practices* (Rev. ed.), by University of Texas Center for Reading and Language Arts, 2003, Austin, TX: Texas Education Agency.

Adapted from *Supplemental Instruction for Third Grade Struggling Readers: A Guide for Tutors,* by University of Texas Center for Reading and Language Arts, 2001, Austin, TX: Texas Education Agency.

Using a Story Map (During Reading)

Objective. Students will learn how to use a story map to improve their comprehension of narrative texts.

Materials. Student copies of narrative text, overhead projector, overhead marker, student copies of a story map (see Figure 6.12), a transparency of the story map

1. Give a copy of the narrative text to each student.
2. Read and discuss the title.
3. Identify any challenging words in the text and preteach their meaning.
4. Explain that the cooking ingredients used in recipes are like the story elements used in stories. Raw rice, water, salt, and butter are some of the ingredients that may be used to make rice. Stories also have critical ingredients that make them effective.
5. Introduce and discuss the common story elements of narrative text:
   - Setting (where and when)
   - Characters (key person or persons in the story)
   - Problem or goal (what the characters are trying to accomplish or solve)
   - Plot (series of events in which the characters try to solve a problem or achieve a goal)
   - Resolution (solution or achievement of a goal)
6. Using previous stories read with the class, discuss each of the story elements, giving students opportunities to provide examples of each element from previous stories.
7. Introduce a story map template and the common story elements of narrative text.
8. Read the text aloud.
9. While reading aloud, stop periodically to model how to identify each story element. Record the information on the transparency.
10. Provide opportunities for guided practice. For example:
    - Give copies of the text to each student.
    - Have students take turns reading the text aloud.
    - Periodically stop students. Ask several students to identify story elements.

    Discuss responses, and record information on a story map transparency.
11. Provide opportunities for independent practice. For example:
    - Give copies of the text and a story map template to each student.
    - Remind students to look for story elements while reading.
    - Pair students. Have them take turns reading.
    - While reading, have each pair record story elements on their story map template.
    - Monitor students to ensure that they take turns reading and correctly identify story elements.
    - As a whole group, discuss story maps.

FIGURE 6.12 ➤ Story Map

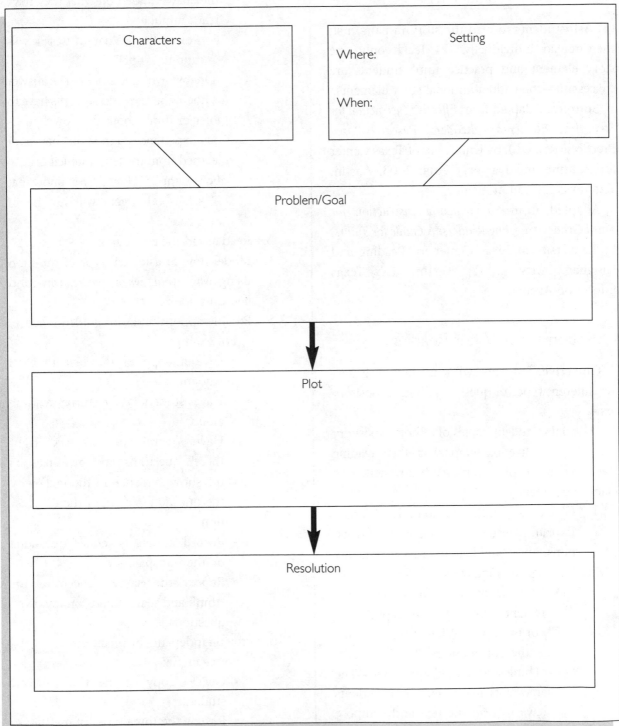

Adaptations

(1) Ask students to read the story in pairs first; then reread individually. (2) Teach only one story element and practice until students are successful—then add additional story elements.

Sources. Adapted from *Effective Instruction for Struggling Elementary Readers: Research-Based Practices* (Rev. ed.), by University of Texas Center for Reading and Language Arts, 2003, Austin, TX: Texas Education Agency.

Adapted from *Supplemental Instruction for Third Grade Struggling Readers: A Guide for Tutors*, by University of Texas Center for Reading and Language Arts, 2001, Austin, TX: Texas Education Agency.

Question Types (After Reading)

Objective. Students will learn how to generate different types of questions about expository texts.

Materials. Student copies of a short expository text (three to five paragraphs) at their reading level, overhead projector, overhead marker, a blank transparency.

1. Give a copy of the text to each student.
2. Explain that there are three types of questions, numbered here in order of difficulty for English language learners.
   (1) "Right there" questions—The answer is right there in the text: explicit.
      For example: "What is the name of the poisonous fish?"
   (2) "Think and search" questions—The answer is in the text, but students have to read the text and compose the answer based on what they have read: implicit.
      For example: "What causes a volcano to erupt?"
   (3) "On my own" questions—The answer is not in the text, and students have to infer or think about their own previous experiences and what they have learned from the text: implicit only.
      For example: "How do you know that sabertooth tigers will not be in a zoo?"
3. Read aloud the entire text.
4. Model how to ask each type of question using *who, what, when, where, why*, and *how* questions.
5. Provide opportunities for guided practice.
   For example:
   - Give a copy of the text to each student.
   - Have students take turns reading aloud.
   - Have several students ask "right there" questions and give reasons (or show evidence in the text) why the question is a "right there" question.
   - Record student-generated questions on the transparency.
   - Repeat the same procedure for "think and search" and "on my own" questions.
6. Provide independent practice.
   For example:
   - Give a copy of the text to each student.
   - Review the three types of questions.

136

- Pair students. Have them take turns reading aloud.
- After reading the entire text, have pairs write a question for each type.
- Monitor to ensure that students take turns reading and correctly generate the three types of questions.
- As a whole group, discuss questions generated by student pairs.

Source. From *From Clunk to Click: Collaborative Strategic Reading,* by J. K. Klingner, S. Vaughn, J. Dimino, J. S. Schumm, & D. P. Bryant, 2001, Longmont, CO: Sopris West.

Who Has the Evidence?

Objective. Students will generate questions that can be answered in the text.

Materials. Instructional-level narrative or expository text

1. Distribute text to students.
2. With younger students, read the text aloud while they follow along. With older students, ask them to choral read or read silently.
3. Tell students you are going to teach them to ask questions that allow for the "evidence" in the story to answer the question.
4. Teach students the meaning of evidence. "Evidence is information in the text that clearly answers the question." Provide an example of a question whereby the evidence cannot be located in the text. Provide an example of a question whereby the evidence can be located in the text.
5. Model how to generate questions.

For example:
- "How did the grandparents find their lost grandchild?"
6. Write the question on the board.
7. Ask students to find the answer to the question in the text.
8. Have students give the answer and identify the words in the text that helped them determine the answer.
9. Write the answer next to the question.
10. Ask students to generate a question from the text. On paper, have students write the question, its answer, and the page number where the answer is located in the text.
11. Have students ask their questions (without giving their answers).
12. After other students respond, have the student who asked the question confirm whether the answer is correct or incorrect. If incorrect, then the student gives the correct answer and the page number in the text where the answer is located. Other students locate the answer in the text.
13. Have students read the next section of text.
14. Ask students to generate three to four questions, the answers, and the page numbers where the answers are located in the text.
15. Assign one student to pretend to be the "teacher." This student asks one question and then calls on students to answer the question and give the page number in the text where the answer is located. Have the

student repeat the procedure with other questions.

16. Have students take turns being the "teacher."

Adaptations

(1) After generating questions, students ask the teacher to answer their questions without using the text. Then, students confirm whether the teacher's answers are correct by looking in the text. (2) Give students opportunities to express their ideas to each other and to the class. (3) Be sure students understand the main idea of the story prior to asking and answering evidence-based questions. (4) Ensure that students are familiar with sentences that refer to previous persons or objects. For example, "He was the same one who returned from the monastery." Be sure students know to whom one is referring. Also be sure students know key words like *monastery*.

Guided Story Response

Objective. Given a narrative text, students will identify the story elements (characters, setting, problem, important events, and solution).

Materials. Instructional-level narrative text, story log on chart paper, student copies of story logs (see Figure 6.13)

1. Give a copy of the text to each student.
2. Introduce the story log on the chart paper.
3. Describe each story element. Be sure English language learners know what you mean by character, setting, problem, important events, and solution. You may want to describe these key words and ask

students to refer to previous stories to ensure they know the meaning. For example, the character is the key person or persons in the story. "Do you remember the story about *la casa* that we read last week? Who was the key person or character in that story? Yes, ___ was the key person or character." Follow this same procedure when introducing all story elements, including setting (where the story takes place), problem (story difficulty), important events (most important things that happen in the story), and solution (how the problem or story difficulty is solved).

4. Have students read the text aloud.
5. As story elements are introduced, model by thinking aloud to help students identify each story element.

    For example:
    - "The characters are lost in the desert. The setting is the desert. I wonder if this will be the setting for the whole story. Do you think the setting will change?"

6. After reading, model completing the story log. Have students contribute their ideas. List the characters, setting, problem, important events, and solution.
7. Give a copy of another instructional-level narrative text and a story log to each student.
8. With students, read each story element on the log. Ask students to define each one.
9. Pair students. Have students take turns reading aloud each paragraph in the story.

FIGURE 6.13 ➤ **Guided Story Prompt Sheet**

Setting

Where did   happen?

When did   happen?

When did the story take place?

Characters

Whom is the story about?

Who are the main characters?

Who else is in the story?

What is _____ like?

Problem

What is   's problem?

What does   have to try to do?

What was the problem in the story?

What did   want (or not want) to do?

Important Events

What did   do about   ?

What did   do now?

What did   do to try to get what he or she wanted?

How did   try to solve the problem?

Solution

Did   get what she or he wanted? Why did   have trouble getting what she or he wanted?

How did   solve the problem?

Why was it hard to solve the problem?

Was the problem solved? How did   achieve his or her goal?

Theme

What did _____ learn at the end of the story?

What is the moral?

What lesson did the story try to tell you?

What is the author's message?

10. Encourage students to look for each story element as they read.

11. After reading the story, have each pair complete a story log.

Adaptations

(1) If there is time, allow students to draw their favorite character or setting on the back of the story log. (2) Ask students to describe to their partner a character they would like to add to the story if they were writing it.

KKWL for Information Texts: Modified for English Language Learners

Objective. ELLs benefit from reading and learning from information texts. Students will be taught key words in the passage and identify what they know, what they want to learn, and, after reading, what they have learned.

Materials. Instructional-level information text with multiple sections or chapters and student copies of the modified KKWL chart (Ogle, 1986). See Figure 6.14.

1. Provide a copy of information text to each student.

2. Introduce the modified KKWL chart by explaining each column:

   "The first *K* stands for **key words** in the passage."

   "The second *K* stands for what you **know**."

   "The *W* stands for what you **want** to learn."

   "The *L* stands for what you **learned**."

3. Preread the chapter and select the key words that you think students will need to know to understand the chapter. Select three or four words and write them on the whiteboard. Briefly describe what each word means and check with students to ensure understanding.

4. Read the first chapter aloud.

5. Model and explain that after reading the first part of the chapter, students should list what they know about the topic (up to this point) in the second *K* column on the chart. For example:
   • List the subject of title, chapter heading, picture ideas, new words, and things learned up to this point. If students have heard any of the key words in the story, they can indicate this in the column as well.

6. Model and explain that the next step is to generate questions that they may have about the subject and what it may mean. With students, generate several questions and write them in the *W* column.
   For example:
   • "Does the text make sense?"
   • "Does this concern me?"

7. Have students read aloud the next section or chapter.

8. Ask students if they have learned any of the answers to the questions that they wrote in the W column. Write their responses in the L column of the chart.

9. Ask students to tell what they know about the subject from the second chapter. List their responses on the chart.

FIGURE 6.14 ➤ **KKWL Chart**

K Key Words	K What I Know	W What I Want to Learn	L What I Learned

10. Have students generate questions they have about the story that they hope will be answered in the next chapter. On the chart, list their questions in the W column.

11. After each chapter is read, look at the questions previously listed in the W column, and ask students whether any of the questions were answered in the chapter they just read. On the chart, write answers to these questions in the L column. Continue to add important points to the K column and list students' questions in the W column.

Adaptations

(1) Use KKWL charts for narrative text. (2) Use KKWL charts to ask students to identify key words that they do not know.

Annotated Bibliography

Blackowicz, C., & Ogle, D. (2001). *Reading comprehension: Strategies for independent learners.* New York: Guilford Press.

This book presents a variety of strategies and examples for teaching comprehension. Based on the authors' classroom experiences, the book describes important components of comprehension instruction. Chapters include creative ways to help students monitor their own understanding, engage in research, and successfully read informational texts. The final chapter focuses on what teachers can do to encourage lifelong reading.

Block, C. C., Rodgers, L. L., & Johnson, R. B. (2004). *Comprehension process instruction.* New York: Guilford Press.

This book provides an excellent overview of when and how to teach reading comprehension processes. Of special note is the focus on teaching comprehension prior to students having difficulties, and how to use and modify comprehension practices for students with difficulties. The appendices provide numerous reproducible forms and posters to assist teachers in implementing identified practices in the book.

Duke, N. K., & Bennett-Armistead, V. S. (2003). *Reading and writing informational text in the primary grades: Research-based practices.* New York: Scholastic.

This book addresses the uses of and instructional methods for information texts for young children. The activities and practices in this book are ideally suited for English language learners, because information text is a rich source for both world knowledge and word knowledge. A rationale for using information texts with young children as well as practices for how to weave information texts into instruction is provided.

Haley, M. H., & Austin, T. Y. (2004). *Content-based second language teaching and learning: An interactive approach.* Boston: Pearson, Allyn and Bacon.

The entire book provides practices and procedures relevant for instruction for second-language learners. The last section of the book specifically addresses comprehension, including practical exercises for using graphic organizers, application activities, and assessments to determine learning.

Herrell, A., & Jordan, M. (2004). *Fifty strategies for teaching English language learners* (2nd ed.). Upper Saddle River, NJ: Pearson.

This book was designed with teachers in mind and provides well-organized practical ideas for teaching English language learners. Section V addresses strategies for building comprehension and provides specific ideas for enhancing understanding of text that are linked to the Teachers of English to Speakers of Other Languages (TESOL) standards.

Klingner, J. K., Vaughn, S., Dimino, J., Schumm, J. S., & Bryant, D. (2001). *From clunk to click: Collaborative strategic reading.* Longmont, CO: Sopris West.

This book describes implementation of the comprehension strategy, or collaborative strategic reading (CSR). A special focus is the use of CSR with English as a second language (ESL) students. An introduction to the strategy and its effectiveness in developing comprehension are provided. Includes a detailed plan for teaching collaborative strategic reading to students, with complete lesson plans and sample materials. Steps for developing cooperative learning groups and adapting CSR for secondary students are also included.

RAND Reading Study Group. (2002). *Reading for understanding: Toward an R&D program in reading comprehension.* Santa Monica, CA: RAND Corporation.

This report reflects the thinking of key researchers around the country on what we know and need to know about teaching reading comprehension. Though it is not designed as a book for teachers, it provides background knowledge on the theory and research underlying reading comprehension instruction. This book also describes the unacceptable gaps in reading comprehension performance for minority students.

Wilhelm, J. D. (2001). *Improving comprehension with think-aloud strategies.* New York: Scholastic.

Comprehension instruction through thinking aloud is described in this book. Strategies for helping students recognize and make meaning from text are also presented. Instructional steps for modeling think-alouds, lesson ideas, and examples of think-alouds in action are provided for teachers. Student checklists and a teacher assessment checklist are included.

◆   ◆   ◆

Web Sites That Teach

www.readingrockets.org/lp.php?SCID=15

This Web site provides an overview of reading comprehension, research findings on reading comprehension, and practical tips for teachers.

www.readingrockets.org/lp.php?CID=59

This section of the Reading Rockets Web site describes current research on teaching reading to English language learners, including instructional strategies for teaching reading comprehension.

www.readingonline.org/articles/handbook/pressley/index.html

This article by Michael Pressley introduces well-validated ways to increase comprehension skills in students through instruction.

www.readingonline.org/electronic/elec_index.asp?HREF=/editorial/may2001/index.html

This site provides 20 articles and resources on reading comprehension and engagement, including book lists, Web sites, and information on research and instruction.

http://curry.edschool.virginia.edu/go/readquest

The Reading Quest Web site focuses on teaching social studies and provides links to reading comprehension resources and reading comprehension strategies that can be used in a variety of subject areas (most include blackline masters and handouts).

www.aera.net/uploadedFiles/Journals_and_Publications/Research_Points/RP_Winter04.pdf

This article, "English Language Learners: Boosting Academic Achievement," provides an overview of current research on teaching reading and literacy to English language learners, with information about comprehension instruction for this population of students.

www.literacy.uconn.edu/compre.htm

The reading comprehension section of the University of Connecticut Literacy Web provides a wealth of resources on comprehension instruction, strategies, and activities, including resources for English language learners.

http://readwritethink.org/index.asp

The Read Write Think Web site provides a variety of reading information, including lessons, standards, resources, and student materials. Reading comprehension information is contained in the "Learning About Language" section.

Questions and Answers for Teachers

THIS SECTION IS INCLUDED FOR THREE REASONS. FIRST, THE QUESTIONS REFLECT the most frequent queries we get at workshops, presentations, and our own college classes. Second, the questions and answers allow us to highlight material presented in this book. Finally, we know that many prospective purchasers of this book will turn to this section to see if the book is worthwhile.

1. What are some factors to consider when assessing or designing instruction for English language learners?

The rate at which English language learners (ELLs) will develop proficiency in English will vary considerably among students, based on factors such as motivation, age, exposure to English, parents' English proficiency, and quality of educational experiences before coming to the United States and once here.

2. Just how valid are assessment tools for English language learners?

For all measures you use, consider the populations on whom the measures were normed. If the measures were normed on English language learners who are similar descriptively to the students you are testing, then you can have reasonable confidence in the findings from the measures. If you are using measures that were normed on monolingual English students, then use of the test and confidence in the findings for ELLs are reduced. With beginning reading assessments that do not have norms, consider students' progress over time, charting their progress on curriculum-based measures. In effect, teachers will create their own measures of progress until students are at a point where normed measures can be used. There is material in this book that will help teachers do this.

3. What is the research behind the material in this book? We have all the bibliographic entries in "References," but to what degree is the research really scientific and proven?

The information we have provided in this book is based on the best scientific research available on teaching reading to English language learners. When research knowledge on English language learners was limited, we interpreted the appropriate findings from monolingual students, so teachers using this book would have access to instructional practices that have a high level of probability of working. While our book provides a great deal of research-based, useful material, we recognize that the research in this area including our own work, is burgeoning, and that in three to five years much more will be known.

4. How can we capitalize on the knowledge and skills students have in their first language?

We can extend students' knowledge and skills in their first language in several critical ways: (1) we can build on meaning by linking the meaning of new words they are learning in English to word meanings they already know; (2) we can build on what they know about the sounds and letters in their first language to similar sounds and letters in English; (3) we can

build on what they know about comprehension in their first language to increase comprehension in English; and (4) we can honor and appreciate the additional knowledge and skills they bring to our classrooms by recognizing their abilities in their first language.

5. Is phonemic awareness appropriate for all language backgrounds? Does it make a difference if the native language is alphabetic? What are the three or four languages that are easiest to use as a base from which to transfer to English?

Because all languages are based on sounds and connecting those sounds in ways that make words, phonological awareness and instruction related to it is appropriate for all language backgrounds. This is true whether or not the language is alphabetic. However, if students are phonologically aware in an alphabetic language like Spanish, the most common language by far of ELLs, we know that there is some transfer to phonological awareness in English.

6. How can we maximize vocabulary development?

Consistent and continual focus on building meaning is the essence of developing and extending vocabulary development in English language learners. Also, wide reading and listening in English promotes vocabulary development. ELLs should be encouraged to read English language magazines, watch age-appropriate and parent-approved English language television, and seek out any other sources in English that will extend their English vocabulary. This book provides an entire chapter on building vocabulary with English language learners.

7. What is the role of cognates in ELL instruction?

It is intuitive that students who speak and/or read a language that has cognates related to English (e.g., Spanish, Italian, French, German) would benefit from systematic instruction that links and extends those cognates. In fact, research supports this. Making connections between words and parts of words in a student's first language to words and types of words in the second language provides valuable linkages for English language learners. This is particularly helpful for students whose first language has many words with Latin and Greek roots and affixes.

8. Do children need to know how to read before we teach vocabulary and comprehension in English?

Like all students, ELLs do not need to know how to read before we teach vocabulary and comprehension. In fact, parents can be exceedingly helpful in building and extending vocabulary and listening comprehension with their children in the home even before they come to school and even if the parents do not speak English. Developing these skills in the first language will be helpful in learning English. From the first day of school and throughout the grades, practices that improve students' knowledge of words and concepts should be promoted.

9. What are the three or four best motivators for English language learners to maintain their interest in learning to read?

All students, including ELLs, are motivated when they have success and when we provide

them with new opportunities to be successful. Students are motivated when they perceive they are making progress. Students are motivated when they are accepted for what they know and not excluded because of their language differences. Teachers should challenge ELLs as much as possible, but not get too far ahead of them and thereby provoke feelings of frustration.

10. Is there any central agency, university, Web site, or other resource that accumulates information on English language learners, such as background, statistics, research, and lesson plans?

There are many places that have information that will help teachers of ELLs, but there is no single repository for this information. This book is a beginning toward providing research-based practices, best practices in areas where the research is still thin or nonexistent, and both bibliographic and Web site resources. The end of each chapter provides extensive information and resources to assist decision makers and teachers.

11. What should the school do when a student who has had good ELL instruction is still making inadequate progress in reading? What are the next steps?

We suggest that you provide additional and more intensive instruction using effective reading intervention practices (such as those described in this book). We suggest that this more intensive instruction be provided in small groups or one on one and that each student's response to this instruction be carefully monitored to assure that growth is occurring at a pace the teacher deems reasonable for a particular student. If the student continues to respond very poorly to this more intensive instruction, we suggest that you consider discussing the student's progress with the school psychologist, parents, and other school specialists.

12. Do English language learners need to have some level of proficiency in spoken English to begin instruction? How do you judge where to begin?

In those situations when the school is not providing literacy instruction in the students' first language, begin literacy instruction in English for students who have limited English proficiency when they enter school. Assess students' literacy and knowledge in both the home language, if possible, and English to determine their literacy level. This does not mean that a particular ELL would be provided with the same literacy instruction as another student, just that the literacy instruction should not be delayed.

13. What are common mistakes, albeit innocent and with good intentions, that some teachers make when working with English language learners?

Perhaps one of the biggest mistakes that some teachers make is delaying literacy instruction because they are concerned that the language development of the student is not fully mature. Students benefit from literacy instruction even when their proficiency in English is below age-level expectations.

Teachers may erroneously assume that students who have limited English abilities are also cognitively limited and therefore provide limited access to higher-level thinking tasks.

Teachers may also lack confidence in their knowledge and skills for teaching English language learners and thus deny these students access to education. We believe that this book will provide teachers with the needed materials and strategies for success with ELLs as well as the confidence that they are doing the right thing.

14. What tools do we need to teach reading to English language learners? Are there some "magic tools" that we, as teachers, can use to teach reading to this population? What tools or tricks can you give me?

There are no "magic tools" for teaching ELLs any more than there are "magic tools" for teaching any other students or subjects. We now know that learning to read in English as a native language and learning to read in English as a second language have a lot of similarities. Therefore, we can apply many of the principles about what we know about learning to read in English as a native language to learning to read in English as a second language. However, unlike English monolingual speakers, ELLs will not have many of the receptive and expressive language skills, and they will not be familiar with the structure of English. Therefore, it will be important to promote the development of students' English proficiency.

This book provides many suggestions for how to adapt instructional practices in reading for ELLs. Solid research and the best practices available, when there is insufficient research, undergird all of our suggestions and practical lessons.

15. How do English language learners learn to read? Do they learn to read differently than monolingual English students?

Students learning to read a second language follow a path similar to those learning English as monolingual readers. However, there are practices and materials that must be modified until the ELL makes considerable progress. Consider whether the student is a reader in any language. If yes, then capitalize on what he or she knows about reading and assist the student in building bridges to reading English. There are several skills that transfer across languages, such as phonemic awareness and use of comprehension strategies.

If the student is an ELL and acquiring initial reading skills in English, then many of the practices used for teaching monolingual students to read in English are required.

This book provides both methods that work well with ELLs and the many modifications and adaptations necessary to boost the abilities of ELLs in English. An example would be to ensure that meaning is emphasized and that students can discern the sounds in English when teaching phonics-related activities.

16. Who should be in charge of teaching and developing students' English language skills: the ESL teacher, the classroom teacher, the speech and language specialist, the special education teacher, or other professional?

Everyone should be responsible for teaching English language skills to English language learners. There should be a schoolwide plan where everyone is providing ELLs with English language models and English language scaffolding. It is critical that districts and schools have a well-defined plan, including adequate professional development, to meet these children's language needs. Many schools have or soon will have ELL specialists on staff who can provide help to other teachers and aid in coordinating a schoolwide plan.

17. Some Spanish-speaking students learn to decode very easily and become good and quick decoders, but they do not understand what they are reading. What should teachers do?

Teachers have to be sure that at the same time they are teaching the technical aspects of reading, they are infusing reading instruction with vocabulary instruction and developing background knowledge, so ELLs can understand different texts. Teachers must make sure that they develop vocabulary and background knowledge by providing instruction and activities throughout the day and that vocabulary, fluency, and comprehension are monitored for progress. Remember, understanding what you read—comprehension—is the point of reading.

18. How can I determine if an English language learner's accent is interfering with his or her decoding? How much should teachers worry about or attempt to correct the accent? Is it all right to just leave the accent as it is?

You can be a great reader and have an accent. Everyone has an accent. Monolingual English readers have an accent. It just depends on whether the way you speak conforms to what people are accustomed to hearing: British English, American English, Irish English, and other accents in English. Albert Einstein's native language was German; he spoke English with an accent; but he was able to comprehend scientific research in English!

19. Some ELLs cannot improve their reading fluency. They are slow. What can we do?

Reading fluency with ELLs is a difficult area to impact with instruction and intervention, but we know it can be done with considerable success. If a student is genuinely a slow learner, it will be harder for that student, but the same would be true for a monolingual English student who reads slowly.

Make sure you provide sufficient practice and models of fluent English reading. Provide ample opportunities for students to read texts, including some text that is easier than their reading level and some text that is a bit more challenging. Give students a chance to read aloud with feedback. For many English language learners, lack of knowledge of vocabulary and syntax can reduce speed of reading. Ensure that students know the meaning of words and understand conceptually the topic they are reading. When sentences contain complex syntactic structures, preteach these aspects of the text and discuss them as part of reading comprehension practices. See Chapter 4, "Fluency for English Language Learners," for many activities designed to promote fluency with ELLs.

20. What do we do with students who are recent immigrants and have arrived at school with no English? What can we do to help them?

First, we have to determine what they can do, what strengths they are bringing to their schooling. They might be literate in their native language. Second, at the district and school level, there needs to be a plan on how to accommodate students who speak no English, and some professional—often the ESL teacher—has to be at the center of that plan.

21. What can we do about the lack of resources and materials? What can we do with so few intervention programs?

It is true that there are fewer resources and materials designed specifically for ELLs. That, of course, is what motivated us to write this book. Teachers need to take advantage of the resources provided in this book on instructing ESL students and ELLs. We can all have success if the principles and practical examples in this book are integrated into daily instruction.

Final Word

We believe that this book will provide enough material for any teacher to make progress with English language learners. However, we do understand that more research and real-world testing of that research needs to be done. If you have a question that we might add to our list, or if you wish to call attention to an area that urgently needs more attention, please contact us.

Glossary

Accuracy. Ability to perform a skill, such as reading words, correctly.

Additive bilingualism. Additive bilingualism occurs in a setting in which the first language and culture are enhanced and maintained, as in dual language programs. Therefore, the first language and culture are not replaced by the addition of a second language and culture.

Affix. Word element attached to the beginning or ending of a word. See also *prefix* and *suffix*.

Alphabetic principle. Understanding that letters in written words represent sounds in spoken words.

Analogy. Analyzing letter-sound patterns in previously learned words for use in reading new words. For example, using the *-ing* in *ring* and *sing* to read the new words *king* and *sting*.

Analytic phonics. Teaching letter-sound correspondences through previously learned words. For example, using the known word *cat* to analyze the individual letters and sounds /c/ /a/ /t/.

Aprenda. A Spanish achievement test that aligns with the objectives of the Stanford Achievement Tests (SAT 9). Numerous forms are used to assess preprimary, primary, and intermediate grades.

At-risk. A term used to describe students who demonstrate low performance in one or more areas related to reading development, including language deficits or low phonological awareness.

Automaticity. Quick and accurate recognition of letters, sounds, and words without hesitation.

Basal reader. A book of graded stories developed as an accompaniment for a reading program to assist teachers with reading instruction.

Base word. A meaningful word to which prefixes, suffixes, and endings can be added. For example, *read* is a base word for *reread, readable, reading*. Sometimes referred to as root word.

Bicultural. Identifying with the language and culture of two different groups.

Bilingual classroom. Setting in which students receive native language literacy instruction based on their primary language.

Bilingual education. An educational setting where students are instructed for some part of the day in their native language.

Bilingualism. The ability to speak, listen to, read, write, and understand more than one language.

Blending. Combining individual sounds or word parts to form whole words. Can be done orally or with print. For example, the speech sounds /c/ /a/ /t/ = cat. Likewise, the printed word *cat* can be read by combining the sounds /c/ /a/ /t/.

CCVC word. A word consisting of the consonant-consonant-vowel-consonant pattern (e.g., *crab, stop*).

Choral reading. Reading of text by several students in unison.

Chunking. Reading phrases, clauses, sentences, and words by dividing word or text into chunks.

Code mixing. A term used to describe the mixing of two languages, where one word in the sentence is substituted in a different language.

Code switching. Process in which words from one language are substituted with words from a second language while speaking. This can be at both the word and sentence level or within blocks of speech.

Cognates. Words that are similar in form and meaning in both English and another language.

Comprehension. Ability to understand and get meaning from spoken and written language.

Comprehension strategies. Techniques students can use to improve understanding of text.

Computer-assisted instruction. Instruction designed to be delivered via computer.

Consonant blend. Two or more consecutive consonant letters at the beginning or end of a word, each of which represents its own distinct sound when the word is pronounced. For example, *st* in *rust* or *str* in *strain*.

Consonant digraph. Two consonant letters that represent a single sound when the word is pronounced. For example, *th* in *that* or *ch* in *much*.

Consonant letters and sounds. All letters and their corresponding sounds that are not vowels: *b, c, d, f, g, h, j, k, l, m, n, p, q, r, s, t, v, w, x, y, z.*

Content-based ESL. The use of learning tasks, classroom techniques, and instructional materials from academic content areas as the means for enhancing content, cognition, language, and study skills for English as a second language (ESL) students.

Content words. Words, usually nouns or verbs, important to the understanding of a concept or text.

Context. The words and sentences occurring before and after an unknown word that provide hints about its meaning.

Conventional spelling. The standard spelling of a word in the English language.

Cooperative learning. An instructional process wherein groups of students work together to learn academic content.

Cross-age tutoring. Pairing older students with younger students for reading instruction, with one student serving as the teacher for the other student.

CVC word. A word consisting of a consonant-vowel-consonant pattern (e.g., *bat, men*).

CVCC word. A word consisting of the consonant-vowel-consonant-consonant pattern (e.g., *tent, lump*).

CVCe word. A word consisting of a consonant-vowel-consonant-silent e pattern (e.g., *make, note*).

Decodable texts. Connected text in which most of the words are composed of letter-sound correspondences previously taught.

Decoding. Using letter-sound relationships and word knowledge to convert printed words into spoken language. For example, converting the *c, a, t,* into the sounds /c/ /a/ /t/ to read the word *cat.*

Dialect. Regional language variations, including differences in pronunciation, grammar, and vocabulary.

Dominant language. The language used more often and with more proficiency.

Dual language program. Also known as two-way bilingual education or two-way immersion. An educational setting where all students are expected to attain literacy and oracy in two languages.

Dyslexia. Neurological disorder characterized by difficulties with written language, including reading, writing, spelling, and handwriting.

Early-exit bilingual education. The process by which students move from bilingual education programs to English-only classes during their first or second year of school.

ELL. English language learner. Denotes a student who is learning English as a second (or additional) language and is not yet proficient in English.

English-only. This term refers to efforts made by federal and state legislators to make English the official language of the United States. Within schools, this term refers to classes in which no accommodations or additional assistance is provided for limited-English-proficient students and all instruction is in English.

Equal Opportunity Act of 1974. In this act, Congress upheld the principle of the *Lau v. Nichols* decision that prohibited environments in which English language learners were left to "sink or swim."

ESL. English as a second language. ESL represents those instructional practices used by teachers for supporting English acquisition and instruction for English language learners. ESL instruction is primarily in English. Also known as English language development (ELD).

ESL classroom. Setting in which students receive literacy instruction in English and where the focus is often English language development using ESL practices.

ESOL. English for speakers of other languages. Used interchangeably with English as a second language (ESL).

Explicit instruction. Overtly teaching the steps required for completing a task.

Explicit questions. Literal comprehension questions that can be answered directly from printed or spoken language without making inferences.

Expository text. Informational text that is designed to teach or explain to the reader about a specific topic.

Expressive language skills. Speaking. Students tend to function at a slightly higher level in receptive language skills than in expressive language skills.

FEP. Fluent English proficient.

Fluency. Ability to perform reading skills (e.g., naming letters, reading words, reading connected text) quickly, smoothly, and automatically.

Frustrational reading level. Text level in which the reader does not have sufficient skills for accurate word recognition and comprehension. Frustration-level text is often defined as text in which the reader is able to read fewer than 90 percent of the words accurately.

Genre. A text structure that is identified by a unique set of characteristics, such as science fiction, mystery, or poetry.

Grade-level text. Text that has been analyzed to determine its difficulty. The level is based on the point in time during the school year that a typical student has the word recognition, vocabulary, and comprehension skills necessary to read the text independently.

Grapheme. The smallest unit of written language (e.g., letter or group of letters) representing the sounds in words. For example, the sound /ai/ in *rain* is represented by the grapheme *ai*.

Graphic organizers. Diagrams or other pictorials illustrating text organization and/or relationships among concepts or events presented in text.

Graphophonemic knowledge. Understanding of the relationship between letters and their sounds.

Guided reading. Teaching strategy wherein teachers support student reading and rereading of leveled books. Explicit phonics and decoding instruction are not taught; rather, incidental word recognition instruction is provided within the context of reading.

Implicit questions. Inferential comprehension questions that require the reader to connect information in text and use prior knowledge to deduce the answer.

Independent reading level. Text level in which the reader has sufficient word recognition and comprehension skills to read the text easily and fluently without assistance. Independent-level text is often defined as text in which the reader is able to read at least 95 percent of the words accurately.

Instructional reading level. Text level in which the reader has sufficient word recognition and comprehension skills to read the text with few errors and some assistance. Instructional-level text is often defined as text in which the reader is able to read between 90 and 94 percent of the words accurately.

Invented spelling. Attempts by young children with limited knowledge to spell words using their own conventions. For example, the word *does* may be spelled using the sounds in the word /d/ /u/ /z/ and the matching letters *duz*.

IPT. IDEA Proficiency Test. An assessment of oral and written language proficiency in English or Spanish.

Irregular words. Words in which some or all of the letters do not represent their most common sounds.

L1. The student's native language or first language.

L2. The second language the student is attempting to learn. For English language learners, L2 is English.

Language acquisition. The development of language skills.

Language dominance. The measurement of the degree of bilingualism, involving a comparison of the proficiencies in two or more languages.

Language maintenance. The process by which one's native language is protected and promoted.

Language minority. A person or community from the nondominant language group.

Language proficiency. The ability to speak or understand language content at levels similar to the native language.

Language submersion. Programs in which academic instruction is taught only in the dominant language of the country, without language scaffolds or support. Also called the "sink or swim" approach.

Late-exit bilingual education. Programs that consist of three or more years of bilingual instruction.

Lau v. Nichols. In 1974 this Supreme Court decision required schools to take proactive steps in helping language-minority students in accessing the curriculum.

LCD. Linguistically and culturally diverse.

Learning disability. Disorder characterized by achievement not commensurate with ability levels in one or more academic areas.

LEP. Limited English proficient. Language-minority students who have not acquired reading, understanding, speaking, or writing the English language at age- and grade-appropriate levels.

Letter knowledge. Ability to automatically identify the names and the most common sounds of the letters of the alphabet.

Letter-sound correspondence. Association between a specific letter and its corresponding sound. For example, the letter *m* and the sound /m/, as in *man*.

Listening comprehension. Ability to understand and get meaning from spoken language.

Listening vocabulary. Words a person understands when they are heard.

Long vowels. Vowel sounds that are the same as the names of the letters. For example, the sound /a/ in the word *make*.

Main idea. Most important point or idea in a text.

Maintenance bilingual education (MBE). Instruction in both English and the student's primary language. Students' primary language skills are used as a foundation and their English language skills are enhanced so that they eventually are competent in both languages.

Matthew effect. As used in reading, a term used to describe the effect of good readers reading more print and, therefore, improving their reading skills faster than poor readers who may have less contact with print.

Morpheme. The smallest meaningful unit of language. A morpheme may be a word or a word element. For example, the *-ed* in *jumped* is a morpheme that conveys past tense.

Morphology. Refers to the condition of the smallest units of language that convey meaning. For example, a base word or a root word is a morphological unit (e.g., *cat, small, pretty*) because it conveys meaning. A prefix such as *un-* in *unhappy* is a morphological unit, as is *happy*.

Mother tongue. This term is used interchangeably with the term native language, referring to the primary language used, the most dominant language learned, or the first language learned.

Multilingualism. The ability to speak, listen to, read, write, and understand three or more languages.

Narrative text. Text that tells a story and follows a common story structure.

Native language/primary language. This is the language a student learned in the home.

Native language instruction. The practice of teaching students in their native language.

Native language support. Clarifying lessons taught in English by using students' native language.

NEP. Non–English proficient.

Newcomer program. Self-contained programs designed to help newly arrived immigrants with educational and transitional needs before they enter traditional English language learner programs.

Onset-rime instruction. Use of word patterns to read unfamiliar words. The word pattern or rime involves the vowel and final consonants of the word (e.g., the /at/ in *sat* or the /ain/ in *train*). The onsets are the initial consonants of the word (e.g., the /s/ in *sat* or the /tr/ in *train*).

Orthography. System of written language, including the formation of letters and spelling of words.

Partner reading. Pairing of students to read aloud to each other.

Peer tutoring. Pairing of students to teach each other academic skills.

PHLOTE. Primary home language other than English.

Phoneme. The smallest unit of sound.

Phonemic awareness. Ability to recognize and manipulate the individual sounds (phonemes) in spoken words. Skills include orally blending, segmenting, adding, and deleting phonemes in words.

Phonics. Systematic teaching of sound-symbol relationships to decode words.

Phonological awareness. Ability to manipulate the sound system of spoken language, including words, rhymes, syllables, onset-rimes, and phonemes. Phonological awareness is a broad term encompassing phonemic awareness.

Phonology. The study of the sound system of a language and the use of sounds in forming words and sentences.

Prediction. Using context and syntax clues to support word identification and confirm word meaning.

Prefix. Meaningful word element attached to the beginning of a word. For example, *un-* and *re-* are prefixes in *unlock* and *refill.*

Print concepts. Skills beginning readers need to understand the concepts of written language. Examples include the concepts of words, sentences, and print moving from left to right.

Progress monitoring. System of frequent, dynamic assessment to measure student progress in a skill area.

Prosody. Use of appropriate intonation and phrasing when reading; reading with expression.

Rate. Speed at which a person reads with comprehension.

Reading. Process of transforming print into meaning.

Reading comprehension. Ability to understand and get meaning from written language.

Reading level. Information for teachers about the difficulty of a text for a particular student. Reading levels are categorized as instructional, independent, and frustrational.

Receptive language skills. Language skills that do not require the student to produce language (listening and reading). Students tend to function at a slightly higher level in receptive language skills than in expressive language skills.

Repeated reading. Reading of text several times with feedback to develop speed and accuracy.

Rhyme. Two or more words that have the same ending sounds, but not necessarily the same letters. For example, *state, straight,* and *bait* rhyme because they all end with the same sound unit.

Rime. The part of a syllable involving the vowel and final consonants of the word (e.g., the /at/ in *sat* or the /ain/ in *train*).

Scaffolded instruction. Temporary supports provided during initial skill instruction. Each task becomes increasingly more difficult until the skill is mastered. Scaffolds can be put in place by changing the difficulty of the content or task as well as changing the amount of support provided by materials or teacher guidance.

Segmenting. Breaking whole words into individual sounds or word parts. For example, the spoken word *cat* can be broken into the speech sounds /c/ /a/ /t/.

Semilingualism. This term refers to bilingual students who are not proficient in any language.

Sheltered English instruction. An approach used in sheltered classrooms intended to make instruction in English comprehensible for ELL students.

Sight words. Words that are read fluently and automatically at first sight.

Sounding out. See *decoding*.

Speaking vocabulary. Words a person uses when he or she speaks.

Story structure. Component parts of a story (narrative text), including characters, setting, events, problem, and resolution.

Structured immersion. The process by which all subject matter is taught to students in their second language using an easier form of the second language.

Students acquiring English (SAE). A less derogatory term than LEP that is used to describe students who are in the process of learning a second language.

Suffix. Meaningful word element attached to the end of a word. For example, *-less-* and *-ly* are suffixes in *restless* and *happily*.

Summarizing. Synthesis of the main ideas in a text.

Syllable. A unit of pronunciation usually containing a vowel.

Syntax. The order of words in a sentence and the rules of language for determining their order.

Synthetic phonics. Systematic teaching of word reading through blending known letter-sound correspondences. For example, using the known sounds /c/ /a/ /t/ to read the word *cat*.

Systematic instruction. Planned, sequential program of instruction.

Tape-assisted reading. Reading text along with an audiotape of a fluent reader.

Target language. The second language that students are learning.

TESL. Teaching English as a second language.

Text. The words that make up written material, such as a story, newspaper article, or sections of a textbook.

Text structure. Organization of the content in written material.

Think-aloud. Modeling of independent comprehension monitoring by stopping periodically during reading to say aloud what the reader is thinking.

Title I. Improving the Academic Achievement of the Disadvantaged, authorized under the Elementary and Secondary Education Act (ESEA) of 1965, as amended in 2001. Under Title I, support is provided to programs that aid at-risk and low-socioeconomic-level students.

Title II. Preparing, Training and Recruiting High Quality Teachers and Principals, authorized under the Elementary and Secondary Education Act (ESEA) of 1965. Under Title II, funds can be allocated to provide training to teachers working with limited-English-proficient students.

Title III. Language Instruction for Limited English Proficient Students and Immigrants, authorized under the Elementary and Secondary Education Act (ESEA) of 1965. Under Title III, school districts are provided aid for teachers of limited-English-proficient students to help the students meet state standards.

Transfer. The idea that skills and knowledge in the primary language can be transferred to English.

Vowel diphthong. A vowel formed by two vowels placed together in a single syllable. For example, *ue* as in *juego* and *uo* as in *cuota*.

Vowel triphthong. A vowel formed by three vowels placed together in a single syllable. For example, *uay* as in *Paraguay*.

WCPM. Words correct per minute. The number of words read correctly per minute is often used to determine a student's fluency level.

Word analysis. Strategies used by readers to decode written words.

Word family. A group of words sharing the same rime. For example, *cat, bat, sat, mat,* and *flat* form a word family.

Word recognition. Strategies readers use to identify written words.

Written expression. Expression of thoughts, feelings, and ideas through writing.

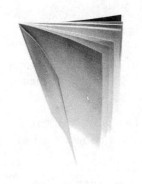

References

Adams, M. J. (1990). *Beginning to read: Thinking and learning about print.* Cambridge, MA: MIT Press.

Adams, M. J. (2000). *Fox in a box.* Monterey, CA: CTB McGraw-Hill.

Adams, M. J. (2001). Alphabetic anxiety and explicit, systematic phonics instruction: A cognitive science perspective. In S. B. Neuman & D. K. Dickinson (Eds.), *Handbook of early literacy research* (pp. 66–80). New York: Guilford Press.

Adams, M. J., Foorman, B. R., Lundberg, I., & Beeler, T. (1998). *Phonemic awareness in young children: A classroom curriculum.* Baltimore: Paul H. Brookes.

Allington, R. L., & Cunningham, P. M. (2002). *Schools that work: Where all children read and write* (2nd ed.). Boston: Allyn & Bacon.

Au, K. H. (1993). *Literacy instruction in multicultural settings.* Orlando, FL: Holt, Rinehart & Winston.

August, D., Carlo, M., Lively, T. J., McLaughlin, B., & Snow, C. (2006). Promoting the vocabulary growth of English learners. In T. A. Young & N. L. Hadaway (Eds.), *Supporting the literacy development of English learners* (pp. 96–112). Newark, DE: International Reading Association, Inc.

August, D., & Hakuta, K. (Eds.). (1997). *Improving schooling for language-minority children: A research agenda.* Washington, DC: National Academy Press.

Baker, S. (2003). Enhancing core reading instruction for English language learners in kindergarten and grade 1. Presented at the Institute for Beginning Reading II, Salem, OR.

Baker, S. K., Simmons, D. C., & Kame'enui, E. J. (1998). Vocabulary acquisition: Research bases. In D. C. Simmons & E. J. Kame'enui (Eds.), *What reading research tells us about children with diverse learning needs* (pp. 183–218). Mahway, NJ: Erlbaum.

Ball, E. W., & Blachman, B. A. (1991). Does phoneme awareness training in kindergarten make a difference in early word recognition and development spelling? *Reading Research Quarterly, 26,* 49–66.

Bear, D. R., Invernizzi, M., Templeton, S., & Johnston, F. (2008). *Words their way: Word study for phonics, vocabulary, and spelling instruction.* Upper Saddle River, NJ: Prentice-Hall.

Beck, I. L., McKeown, M. G., & Kucan L. (2002). *Bringing words to life: Robust vocabulary instruction.* New York: Guilford Press.

Beck, I. L., McKeown, M. G., Sandora, C., & Kucan, L. (1996). Questioning the author: A yearlong classroom implementation to engage students with text. *The Elementary School Journal, 96,* 385–414.

Behavioral Research & Teaching. (2005, January). *Oral reading fluency: 90 years of assessment.* (BRT Technical Report No. 33). Eugene, OR: Author.

Bender, W. N., & Larkin, M. J. (2003). *Reading strategies for elementary students with learning disabilities.* Thousand Oaks, CA: Corwin Press.

Biemiller, A. (1999). *Language and reading success.* Cambridge, MA: Brookline Books.

Blachman, B. A., Ball, E. W., Black, R., & Tangel, D. M. (2000). *Road to the code: A phonological awareness program for young children.* Baltimore: Paul H. Brookes.

Black, E. B. (1952). A study of the consonant situations in a primary reading vocabulary. *Education, 72*(9), 618–623.

Blackowicz, C. L., & Fisher, P. (2002). *Teaching vocabulary in all classrooms* (2nd ed.). Upper Saddle River, NJ: Pearson.

Blackowicz, C. L., & Ogle, D. (2001). *Reading comprehension: Strategies for independent learners.* New York: Guilford Press.

Blevins, W. (1998). *Phonics from A to Z: A practical guide.* New York: Scholastic Professional Books.

Blevins, W. (2001). *Building fluency: Lessons and strategies for reading success.* New York: Scholastic.

Block, C. C., & Pressley, M. (2003). Best practices in comprehension instruction. In L. M. Morrow, L. B. Gambrell, & M. Pressley (Eds.), *Best practices in literacy instruction* (2nd ed., pp. 111–126). New York: Guilford Press.

Block, C. C., Rodgers, L. L., & Johnson, R. B. (2004). *Comprehension process instruction.* New York: Guilford Press.

Bos, C. S. (1987). *Promoting story comprehension using a story retelling strategy.* Paper presented at the Teachers Applying Whole Language Conference, Tucson, AZ.

Bos, C. S., & Reyes, E. I. (1996). Conversations with a Latina teacher about education for language-minority students with special needs. *Elementary School Journal, 96,* 343–352.

Bos, C. S., & Vaughn, S. (2006). *Strategies for teaching students with learning and behavior problems* (6th ed.). Boston: Allyn and Bacon.

Bowers, L., Huisingh, R., LoGiudice, C., Orman, J., & Johnson, P. F. (2000). *125 vocabulary builders.* East Moline, IL: LinguiSystems.

Bradley, L., & Bryant, P. E. (1985). Rhyme and reason in reading and spelling. *International Academy for Reading in Learning Disabilities, Monograph Series, 1,* 75–95. Ann Arbor: University of Michigan Press.

Brown, R., El-Dinary, P. B., Pressley, M., & Coy-Ogan, L. (1995). A transactional strategies approach to reading instruction (National Reading Research Center). *The Reading Teacher, 49,* 256–258.

Byrne, B. (1998). *The foundation of literacy: The child's discovery of the alphabetic principle.* Hove, UK: Psychology Press.

Byrne, B., & Fielding-Barnsley, R. (1989). Phonemic awareness and letter knowledge in the child's acquisitions of the alphabetic principle. *Journal of Educational Psychology, 81,* 313–321.

Calderon, M. (1998). *Cooperative learning for bilingual instruction: Manual for teachers and teacher trainers.* El Paso, TX: MTTI.

Calderon, M. E., Hertz-Lazarowitz, R., & Slavin, R. (1996). *Effects of bilingual cooperative integrated reading and composition on students transitioning from Spanish to English reading.* Unpublished paper for the Office of Educational Research and Improvement, U.S. Department of Education, Washington, DC.

Calderon, M. E., & Minaya-Rowe, L. (2003). *Designing and implementing two-way bilingual programs: A step-by-step guide for administrators, teachers, and parents.* Thousand Oaks, CA: Corwin Press.

Carnine, D. (1999). Perspective: Campaigns for moving research to practice. *Remedial and Special Education, 20,* 2–9.

Carnine, D. W., Silbert, J., & Kame'enui, E. J. (1997). *Direct instruction reading* (3rd ed.). Upper Saddle River, NJ: Merrill.

Center for the Improvement of Early Reading Achievement (CIERA). (2001). *Put reading first: The research building blocks for teaching children to read.* Washington, DC: Partnership for Reading.

Chall, J. S. (2000). *The academic achievement challenge: What really works in the classroom?* New York: Guilford Press.

Chamot, A., & O'Malley, J. M. (1994). *The CALLA handbook.* Reading, MA: Addison-Wesley.

Chard, D. J., & Dickson, S. V. (1999). Phonological awareness: Instructional and assessment guidelines. *Intervention in School and Clinic, 34,* 261–270.

Chard, D. J., & Osborn, J. (1999). Word recognition instruction: Paving the road to successful reading. *Intervention in School and Clinic, 34,* 271–277.

Chard, D. J., Simmons, D. C., & Kame'enui, E. J. (1998). Word recognition: Research bases. In E. J. Kame'enui & D. C. Simmons (Eds.), *What reading research tells us about children with diverse learning needs: Bases and basics* (pp. 141–167). Mahwah, NJ: Erlbaum.

Chiappe, P. R., Siegel, L. S., & Wade-Woolley, L. (2002). Linguistic diversity and the development of reading skills: A longitudinal study. *Scientific Studies of Reading, 6,* 369–400.

Children's Educational Services, Inc. (1987). *Test of oral reading fluency.* Minneapolis, MN: Author.

Cicero, C. A., & Royer, J. M. (1995). The development of cross-language transfer of phonological awareness. *Journal of Contemporary Educational Psychology, 20,* 275–303.

Clay, M. (1993). *Reading recovery: A guidebook to teachers in training.* Portsmouth, NH: Heinemann.

Clay, M. (2002). *Three into one will go: Putting Humpty Dumpty together again.* Paper presented at the Canadian Regional IRA Conference, Vancouver, BC.

Comeau, L., Cormier, P., Grandmaison, E., & Lacroix, D. (1999). A longitudinal study of phonological processing skills in children learning to read in a second language. *Journal of Educational Psychology, 91,* 29–43.

Cooper, H. (1996). Speaking power to truth: Reflections of an educational researcher after 4 years of school board service. *Educational Researcher, 25,* 29–34.

Cunningham, A., & Stanovich, K. E. (1998). What reading does to the mind. *American Educator, 22*(1–2), 8–15.

Cunningham, P. M. (1998). The multisyllabic word dilemma: Helping students build meaning, spell, and read "big" words. *Reading and Writing Quarterly: Overcoming Learning Difficulties, 14,* 189–218.

Cunningham, P. M. (1999). *Phonics they use: Words for reading and writing* (3rd ed.). Boston: Addison-Wesley.

Cunningham, P. M. (2004). *Phonics they use: Words for reading and writing* (4th ed.). Boston: Allyn and Bacon.

Dale, E. (1965). Vocabulary measurement: Techniques and major findings. *Elementary English, 42,* 82–88.

Davis, F. B. (1942). Two new measures of reading ability. *Journal of Educational Psychology, 33,* 365–372.

Denton, C., Anthony, J. L., & Parker, R. (2004). Effects of two tutoring programs on the English reading development of Spanish-English bilingual students. *Elementary School Journal, 104,* 289–305.

Dianda, M., & Flaherty, J. (1995). *Effects of Success for All on the reading achievement of first graders in California bilingual programs.* Los Alamitos, CA: Southwest Regional Educational Laboratory.

Diaz-Rico, L. T. (2004). *Teaching English learners: Strategies and methods.* Boston: Allyn and Bacon.

Dickson, S. V., Simmons, D. C., & Kame'enui, E. J. (1995a). *Text organization and its relation to reading comprehension: A synthesis of the research.* (Tech. Rep. No. 17). Eugene: University of Oregon, National Center to Improve the Tools of Educators.

Dickson, S. V., Simmons, D. C., & Kame'enui, E. J. (1995b). *Text organization: Curricular and instructional implications for diverse learners.* (Tech. Rep. No. 18). Eugene: University of Oregon, National Center to Improve the Tools of Educators.

Donat, D. J. (2003). *Reading their way: A balance of phonics and whole language.* Lanham, MD: Rowman & Littlefield.

Donovan, M. S., & Cross, C. T. (2002). *Minorities in special and gifted education.* Washington, DC: National Research Council.

Duke, N. K., & Bennett-Armistead, V. S. (2003). *Reading and writing informational text in the primary grades: Research-based practices.* New York: Scholastic.

Durgunoglu, A. Y., Nagy, W., & Hancin-Bhatt, B. (1993). Cross-language transfer of phonological awareness. *Journal of Educational Psychology, 85,* 453–465.

Durkin, D. (1978–1979). What classroom observations reveal about reading instruction. *Reading Research Quarterly, 14*(4), 481–533.

Ebbers, S. M. (2004). *Vocabulary through morphemes: Suffixes, prefixes, and roots for intermediate grades.* Longmont, CO: Sopris West.

Echevarria, J., Vogt, M., Short, D. J. (2004). *Making content comprehensive for English learners: The SIOP model.* Pearson: Boston.

Edelsky, C. (1981a). Conversational analysis: New perspectives. In C. Edelsky (Ed.), *Conversational analysis: New perspectives, Special issue of the Journal of the Linguistic Association of the Southwest, 4*(1).

Edelsky, C. (1981b). Having the floor: Two general ways. In C. Edelsky (Ed.), *Conversational analysis: New perspectives, Special issue of the Journal of the Linguistic Association of the Southwest, 4*(1), 56–75.

Edelsky, C., Casanova, U., Guzzetti, B., Hudelson, S., Kansy, H., & Y Serna, I. (1993). Lost & found, review of E. Hoffman, "Lost in Translation." *Review of Education, 15,* 307–315.

Ehri, L. C. (1991). Learning to read and spell words. In L. Rieben & C. A. Perfetti (Eds.), *Learning to read and its implications* (pp. 57–73). Hillsdale, NJ: Erlbaum.

Ehri, L. C., Nunes, S. R., Willows, D. M., Schuster, B., Yaghoub-Zadeh, Z., & Shanahan, T. (2001). Phonemic awareness instruction helps children learn to read: Evidence from the National Reading Panel's meta-analysis. *Reading Research Quarterly, 36,* 250–287.

Fashola, O. S., Drum, P. A., Mayer, R. E., & Kang, S. (1996). A cognitive theory of orthographic translations: Predictable errors in how Spanish-speaking children spell English words. *American Educational Research Journal, 33,* 825–844.

Fitzgerald, J., & Noblit, G. (2000). Balance in the making: Learning to read in an ethnically diverse first-grade classroom. *Journal of Educational Psychology, 92,* 3–22.

Foorman, B. R., & Torgesen, J. (2001). Critical elements of classroom and small-group instruction promote reading success in all children. *Learning Disabilities Research and Practice, 16,* 203–212.

Fuchs, D., Fuchs, L. S., Mathes, P. G., & Simmons, D. C. (1997). Peer-assisted learning strategies: Making classrooms more responsive to diversity. *American Educational Research Journal, 34*(1), 174–206.

Fuchs, D., Fuchs, L., Thompson, A., Al Otaiba, S., Yen, L., Yang, N., Braun, M., & O'Connor, R. E. (2001). Is reading important in reading-readiness programs? A randomized field trial with teachers as program implementers. *Journal of Educational Psychology, 93,* 251–267.

Fuchs, L., Fuchs, D., & Hamlett, C. (1989). Monitoring reading growth using student recalls: Effects of two teacher feedback systems. *Journal of Educational Research, 83,* 101–111.

Fuchs, L. S., Fuchs, D., Hosp, M. K., & Jenkins, J. R. (2001). Oral reading fluency as an indicator of reading competence: A theoretical, empirical, and historical analysis. *Scientific Studies of Reading, 5,* 239–256.

Fuchs, L. S., Hamlett, C. L., & Fuchs, D. (1997). *Monitoring basic skills progress: basic reading* (2nd ed.) [Computer software and manual]. Austin, TX: Pro-ED.

Garcia, G. E. (2003). The reading comprehension development and instruction of English-language learners. In A. P. Sweet & C. E. Snow (Eds.), *Rethinking reading comprehension* (pp. 30–50). New York: Gulliford.

Gersten, R., & Baker, S. (2003). English-language learners with learning disabilities. In H. L. Swanson, K. R. Harris, & S. Graham (Eds.), *Handbook of learning disabilities* (pp. 94–109). New York: Guilford Press.

Gersten, R., Fuchs, L., Williams, J. P., & Baker, S. (2001). Teaching reading comprehension strategies to students with learning disabilities. *Review of Educational Research, 279–320.*

Gersten, R., & Geva, E. (2003). Teaching reading to English language learners. *Education Leadership, 60*(7), 44–49.

Gersten, R. M. & Jimenez, R. T. (1994). A delicate balance: Enhancing literacy instruction for students of English as a second language. *The Reading Teacher, 47*(6), 438–449.

Geva, E. (2000). Issues in the assessment of reading disabilities in L2 children: Beliefs and research evidence. *Dyslexia, 6,* 13–28.

Geva, E., Yaghoub-Zadeh, Z., & Schuster, B. (2000). Understanding individual differences in word recognition skills of ESL children. *Annals of Dyslexia, 50,* 123–154.

Gilbert, J. (2001). *The well-read cook's book.* Self-published.

Goldenberg, C., & Gallimore, R. (1991). Local knowledge, research knowledge, and educational change: A case study of first-grade Spanish reading improvement. *Educational Researcher, 20*(8), 2–14.

Goldenberg, C., & Sullivan, J. (1994). *Making change happen in a language-minority school: A search for coherence.* EPR #13. Washington, DC: Center for Applied Linguistics.

Good, R. H., Kaminski, R. A., Smith, S., Laimon, D., & Dill, S. (2003). *Dynamic indicators of basic early literacy skills* (6th ed.). Eugene, OR: University of Oregon. Available: http://dibels.uoregon.edu

Goswami, U. (2000). Casual connections in beginning reading: The importance of rhyme. *Journal of Research in Reading, 22,* 217–240.

Goswami, U. (2006). Neuroscience and education: From research to practice. *Nature Reviews Neuroscience, 7,* 406–413.

Goswami, U., & Bryant, P. (1990). *Phonological skills and learning to read.* Mawah, NJ: Erlbaum.

Gottardo, A., Yan, B., Siegel, L. S., & Wade-Woolley, L. (2001). Factors related to English reading performance in children with Chinese as a first language: More evidence of cross-language transfer of phonological processing. *Journal of Educational Psychology, 93,* 530–542.

Gough, P., & Tumner, W. (1986). Decoding, reading, and reading disability. *Remedial and Special Education, 7,* 6–10.

Grabe, W. (1991). Current developments in second language reading research. *TESOL Quarterly, 25,* 375–406.

Graves, A. W. (1986). Effects of direct instruction and metacomprehension training on finding main ideas. *Learning Disabilities Research and Practice, 1*, 90–100.

Graves, A., Gersten, R., & Haager, D. (2004). Literacy instruction in multiple-language first-grade classrooms: Linking student outcomes to observed instructional practice. *Learning Disabilities Research and Practice, 19*, 262–272.

Graves, M. F., Juel, C., & Graves, B. B. (1998). *Teaching reading in the 21st century*. Needham Heights, MA: Allyn and Bacon.

Graves, M. F., Juel, C., & Graves, B. B. (2001). *Teaching reading in the 21st century* (2nd ed.). Boston: Allyn and Bacon.

Graves, M. F., Prenn, M., & Cooke, C. L. (1985). The coming attractions: Previewing short stories. *Journal of Reading, 28*, 594–598.

Graves, M. F., & Slater, W. H. (1996). Vocabulary instruction in content areas. In D. Lapp, J., Flood, & N. Farnan (Eds.), *Content area reading and learning*. Needham Heights, MA: Allyn and Bacon.

Greaney, K. T., Tunmer, W. E., & Chapman, J. W. (1997). Effects of rime-based orthographic analogy training on the word recognition of children with reading disability. *Journal of Educational Psychology, 89*, 645–651.

Gunn, B., Biglan, A., Smolkowski, K., & Ary, D. (2000). The efficacy of supplemental instruction in decoding skills for Hispanic and non-Hispanic students in early elementary school. *The Journal of Special Education, 34*(2), 90–103.

Gunn, B., Smolkowski, K., Biglan, A., Black, C., & Blair, J. (2005). Fostering the development of reading skill through supplemental instruction: Results for Hispanic and non-Hispanic students. *The Journal of Special Education, 39*(2), 66–85.

Haager, D., Gersten, R., Baker, S., & Graves, A. (2003). The English-language learner classroom observation instrument: Observations of beginning reading instruction in urban schools. In S. R. Vaughn & K. L. Briggs (Eds.), *Reading in the classroom: Systems for observing teaching and learning* (pp. 111–114). Baltimore: Paul H. Brookes.

Haley, M. H., & Austin, T. Y. (2004). *Content-based second language teaching and learning: An interactive approach*. Boston: Pearson/Allyn and Bacon.

Hart, B., & Risley, T. R. (2003). *The early catastrophe*. Washington, DC: American Federation of Teachers.

Hasbrouck, J. E., & Tindal, G. (1992). Curriculum-based oral reading fluency norms for students in grades 2 through 4. *Teaching Exceptional Children, 24*, 41–44.

Haver, J. J. (2003). *Structured English immersion*. Thousand Oaks, CA: Corwin Press.

Hayes, D. P., & Ahrens, M. G. (1988). Vocabulary simplifications for children: A special case of "motherese"? *Journal of Child Language, 15*, 395–410.

Henry, M. (1997). The decoding /spelling curriculum: Integrated decoding and spelling instruction from pre-school to early secondary school. *Dyslexia, 3*, 178–189.

Henry, M. K. (2003). *Unlocking literacy: Effective decoding and spelling instruction*. Baltimore: Paul H. Brookes.

Hernandez, H. (1997). *Teaching in multicultural classrooms*. Upper Saddle River, NJ: Merrill/Prentice-Hall.

Hernandez, J. S. (1991). Assisted performance in reading comprehension strategies with non-English proficient students. *The Journal of Educational Issues of Language Minority Students, 8*, 91–112.

Herrell, A., & Jordan, M. (2004). *Fifty strategies for teaching English language learners* (2nd ed.). Upper Saddle River, NJ: Pearson.

Hickman, P., Pollard-Durodola, S., & Vaughn, S. (2004). Storybook reading: Improving vocabulary and comprehension for English language learners. *The Reading Teacher, 57*(8), 720–730.

Hiebert, E. H. (2002). *QuickReads: A research-based fluency program*. Parsippany, NJ: Modern Curriculum Press.

Hiebert, E. H., & Sawyer, C. C. (1984). *Young children's concurrent abilities in reading and spelling*. Paper presented at the annual meeting of the American Educational Research Association, New Orleans, LA.

Honig, B. (1999). Reading the right way. In *Reading research: Anthology The why? of reading instruction* (pp. 7–12). Novato, CA: Arena Press (Consortium on Reading Excellence [CORE]).

Honig, B., Diamond, L., & Gutlohn, L. (2000). *CORE teaching reading*. Novato, CA: Arena Press.

Hudelson, S. (1984). Kan yu ret an rayt en ingles: Children become literate in English as a second language. *TESOL Quarterly, 18*, 221–238.

Hudson, R. F., & Smith, S. W. (2001). Effective reading instruction for struggling Spanish-speaking readers: A combination of two literatures. *Intervention in School and Clinic, 37*(1), 36–39.

Institute for Education Sciences. (2005). *National Assessment of Educational Progress (NAEP) 2004 trends in academic progress. Three decades of student performance in reading and mathematics: Findings in brief*. National Center on Educational Statistics, U.S. Department of Education.

Invernizzi, M., & Meier, J. (2002). *Phonological awareness literacy screening (PALS 1–3)*. Charlottesville: University of Virginia Press.

Jenkins, J. R., Heliotis, J., Stein, M. L., & Haynes, M. (1987). Improving reading comprehension by using paragraph restatements. *Exceptional Children, 54*, 54–59.

Jitendra, A. K. (1998). Effects of a direct instruction mail idea summarization program and self-monitoring on reading comprehension of middle school students with learning disabilities. *Reading and Writing Quarterly: Overcoming Learning Disabilities, 14*, 379–396.

Jitendra, A. K., Hoppes, M. K., & Xin, Y. P. (2000). Enhancing main idea comprehension for students with learning problems: The role of a summarization strategy and self-monitoring instruction. *Journal of Special Education, 34*(3), 127–139.

Juel, C. (1988). Learning to read and write: A longitudinal study of 54 children from first through fourth grades. *Journal of Educational Psychology, 80*(4), 437–447.

Kame'enui, E. J., & Simmons, D. C. (2001). Introduction to this special issue: The DNA of reading fluency. *Scientific Studies of Reading, 5*, 203–210.

Kamil, M. L. (2004). Vocabulary and comprehension instruction: Summary and implications of National Reading Panel findings. In P. McCardle & V. Chhabra (Eds.), *The voice of evidence in reading research* (pp. 213–234). Baltimore: Paul H. Brookes.

Kaminski, R. R., & Good, R. (1996). Toward a technology for assessing basic early literacy skills. *School Psychology Review, 25*, 215–227.

Klingner, J. K., Vaughn, S., Dimino, J., Schumm, J. S., & Bryant, D. P. (2001). *From clunk to click: Collaborative strategic reading*. Longmont, CO. Sopris West.

Koskinen, P. S., Blum, I. H., Bisson, S. A., Phillips, S. M., Creamer, T. S., & Baker, T. K. (1999). Shared reading, books, and audiotapes: Supporting diverse students in school and home. *The Reading Teacher, 52*(5), 430–444.

Kress, J. (1993). *The ESL book of lists*. Upper Saddle River, NJ: Prentice-Hall.

Kreuger, E., & Townshend, N. 1997. Reading clubs boost second-language first graders' reading achievement. *The Reading Teacher, 51*, 122–127.

Kuhn, M. R., & Stahl, S. A. (2003). Fluency: A review of development and remedial practices. *Journal of Educational Psychology, 95*, 3–21.

Learning First Alliance. (2000). *Every child reading: A professional development guide*. Washington, DC.

Lee, D. M., & Allen, R. C. (1963). *Learning to read through experience* (2nd ed.). New York: Meredith.

Lenters, K. (2004). No half-measures: Reading instruction for young second-language learners. *The Reading Teacher, 58*(4), 328–336.

Lenters, K. (2005). What reading teachers should know about ESL learners. *The Reading Teacher, 57*, 22–30.

Leslie, L., & Caldwell, J. (2001). *The qualitative reading inventory 3.* New York: Addison-Wesley Longman.

Linan-Thompson, S., & Hickman-Davis, P. (2002). Supplemental reading instruction for students at risk for reading disabilities: Improve reading thirty minutes at a time. *Learning Disabilities Research and Practice, 17*, 241–250.

Linan-Thompson, S., Vaughn, S., Hickman-Davis, P., & Kouzekanani, K. (2003). Effectiveness of supplemental reading instruction for second-grade English language learners with reading difficulties. *The Elementary School Journal, 103*, 221–238.

Lindsey, K., Manis, F., & Bailey, C. (2003). Prediction of first-grade reading in Spanish-speaking English-language learners. *Journal of Educational Psychology, 95*, 482–494.

Lundberg, I., Frost, J., & Peterson, O. (1998). Effects of an extensive program for stimulating phonological awareness in preschool children. *Reading Research Quarterly, 23*, 263–284.

Lundberg, I., Olofsson, A., & Wall, S. (1980). Reading and spelling skills in the first school years predicted from phonemic awareness skills in kindergarten. *Scandinavian Journal of Psychology, 21*, 159–173.

MacGinitie, W. H., MacGinitie, R. K., Maria, K., Dreyer, L. G., & Hughes, K. E. (2000). *Gates-MacGinitie Reading Tests, fourth edition (GRMT-4).* Itasca, IL: Riverside.

Malone, L. D., & Mastropieri, M. (1992). Reading comprehension instruction: Summarization and self-monitoring training for students with learning disabilities. *Exceptional Children, 58*, 270–279.

Mastropieri, M. A., & Scruggs, T. E. (1997). Best practices in promoting reading comprehension in students with learning disabilities: 1976 to 1996. *Remedial and Special Education, 18*, 197–214.

McCormick, C. E., Throneburg, R., & Smitley, J. (2002). *A sound start: Phonemic awareness lessons for reading success.* New York: Guilford Press.

McKenna, M. C., & Stahl, S. A. (2003). *Assessment for reading instruction.* New York: Guilford Press.

McLaughlin, B. (1987). *Theories of second-language learning.* London: Edward Arnold.

Moats, L. (2000). *Speech to print: Language essentials for teachers.* Baltimore: Paul H. Brookes.

Moats, L. (2001). When older students can't read. *Educational Leadership, 58*(6), 36–40.

Muniz-Swicegood, M. (1994). The effects of metacognitive reading strategy training on the reading performance and student reading analysis strategies of third-grade bilingual students. *Bilingual Research Journal, 18*, 83–97.

Nagy, W. E., & Anderson, R. C. (1984). How many words are there in printed school English? *Reading Research Quarterly, 19*, 304–330.

Nagy, W. E., Garcia, G. E., Durgunoglu, A., & Hancin-Bhatt, B. (1993). Spanish-English bilingual children's use and recognition of cognates in English reading. *Journal of Reading Behavior, 25*, 241–259.

National Reading Panel (NRP). (2000). *Teaching children to read: An evidence-based assessment of the scientific research literature on reading and its implications for reading instruction. Reports of the subgroups.* (NIH Publication No. 00-4754). Bethesda, MD: National Institutes of Health, National Institute of Child Health and Human Development.

National Research Council (NRC). (1998). *Preventing reading difficulties in young children.* Washington, DC: National Academy Press.

Newcomer, P. (1999). *Standardized reading inventory, second edition (SRI-2)*. Austin, TX: Pro-Ed.

No Child Left Behind Act of 2001. Public Law 107-110. (2001, August 2). Pub. L. No. 107-110, (H. R. 1). Retrieved from www.nochildleftbehind.gov

Oaks, R. E. (1952). A study of the vowel situations in a primary reading vocabulary. *Education*.

O'Connor, R. E. (2000). Increasing the intensity of intervention in kindergarten and first grade. *Learning Disabilities Research and Practice, 15,* 43–54.

O'Connor, R. E., Notari-Syverson, A., & Vadasy, P. F. (2005). *Ladders to literacy*. Baltimore: Paul H. Brookes.

Ogle, D. M. (1986). KWL: A teaching model that develops active reading of expository text. *The Reading Teacher, 39,* 564–570.

O'Shea, L. J., Sindelar, P. T., & O'Shea, D. J. (1987). The effects of repeated readings and attentional cues on the reading fluency and comprehension of learning disabled readers. *Learning Disabilities Research, 2,* 103–109.

Perfetti, C. A. (1977). Language comprehension and fast decoding: Some psycholinguistic prerequisites for skilled reading comprehension. In J. T. Guthrie (Ed.), *Cognition, curriculum, and comprehension* (pp. 20–41). Newark, DE: International Reading Association.

Perfetti, C. A. (1985). *Reading ability*. New York: Oxford University Press.

Pressley, M. (1998; 2006). *Reading instruction that works: The case for balanced teaching*. New York: Guilford Press.

Pressley, M., & Afflerbach, P. (1995). *Verbal protocols of reading: The nature of constructively responsive reading*. Mahwah, NJ: Erlbaum.

Pressley, M., & El-Dinary, P. B. (1997). What we know about translating comprehension-strategies instruction research into practice. *Journal of Learning Disabilities, 30,* 486–488, 512.

Quiroga, T., Lemos-Britton, Z., Mostafapour, E., & Berninger, V. (2002). Phonological awareness and beginning reading in Spanish-speaking ESL first graders: Research into practice. *Journal of School Psychology, 40,* 85–111.

Rabren, K., Darch, C., & Eaves, R. C. (1999). The differential effects of two systematic reading comprehension approaches with students with learning disabilities. *Journal of Learning Disabilities, 32*(1), 36–47.

RAND Reading Study Group. (2002). *Reading for understanding: Toward an R&D program in reading comprehension*. Santa Monica, CA: RAND Corporation.

Rasinski, T. V. (2003). *The fluent reader: Oral reading strategies for building word recognition, fluency, and comprehension*. New York: Scholastic Professional Books.

Reid, D. K., Hresko, W. P., & Hammill, D. D. (2001). *Test of early reading ability, third edition (TERA-3)*. Austin, TX: Pro-Ed.

Reutzel, D. R., & Cooter, R. B., Jr. (1999). *Balanced reading strategies and practices: Assessing and assisting readers with special needs*. Upper Saddle River, NJ: Merrill.

Saunders, W., O'Brien, G., Lennon, D., & McLean, J. (1996). Making the transition to English literacy successful: Effective strategies for studying literature with transition students. In R. Gersten & R. Jimenez (Eds.), *Effective strategies for teaching language minority students*. Monterey, CA: Brooks Cole.

Schumm, J. S., Moody, S. W., & Vaughn, S. R. (2000). Grouping for reading instruction: Does one size fit all? *Journal of Learning Disabilities, 33,* 477–488.

Scott, J. A., & Nagy, W. E. (2004). Developing word consciousness. In J. F. Baumann & E. J. Kame'enui (Eds.), *Vocabulary instruction: Research to practice* (pp. 201–217). New York: Guilford Press.

Seymour, P. H. K. (2006). Framework for beginning reading in different orthographies. In R. Malatesha Joshi & P. G. Aaron (Eds.), *Handbook of orthography and literacy*. Mahway, NJ: Erlbaum.

Share, D. L. (1995). Phonological recoding and self-teaching: Sine qua non of reading acquisition. *Cognition, 55,* 155–218.

Shaywitz, S. E., & Shaywitz, B. A. (1996). Unlocking learning disabilities: The neurological basis. In S. C. Cramer & W. Ellis (Eds.), *Learning disabilities: Lifelong issues* (pp. 255–260). Baltimore: Paul H. Brookes.

Short, D., & Echevarria, J. (2005). Teacher skills to support English language learners. *Educational Leadership, 62,* 8–13

Sindelar, P. T., Monda, L. E., & O'Shea, L. J. (1990). The effects of repeated readings on instructional and mastery level readers. *Journal of Educational Research, 83,* 220–226.

Smith, M. K. (1941). Measurement of the size of general English vocabulary through the elementary grades and high school. *Genetic Psychological Monograph, 24,* 311–345.

Smith, S. B., Simmons, D. C., & Kame'enui, E. J. (1998). Phonological awareness: Research bases. In D. C. Simmons & E. J. Kame'enui (Eds.), *What reading research tells us about children with diverse learning needs: Bases and basics.* Mahwah, NJ: Erlbaum.

Snow, C. E., Burns, M. S., & Griffin, P. (Eds.). (1998). *Preventing reading difficulties in young children.* Washington, DC: National Academy Press.

Stahl, S. A. (1985). To teach a word well: A framework for vocabulary instruction. *Reading World, 24*(3), 16–27.

Stahl, S. A. (1986). Three principles of effective vocabulary instruction. *Journal of Reading, 29,* 662–668.

Stahl, S. A. (2001). Teaching phonics and phonological awareness. In S. B. Neuman & D. K. Dickinson (Eds.), *Handbook of early literacy research* (pp. 333–347). New York: Guilford Press.

Stahl, S. A. (2004). What do we know about fluency? Findings of the National Reading Panel. In P. McCardle & V. Chhabra (Eds.), *The voice of evidence in reading research* (pp. 187–211). Baltimore: Paul H. Brookes.

Stahl, S. A., & Kapinus, B. (2001). *Word power: What every educator needs to know about teaching vocabulary.* Washington, DC: National Education Association.

Stahl, S. A., & Kuhn, M. R. (2002). Making it sound like language: Developing fluency. *The Reading Teacher, 55,* 582–584.

Stanovich, K. E. (1986). Matthew effects in reading: Some consequences of individual differences in the acquisition of literacy. *Reading Research Quarterly, 21,* 360–406.

Stanovich, K. E. (2000). *Progress in understanding reading: Scientific foundations and new frontiers.* New York: Guilford Press.

Swanson, H. L. (1999). Instructional components that predict treatment outcomes for students with LD: Support for a combined strategy and direct instruction model. *Learning Disabilities Research and Practice, 14,* 129–140.

Texas Education Agency (TEA). (2000). *Guidelines for examining phonics and word recognition programs.* Austin, TX: Author.

Tikunoff, W. J. (1983). *Compatibility of the SBIF features with other research instruction of LEP students.* San Francisco: Far West Laboratory.

Torgesen, J. K. (2000). Individual differences in response to early interventions in reading: The lingering problem of treatment resisters. *Learning Disabilities Research and Practice, 15,* 55–64.

Torgesen, J. K., & Mathes, P. G. (2000). *A basic guide to understanding, assessing, and teaching phonological awareness.* Austin, TX: Pro-Ed.

Torgesen, J., Wagner, R., & Rashotte, C. (1994). Longitudinal studies of phonological processing and reading. *Journal of Learning Disabilities, 27,* 276–286.

Ulanoff, S. H., & Pucci, S. L. (1999). Learning words from books: The effects of reading aloud on second language acquisition. *Bilingual Research Journal, 23,* 409–422.

University of Texas Center for Reading and Language Arts. (2001a). *Essential reading strategies for the struggling reader: Activities for an accelerated reading program. Expanded edition.* Austin, TX: Texas Education Agency.

University of Texas Center for Reading and Language Arts. (2001b). *Second grade teacher academy.* Austin, TX: Texas Education Agency.

University of Texas Center for Reading and Language Arts. (2001c). *Supplemental instruction for third grade struggling readers: A guide for tutors.* Austin, TX: Texas Education Agency.

University of Texas Center for Reading and Language Arts. (2002a). *Reading strategies and activities: A resource book for students at risk for reading difficulties, including dyslexia.* Austin, TX: Texas Education Agency.

University of Texas Center for Reading and Language Arts. (2002b). *Effective fluency instruction and progress monitoring.* Austin, TX: Texas Education Agency.

University of Texas Center for Reading and Language Arts. (2002c). *The secretary's reading leadership academy: Effective reading instruction.* Austin, TX: Author.

University of Texas Center for Reading and Language Arts. (2003). *Effective instruction for elementary struggling readers: Research-based practices* (Rev. ed.). Austin, TX: Texas Education Agency.

University of Texas Systems and Texas Education Agency. (2005a). *Introduction to the 3-tier reading model: Reducing reading difficulties for kindergarten through third grade students* (4th ed.). Austin, TX: Texas Education Agency.

University of Texas System and Texas Education Agency. (2005b). *Texas primary reading inventory 2005.* Austin, TX: Texas Education Agency.

Vaughn, S., & Dammann, J. E. (2001). Science and sanity in special education. *Behavioral Disorders, 27,* 21–29.

Vaughn, S., & Linan-Thompson, S. (2004). *Research-based methods of reading instruction: Grades K–3.* Alexandria, VA: Association for Supervision and Curriculum Development.

Vaughn, S., Linan-Thompson, S., & Hickman, P. (2003). Response to intervention as a means of identifying students with reading/learning disabilities. *Exceptional Children, 69,* 391–410.

Vaughn, S., Mathes, P. G., Linan-Thompson, S., Cirino, P. T., Carlson, C. D., Pollard-Durodola, S. D., et al. (2006). First-grade English language learners at-risk for reading problems: Effectiveness of an English intervention. *Elementary School Journal, 107*(2), 153–180.

Vaughn, S., Mathes, P. G., Linan-Thompson, S., & Francis, D. J. (2005). Teaching English language learners at risk for reading disabilities to read: Putting research into practice. *Learning Disabilities Research & Practice, 20*(1), 58–67.

Vaughn, S., Moody, S., & Schumm, J. S. (1998). Broken promises: Reading instruction in the resource room. *Exceptional Children, 64,* 211–226.

Wagner, R. K., Torgesen, J. K., & Rashotte, C. A. (1994). Development of reading-related phonological processing abilities: New evidence of bidirectional causality from a latent variable longitudinal study. *Developmental Psychology, 30,* 73–87.

Walberg, H. J. (1998). Foreword. In K. Topping & S. Ehly, *Peer-assisted learning.* Mahwah, NJ: Erlbaum.

White, T. G., Sowell, J., & Yanagihara, A. (1989). Teaching elementary students to use word-part clues. *The Reading Teacher, 42,* 302–308.

Wiederholt, J. L., & Blalock, G. (2000). *Gray silent reading tests.* Austin, TX: Pro-Ed.

Wiederholt, J. L., & Bryant, B. R. (2001). *The Gray oral reading tests, fourth edition (GORT-4).* Austin, TX: Pro-Ed.

Wilhelm, J. D. (2001). *Improving comprehension with think-aloud strategies.* New York: Scholastic.

Williams, J. P. (1988). Identifying main ideas: A basic aspect of reading comprehension. *Topics in Language Disorders, 8,* 1–13.

Williams, J. P. (1998). Improving the comprehension of disabled readers. *Annals of Dyslexia, 48,* 213–238.

Wong, B. Y. L., & Jones, W. (1982). Increasing meta-comprehension in learning disabled and normally achieving students through self-questing training. *Learning Disability Quarterly, 5*, 228–240.

Woodcock, R. W. (1998). *The WJ-R and Bacteria-R in neuropsychological assessment: Research report number 1.* Itasca, IL: Riverside.

Yopp, H. K. (1995). A test for assessing phonemic awareness in young children. *The Reading Teacher, 49*, 20–29.

Zehr, M. A. (2005). Bilingual educators ratchet up criticism of federal NCLB [No Child Left Behind] law. *Education Week, 25*(14), 30.

◆   ◆   ◆

Index

Page numbers appearing in *italics* refer to figures and tables

accuracy, definition, 151
adjusting instructional language
    level of English vocabulary, 4
    student acquisition of new skills and strategies and, 4
    using consistent language, 4–5
advanced word analysis
    is it real? activity, 53
    make a new word activity, 52
    word part *Jeopardy!* activity, 52
affixes
    common prefixes, *105*
    common suffixes, *106*
    definition, 151
    phonics and word study and, 38–39, 51–53
AIMSweb Assessment System, 69
AIMSweb Progress Monitoring and Improvement System, 69
alphabetic knowledge
    activities for developing, 37
    progression of, 36
    pronunciation and, 36–37
alphabetic principle, definition, 151
alphabetic understanding
    elements of, 37
    teaching strategies, 37–38
analogy, definition, 151
analogy-based phonics
    strategy use in context activity, 49
    what do I already know? activity, 48–49
analytic phonics, definition, 151

assessments. *See also* specific assessments
 benchmarks to identify students at risk for difficulties, 6
 benefits of, 12
 comprehension, 116–119
 factors to consider, 145
 fluency, 65, 66–70
 importance of, 6
 important characteristics of the measure, 13
 instruction guidance and, 12
 irregular word reading, 44
 oral language proficiency and, 6
 phonemic awareness, 12–13
 prediction of later reading ability and, 12
 reading comprehension assessments examples,
  117–118
 regular word reading, 44
 screening measures in first grade, 6
 validity for English language learners, 145–146
association processing
 concept map activity, 95–96
 definitional knowledge activity, 97
 description, 92, 93
 elaborating words activity, 96–97
 personal vocabulary book activity, 94–95
 say it another way activity, 94
 synonym web activity, 95
at-risk, definition, 152
August, D., seven classroom attributes associated with
 positive student outcomes, 2
automaticity, definition, 152

basal reader, definition, 152
base word, definition, 152
Beck, I. L.
 goal for vocabulary development, 91
 tiers of words, 90
Bender, W. N., phonemic awareness skills hierarchy, 12
bibliographies
 comprehension, 142
 fluency, 84–85
 phonemic awareness, 28–29
 phonics and word study, 54
 vocabulary instruction, 110
bicultural, definition, 152
bilingual classroom, definition, 152
bilingual education
 definition, 152

bilingual education (*continued*)
 early-exit, 153
 late-exit, 155
 maintenance, 156
bilingualism
 additive, 152
 definition, 152
blending
 assessment and, 12
 basic lesson: what did I say?, 18–19
 definition, 152
 description, 10
 followup lesson: guess my picture, 19
 followup lesson: put it together chant, 19
 impact on later reading, 11
 linking sound to letters and print and, 15
 teacher confidence and skills and, 15–16

Calderon M. E., tiers of words, 90
capacity building, vocabulary instruction and, 93
CCVC word, definition, 152
choral reading
 activities for, 63, 73–74
 definition, 152
chunking, definition, 152
classroom activities
 advanced word analysis, 52–53
 alphabetic knowledge, 37
 comprehension, 129–141
 fluency, 70–76, 78–83
 irregular word reading, 48, 49–50
 phonemic awareness, 16–24, 28
 phonics and word study, 44–45, 47–53
 print awareness, 36
 regular word reading, 44–45, 47–48
 structural analysis, 51–52
 vocabulary instruction, 94–110
code mixing, definition, 152
code switching, definition, 152
cognates
 definition, 152
 role of, 91, 147
comprehension
 assessment, 116–119, *117–118*
 before-reading practices, 120–121, 130–131
 bibliography, 142
 check card for, *79*
 classroom activities, 129–141

comprehension *(continued)*

connecting with text: student form, *129*

connecting with text (during reading) activity, 129–130

cooperative learning practices, 120

culturally relevant texts and, 120

decoding and reading practice with decodable text and, 39

definition, 152

description, 114–115

during- and after-reading activities, 121, *129*, 129–133, *131*

explicit skills instruction and, 3, 115, 123

finding the main idea, *125*

fluency and, 79, *79*, 114

format for story read-aloud and comprehension instruction, *128*

frame for answering "5Ws" and "How" questions, *123*

getting the gist or main idea (during reading) activity, 131–133

gist log, *132*

good readers and, 116

graphic and semantic organizers and, 120, *122*

guided practice, 120

guided story prompt sheet, *139*

guided story response activity, 138–140

guidelines for teachers' promotion of, 114–115, 116–128

implicit only information, 115

importance of, 113, 128

informal assessment, 118–119

instructional factors, 119

intervention practices to facilitate, 119–120

KKWL for information texts: modified for English language learners, 140–141, *141*

listening comprehension, 128

main idea and summarization, 123–125, *125*, 131–133, 156, 158

making predictions (before reading) activity, 130

my story retell, *127*

organizer, *122*

phonemic awareness and, 11

poor readers and, 116

practices associated with improved outcomes for ELLs, 115–116

previewing text, 120–121

questioning practices, 115, 120, 121, *124*, 136–137

comprehension *(continued)*

questioning the author: modified procedures for English language learners, *124*

question types (after reading) activity, 136–137

reading comprehension assessments examples, *117–118*

reading with a purpose: information text (before and after reading) activity, 130–131

rote instruction and, 114

rule-based instructional strategy: an example, *126*

selection of reading materials for English language learners, 113–114

as "sense making," 114

skills and strategies for, 114

small-group activities and, 120

Spanish-speaking students and, 149

story graphic, *131*

story read-aloud practice, 125–128

story retelling and, 123–125

strategies for, 152

strategy instruction and, 6

students' stage of development in their first and second language and, 114

teaching strategies, 115–116, 119–128

test selection considerations, 116–117

textually explicit information, 115

textually implicit information, 115

using a story map (during reading) activity, 134–136, *135*

using students' language experience and, 122–123

vocabulary instruction and, 90

Web sites, 143

who has the evidence? activity, 137–138

comprehension processing

can this be right? activity, 100

definitional knowledge activity, 97–98

description, 92

I can name it in three clues activity, 99

is it or isn't it? activity, 101–102

relative connections activity, 99–100

vocabulary word sorts activity, 98–99

Comprehensive Test of Phonological Processing

description, 13

phonological awareness subtest, 13

rapid-naming tasks, 13

computer-assisted instruction, definition, 152

consonant blend, definition, 152

consonant digraph, definition, 152

consonant letters and sounds, definition, 153
content-based ESL, definition, 153
content words, definition, 153
context
    definition, 153
    strategy use in context activity, 49
    vocabulary instruction and, 92
cooperative learning
    comprehension and, 120
    definition, 153
    fluency and, 62
cross-age tutoring, definition, 153
CTOPP. *See* Comprehensive Test of Phonological
    Processing
CVCC word, definition, 153
CVCe word, definition, 153
CVC word, definition, 153

DEAR. *See* drop everything and read
decodable text, definition, 153
decoding, definition, 153
decoding and reading practice with decodable text
    advanced strategies for, 38, 52–53
    affixes and, 38–39, 51–53
    analogy-based phonics and, 38, 48–49
    description, 38
    inflectional endings and, 38–39
    segmenting multisyllable words into decodable
      parts, 38
    students' accents and, 149–150
    vocabulary instruction and, 39
definitions of terms, 151–159
deleting
    assessment and, 12
    deleting syllables followup lesson, 23
dialect, definition, 153
DIBELS. *See* Dynamic Indicators of Basic Early Literacy
    Skills
DIBELS Oral Reading Fluency (DORF) and Retell Fluency,
    69
dominant language, definition, 153
doubling rule
    basic lesson for, 50
    review lesson, 51
drop everything and read, effectiveness of, 64–65
dual language program, definition, 153
Dynamic Indicators of Basic Early Literacy Skills, 13
dyslexia, definition, 153

echo reading activity, 73
ELLs. *See* English language learners
English as a second language, definition, 154
English for speakers of other languages, definition, 154
English language learners
    best motivators for, 147
    definition, vii, 153
    educational background of families and, 1
    factors to consider in designing instruction for, 145
    growth in the number of, vii
    lack of resources and materials for teaching, 150
    learning disabilities and, viii
    limited English proficiency and, 11, 148
    providing additional and more intensive instruction
      for, 147–148
    research behind the book, 146
    resources for teachers, 147
    responsibility for teaching, 149
    socioeconomic level and, 1
    Spanish as the predominant home language for, 1
    tools for teaching reading skills, 148
English-only, definition, 153–154
Equal Opportunity Act of 1974, 154
ESL classroom, definition, 154
explicit skills instruction
    comprehension and, 115
    description, 3, 154
    effectiveness of, 3
    elements of, 3
    fluency and, 61–62
    teacher modeling of skills and strategies, 3
    vocabulary instruction and, 93
expository text, definition, 154
expressive language skills
    definition, 154
    vocabulary development and, 88

FEP. *See* fluent English proficient
fluency
    amount of time to spend on each day, 61
    assessment of, 59, 61, 65, 66–70
    assisted reading log, 75
    beat the clock activity, 70–71
    benefits to English language learners, 58–59
    bibliography, 84–85
    choral reading activities, 63, 73–74
    classroom activities for, 70–76, 78–83
    comprehension check card, 79

fluency (*continued*)

cooperative learning strategies, 62
critical elements for improving, 64
description, 58–59, 154
echo reading activity, 73
effect on reading speed, 59, 150
engaging students and, 62
expressive reading, 70
expressive reading scores, *70*
fast start activity, 71
fluency plus comprehension activity, 79
frustration-level text, 60–61
goal of, 61
good expression and, 58, 60
guidelines for partner repeated reading, *65*
importance of improvements in, 5
importance of teaching, 59–60
independent-level text, 60
instructional-level text, 60
maintaining and generalizing skills, 62
norms for, 66–68
oral reading fluency guidelines for grades 2–4, *68*
oral reading practices that are too challenging or too embarrassing, 64
partner reading, 64
partner reading activities, 76, 78, 79–80
practices associated with improved reading outcomes, 62–68
practices for direct teaching of, 61–62
practice time and, 60, 62
preteaching unfamiliar words, 62
prevalence of problems among English language learners, 57
previewing and fluency activity, 78
prosody and, 58, 60
providing explicit instruction, 61–62
readers' theater or reading performances, 64, 80–81
reading difficult text activity, 82
reading outlaw words fluently activity, 71–73
reading 'round the clock activity, 82–83
reading with a model reader, 63
reading words and phrases fluently activity, 81–82
reasons why English learners struggle with, 59
repeated reading of the same text, 64
repeated readings: using a tape as a model, 74–76
rereading and, 62–63
retell activity, 79–80

fluency (*continued*)

retell cue card, *80*
round-robin reading and, 64
sample irregular word grid, *72*
sample reading fluency chart, *67*
scaffolding fluency practices, 62
selected list of publishers of high-interest texts with controlled reading levels, 77
show time activity, 81
silent reading practice, 60
spotlight readers activity, 80
student examples, 57–58
students working with a tutor and, 61
sustained silent reading without teacher guidance or support and, 64
taking turns in reading and, 64
tape-recorded readings, 63–64
teaching strategies, 60–68
text type and, 61
times measures of the number of words read correctly in a minute, 65–68
Web sites, 85–86
whom I read to chart, *83*
fluent English proficient, definition, 154
frustration reading level
definition, 154
fluency and, 60–61

generative processing
description, 92
possible sentences activity, 102
genre, definition, 154
GORT-4. *See* Gray Oral Reading Tests, 4th ed.
Gough, P., basic processes necessary to learn to read, 32
Grabe, W., strategy instruction and comprehension, 6
grade-level text, definition, 154
grapheme, definition, 154
graphic organizers
comprehension and, 120, *122*
definition, 154
graphophonemic knowledge, definition, 154
Graves, B. B., before-reading practices, 120
Graves, M. F., before-reading practices, 120
Gray Oral Reading Tests, 4th ed., 69–70
guided reading
comprehension and, 120, *139*
definition, 155

Hakuta, K., seven classroom attributes associated with positive student outcomes, 2
Haver, Johanna, *Structured English Immersion*, vii

IDEA Proficiency Test, 155
identification
    basic lesson: what's the sound?, 16
    description, 10
    follow-up lesson: did you hear it?, 17
    follow-up lesson: the first sound is..., 17
    follow-up lesson: which word is different?, 18
    teacher confidence and skills and, 15–16
implicit instruction, vocabulary instruction and, 93
implicit questions, definition, 155
independent reading
    definition, 155
    vocabulary instruction and, 91
inflectional endings, decoding and reading practice with decodable text and, 38–39
instructional reading level, definition, 155
IPT. *See* IDEA Proficiency Test
irregular word reading
    assessment of, 44
    description, 39, 155
    difficulty for English language learners, 39
    irregular word road race activity, 49–50
    reading outlaw words fluently activity, 71–73
    road race gameboard, *50*
    sample irregular word grid, *72*
    teaching strategies, 43
    what's the word? activity, 48

Juel, C., before-reading practices, 120

Kucan, L.
    goal for vocabulary development, 91
    tiers of words, 90

L1, definition, 155
L2, definition, 155
language acquisition, definition, 155
language dominance, definition, 155
language maintenance, definition, 155
language minority, definition, 155
language proficiency, definition, 155
language submersion, definition, 155
Larkin, M. J., phonemic awareness skills hierarchy, 12
Lau v. Nichols, case description, 155

LCD. *See* linguistically and culturally diverse
learning disabilities
    definition, 156
    phonemic awareness and, 11
LEP. *See* limited English proficient
letter knowledge, definition, 156
letter-sound correspondence
    basic lesson, 40, 42, 44
    definition, 156
    phonics and word study and, 32–33, 40, 42
limited English proficient, definition, 156
linguistically and culturally diverse, 156
listening comprehension, definition, 128, 156
listening vocabulary, definition, 88, 156
long vowels, definition, 156

main idea and summarization
    comprehension and, 123–125, *125*, 131–133
    definitions, 156, 158
    finding the main idea, *125*
maintenance bilingual education, definition, 156
manipulation
    adding sounds, 10
    basic lesson: add a sound/take away a sound, 22–23
    deleting sounds, 10, 12, 23
    description, 10
    follow-up lesson: deleting syllables, 23
    follow-up lesson: do the phoneme shuffle, 23–24, 28
maps
    concept maps, 95–96
    semantic maps, 108–110, *109*
    using a story map (during reading) activity, 134–136, *135*
    word maps, *107*, 107–108
Matthew effect, definition, 156
MBE. *See* maintenance bilingual education
McKeown, M. G.
    goal for vocabulary development, 91
    tiers of words, 90
Minaya-Rowe, L., tiers of words, 90
Monitoring Basic Skills Progress: Basic Reading, 69
morphemes
    definition, 156
    number morphemes activity, 103–106
morphology, definition, 156
mother tongue, definition, 156
multilingualism, definition, 156

multimedia methods, vocabulary instruction and, 93

NAEP. *See* National Assessment of Educational Progress
narrative text, definition, 156
National Assessment of Educational Progress, fluency findings, 59
National Reading Panel, effective practices for teaching vocabulary, 93
native language instruction, definition, 156
native language/primary language, definition, 156
native language support, definition, 156
NEP. *See* non-English proficient
Neuhaus Education Center, 16
newcomer program, definition, 157
No Child Left Behind Act, goal of, vii–viii
non-English proficient, 157

onset
    description, 11, 157
    onset-rime level activity for regular word reading, 45, 47
oral language skills
    assessments of, 6
    children who speak no English at all and, 34
    phonics and word study and, 34, 35–36
orthography
    definition, 157
    phonemic awareness and, 5
    phonics and word study and, 32

partner reading
    activities for, 76, 78, 79–80
    definition, 157
    description, 64
    guidelines for partner repeated reading, 65
Peabody CBM Reading Passages, 69
peer tutoring, definition, 157
Perfetti, C. A., slow speed of reading words effect on comprehension, 59
PHLOTE. *See* primary home language other than English
phoneme, definition, 157
phonemic awareness
    appropriateness for all language backgrounds, 146
    assessments for, 12–13
    bibliography, 28–29
    blending, 10, 11, 12, 15–16, 18–19
    classroom activities for, 16–24, 28
    complexity of, 11–12

phonemic awareness *(continued)*
    compound words, 24
    comprehension and, 11
    description, 10, 157
    early grades and, 14
    elements of instruction in, 10, 11–13
    feedback for, 14
    four-phoneme words, 27
    grade level and, 12
    identification, 10, 15–18
    importance of, 9
    learning disabilities and, 11
    lesson planning for, 14, 16–24, 28
    letter-sound correspondences, 5
    linking sounds to letters and print and, 14–15
    manipulation, 10, 12, 23–24, 28
    modeling tasks, 14
    older students and, 14
    onset and, 11
    orthographic patterns and representations, 5
    as a predictor of reading skills, 9, 11
    pronunciation and, 14
    rime and, 11
    role in reading skills, 9
    segmentation, 10, 11, 15–16, 20–22
    skills hierarchy, 12
    spelling and, 11
    teaching strategies, 14–16
    three-phoneme words, 26
    three-syllable words, 25
    transfer from the home language to reading in a second language, 5, 9
    two-phoneme words, 26
    two-syllable words, 25
    use of pictures or brief definitions and, 10
    Web sites, 29
    word types for use in activities, 24–27
phonics and word study
    advanced word analysis, 52–53
    alphabetic knowledge, 36–37
    alphabetic understanding, 37–38
    analogy-based phonics, 48–49
    auditorially similar sounds and, 40
    bibliography, 54
    classroom activities for, 44–45, 47–53
    decoding and reading practice with decodable text and, 38–39, 48–49, 51–53
    description, 32–33, 157

phonics and word study (continued)
early instruction and, 33
elements to include in instruction, 34–39
embedded phonics, 32
guide to pronunciation of English sounds, 41
importance of teaching, 34
inconsistencies in English and, 32, 33, 39
informal assessment of, 43
instructional factors, 40, 42–43
irregular words, 39, 43, 48, 49–50
length of instructional time needed for competence, 33, 35
letter-sound knowledge, 32–33, 40, 42, 44
limited English proficiency and, 33, 39
most common rimes, 46
older students and, 33, 39, 42
oral language skill development and, 34, 35–36
orthographic system of a language and, 32, 33, 39
phonics rules and percentage of exceptions to them, 35
practice reading and, 43
print awareness, 36
progress monitoring, 43–44
regular word reading, 42–43, 44–45, 47–48
review lesson, 50–51
sample answers and questions, 53
sequential teaching of elements, 35
sounds that are difficult for ELLs, 37
structural analysis, 51–52
synthetic approaches, 32–33
teaching strategies, 39–43
visually similar letters and, 40
Web sites for, 55
phonological awareness
definition, 157
importance of, 5
phonological memory, Comprehensive Test of Phonological Processing and, 13
phonology, definition, 157
practice opportunities
for comprehension, 119–121, 128
decoding and reading practice with decodable text, 38–39, 48–49, 51–53
for fluency, 60, 62
importance of, 4
silent reading practice, 60
types of, 4
prediction, definition, 157

prefixes. See also affixes
common prefixes, 105
definition, 157
primary home language other than English, 157
print awareness, activities for developing, 36
print concepts, definition, 157
progress monitoring. See assessments
pronunciation
alphabetic knowledge and, 36–37
guide to pronunciation of English sounds, 41
phonemic awareness and, 14
prosody
definition, 157
fluency and, 58, 60
questions and answers
comprehension, 115, 120, 121, 124, 136–137
implicit questions, 155
phonics and word study, 53
for teachers, 145–150
rapid-naming tasks, Comprehensive Test of Phonological Processing and, 13
rate, definition, 157
reading, definition, 157
reading comprehension, definition, 157
reading level, definition, 157
receptive language skills
definition, 158
vocabulary instruction and, 88
regular word reading
assessment of, 44
basic lesson for, 42
building words activity, 47
changing word activity, 47–48
onset-rime level activity, 45, 47
phoneme level activity, 44–45
teaching strategies, 42–43
repeated reading
definition, 158
guidelines for partner repeated reading, 65
of the same text, 64
using a tape as a model, 74–76
Research-Based Methods of Reading Instruction: Grades K–3, viii
research-based practices
adjusting instructional language, 4–5
appropriate assessments, 6–7

research-based practices (*continued*)

contribution of the critical elements of reading to the reading development of ELLs, 5–6

demographics of English language learners, 1

explicit skills, 2, 3

factors contributing to instructional efficacy, 6

fluency development, 5

goals for the early grades, 1–2

integration of practices for English language learners, 2

most effective instructional practices, 2–5

oral language skills, 1–2, 5

phonemic awareness in the home language, 5

phonological awareness, 5

practice opportunities, 4

similarity of cognitive processes involved in learning to read different alphabetic languages, 2, 6

strategy instruction, 6

student acquisition of English language skills, 2

vocabulary development, 5–6

resources. *See* bibliographies; Web sites

rhyme, definition, 158

rimes

description, 11, 157, 158

list of most common rimes, *46*

onset-rime level activity for regular word reading, 45, 47

SAE. *See* students acquiring English

scaffolded instruction, definition, 158

segmenting

assessment and, 12

basic lesson: break it up!, 20

decoding and reading practice with decodable text, 38

description, 10, 158

follow-up lesson: Elkonin boxes, 21–22

follow-up lesson: syllable split, 20–21

follow-up lesson: two for one, 20

impact on later reading, 11

linking sound to letters and print and, 15

teacher confidence and skills and, 15–16

semantic maps, 108–110, *109*

semilingualism, definition, 158

sheltered English instruction, definition, 158

sight words, definition, 158

sounding out. *See* decoding

speaking vocabulary, definition, 158

spelling

conventional, 153

invented, 155

phonemic awareness and, 11

Stahl, S. A., principles for vocabulary instruction, 91

story structure, definition, 158

structural analysis

go fish for word parts, 106–107

let's add word parts activity, 51–52

number morphemes activity, 103–106

roots plus activity, 102–103

skills development, 91

structured immersion, definition, 158

students acquiring English, definition, 158

suffixes. *See also* affixes

common suffixes, *106*

definition, 158

summarization. *See* main idea and summarization

sustained silent reading without teacher guidance or support, effectiveness of, 64

syllable, definition, 158

syntax, definition, 158

synthetic phonics

approaches to teaching, 32–33

definition, 158

systematic instruction, definition, 158

tape-assisted reading, definition, 158

target language, definition, 159

teaching English as a second language, 159

teaching strategies

alphabetic understanding, 37–38

capitalizing on knowledge and skills of students' first language, 146

common mistakes made by teachers, 148

comprehension, 115–116, 119–128

fluency, 60–68

irregular word reading, 43

modifications for English language learners, 149

phonemic awareness, 14–16

phonics and word study, 39–43

questions and answers for teachers of English language learners, 145–150

regular word reading, 42–43

students with no English, 150

vocabulary instruction, 93–94, 115

TESL. *See* teaching English as a second language

Test of Phonological Awareness
    description, 12
    elementary version, 13
    kindergarten version, 12–13
Texas Primary Reading Inventory Fluency Probes, 69
text, definition, 159
text structure, definition, 159
think-aloud, definition, 159
Title I, description, 159
Title II, description, 159
Title III, description, 159
TOPA. *See* Test of Phonological Awareness
transfer, definition, 159
Tumner, W., basic processes necessary to learn to read, 32

vocabulary instruction
    association processing, 92, 94–97
    bibliography, 110
    classroom activities, 94–110
    complexity of skills associated with comprehension
        and vocabulary development, 87–88
    comprehension processing, 92, 97–102
    context and, 92
    decoding and reading practice with decodable text
        and, 39
    deep processing and, 92, 93
    definitional knowledge and, 91–92
    description, 88–90
    determining which words to teach, 90–91
    direct instruction and, 94
    elements of, 91–92
    engaging students and, 93
    explicit skills instruction and, 3
    expressive vocabulary, 88
    generative processing, 92, 102
    goal, 89
    importance of, 5–6, 90–91
    importance of reading to, 91
    independent reading and, 91
    knowing how to read and, 147
    Latin and Greek word parts, *104*
    Latin roots and Greek combining forms, *103*
    listening vocabulary, 88
    maximizing vocabulary development, 146
    morphological cues, 91

vocabulary instruction (*continued*)
    multiple exposures to target words and, 92, 93
    need for oral vocabulary, 87
    number of new words children need to learn each
        year, 87
    older, literate students and, 89
    oral vocabulary, 88
    reading comprehension and, 90
    reading opportunities and, 93–94
    reading vocabulary, 88
    receptive vocabulary, 88
    reciprocal teaching and, 94
    role of cognates, 91, 147
    role of vocabulary in reading, 87
    semantic maps, 108–110, *109*
    stages of word knowledge, 88–89
    structural analysis, 91, 102–107
    teaching strategies, 93–94, 115
    tiers of words, 90
    Web sites, 111
    word consciousness and, 93
    word maps, *107*, 107–108
    writing vocabulary, 88
vowel diphthong, definition, 159
vowel triphthong, definition, 159

WCPM. *See* words correct per minute
Web sites
    comprehension, 143
    fluency, 85–86
    phonemic awareness, 29
    phonics and word study, 55
    vocabulary instruction, 111
word analysis
    advanced, 52–53
    definition, 159
word family, definition, 159
word maps, *107*, 107–108
word recognition, definition, 159
words correct per minute
    definition, 159
    fluency and, 65–68
word study. *See* phonics and word study
written expression, definition, 159

About the Authors

Sylvia Linan-Thompson is an associate professor in special education at the University of Texas in Austin, a fellow in the Mollie V. Davis Professorship in Learning Disabilities, and director of the Vaughn Gross Center for Reading and Language Arts. She has investigated reading interventions for struggling monolingual English readers in primary grades, literacy acquisition of English language learners, and Spanish literacy development. Currently she is co-principal investigator on three longitudinal, large-scale research projects, two of which are investigating effective reading instruction for English language learners. She has authored articles on these topics and has developed instructional guides.

Sharon Vaughn is the H. E. Hartfelder/Southland Corporation Regents Chair in Human Development at the University of Texas and is on the University's Board of Directors for the Vaughn Gross Center for Reading and Language Arts. Dr. Vaughn was the editor-in-chief of the *Journal of Learning Disabilities* and *Learning Disabilities Research and Practice* and is the author of numerous books and research articles on learning and reading difficulties; she is also a consultant on translating research into practice for school districts and state departments of education. She co-authored (with Sylvia Linan-Thompson) *Research-Based Methods of Reading Instruction, Grades K–3* (2004), also published by ASCD.

Related ASCD Resources

Research-Based Methods of Reading Instruction for English Language Learners

At the time of publication, the following ASCD resources were available; for the most up-to-date information about ASCD resources, go to www.ascd.org. ASCD stock numbers are noted in parentheses.

Audio

Improving Reading Is Everyone's Business by Brenda Hunter (#203122 audiotape; #503215 CD)

Literacy Matters Across the Curriculum by Robin Fogarty and Brian Pete (#204280 audiotape; #504414 CD)

Teaming for Personalized Literacy Learning by Garry Bueckert (#505271 CD)

What Works for Boys: Action Research on Closing the Literacy Gender Gap by Marilyn Dolbeare-Mathews (#203178 audiotape; #503271 CD)

Networks

Visit the ASCD Web site (www.ascd.org) and search for "networks" for information about professional educators who have formed groups around topics like "Language, Literacy, and Literature." Look in the "Network Directory" for current facilitators' addresses and phone numbers.

Online Resources

Visit ASCD's Web site (www.ascd.org) for the following professional development opportunities:

Professional Development Online: *Helping Struggling Readers* and *Successful Strategies for Literacy and Learning,* among others (for a small fee; password protected)

Mixed Media

Literacy Across the Curriculum Professional Development Planner and Resource Package (#703400)

Reading Strategies for the Content Areas, volumes 1 and 2 (ASCD Action Tool) by Sue Beers and Lou Howell (Volume 1: 703109; Volume 2: #705002)

Print Products

Literacy Leadership for Grades 5–12 by Rosemarye Taylor and Valerie Doyle Collins (#103022)

Literacy Strategies for Grades 4–12: Reinforcing the Threads of Reading by Karen Tankersley (#104428)

The Multiple Intelligences of Reading and Writing: Making the Words Come Alive by Thomas Armstrong (#102280)

Research-Based Methods of Reading Instruction, Grades K-3 by Sharon Vaughn and Sylvia Linan-Thompson (#104134)

Teaching Reading in the Content Areas: If Not Me, Then Who? 2nd Edition by Rachel Billmeyer and Mary Lee Barton (#397258)

The Threads of Reading: Strategies for Literacy Development by Karen Tankersley (#103316)

Using Data to Assess Your Reading Program by Emily Calhoun (book with CD-ROM) (#102268)

Video

The Lesson Collection: Literacy Strategies (Tapes 49–56) (#405160 VHS)

The Lesson Collection: Reading Strategies (Tapes 1–8) (#499257 VHS)

The Lesson Collection: Reading Strategies 2 (Tapes 25–32) (#402034 VHS)

The Multiple Intelligences of Reading and Writing: Making the Words Come Alive Books-in-Action (#403325 VHS)

Reading in the Content Areas Video Series (3 videotapes) (#402029)

For more information, visit us on the World Wide Web (http://www.ascd.org), send an e-mail message to member@ascd.org, call the ASCD Service Center (1-800-933-ASCD or 703-578-9600, then press 2), send a fax to 703-575-5400, or write to Information Services, ASCD, 1703 N. Beauregard St., Alexandria, VA 22311-1714 USA.